THE GATHERING PLACE

THE GATHERING PLACE

AN ILLUSTRATED
HISTORY OF
SALT LAKE CITY

BY JOHN S. McCORMICK

Signature Books
Salt Lake City

Cover design by Ron Stucki

© Signature Books 2000. All rights reserved.
Signature Books is a registered trademark of
Signature Books, Inc.

The Gathering Place: An Illustrated History of Salt Lake City
was manufactured in the United States of America and
was printed on acid-free paper.

Portions of an earlier version of *The Gathering Place:*
An Illustrated History of Salt Lake City were
published in 1980 under the title *Salt Lake City:*
The Gathering Place, An Illustrated History
by Windsor Publications, Inc.,
Woodland Hills, California.

04   03   02   01   00   6   5   4   3   2   1

Library of Congress Cataloging-in-Publication Data
McCormick, John S.
The gathering place : an illustrated history of
Salt Lake City / by John S. McCormick
p.   cm.
Includes bibliographical references and index.
ISBN 1-56085-132-5 (cloth)
1. Salt Lake City (Utah)—History—Pictorial works.
2. Salt Lake City (Utah)—History.
I. McCormick, John S., Salt Lake City.   II. Title.
F834.S257 M38   2000
979.2'258—dc21   99-041904
CIP

CONTENTS

FOREWORD

Rod Decker

The 1960s movie *Spartacus* features a scene between Kirk Douglas, in the title role, and Laurence Olivier, who plays Crassus, the general who has defeated Spartacus and his slave revolt. Crassus wishes to give his prisoner a lesson in the philosophy of history before crucifying him. "What is Rome?" he asks with icy arrogance. "A city," replies Spartacus, his cleft chin jutting at an especially defiant angle. "No," says Crassus, "Rome is not a city. Rome is an idea in the mind of God."

Salt Lake City might be thought of as an idea in the mind of God. At least, that is one way to look at it, and one way some historians have written about it. It was founded to be a sacred city, and remains a religious center. And while most cities are just cities, over Salt Lake City there seems to hover—floating, perhaps, on a cloud of ozone—an ideal city, towards which the undistinguished office buildings and ordinary neighborhoods strive throughout their history, as toward a final cause.

In Rome or Jerusalem, God had several ideas, and they conflict. In Salt Lake City, as in Mecca, God had one idea. The 24th of July Parade through the city celebrates the idea and its continuing power to inform the city. There are high school bands, sheriff's posses, floats from businesses, Mormon congregations, but no place in the parade for the Budweiser Clydesdales or a float advocating the Equal Rights Amendment.

Few cities in the world have such a powerfully defining story. Salt Lake City was founded by Mormons who moved to the "wilderness" to escape religious persecution, struggled against nature and national opinion, and saw their city grow prosperous and respectable through faithfulness—more or less—to its original principles. That's the story that defines Salt Lake City.

The original layout of the city reinforces the imposing power of its story. Following Mormon church founder Joseph Smith, Brigham Young made the city in square blocks separated by wide streets, no meandering lanes or crosscutting boulevards, no hidden nooks or enclaves as refuge from the orderly plan. Though Salt Lake City was meant to be a sacred city, it was laid out in marching squares for business, and that contributes to a sober working ethos. Magazines or scholars survey cities from time to time to rank them. Salt Lake City always surprises such observers with the paucity of its nightlife. There is no café society, no cabaret row or air of revelry, no urban bohemia. More than residents of other cities, Salt Lakers work and stay with their families. The grid of blocks and streets holds Salt Lake life like a corset and keeps the city upright, prim, and attentive to duty.

John S. McCormick writes to change the defining story of Salt Lake City. For him, the history of Salt Lake City is not a striving toward some ozone-borne ideal, but rather the outcome of conflicts between contending peoples and contradictory ideas. For example, he tells the story of how the Mormons came to settle Salt Lake City, but notes that they were persecuted in large part because they rejected American capitalism. Salt Lake City and the Mormons both prospered, but not entirely because of superior virtue. Rather they were accepted by America only after they changed from a reproach against American capitalism to a pillar of that system.

Even more, *The Gathering Place* is a gathering of stories of people and groups who did not agree with the regnant ideal of the city. McCormick tells of Native Americans, later immigrants, African Americans, Hispanics, communists, labor agitators, radicals, gays, lesbians, hippies, and non-conformists. He sympathizes with their struggles and celebrates their victories, especially their victories against Salt Lake respectability and the institutions that dominate traditional Salt Lake history. Readers will find Salt Lake stories here that are found nowhere else.

This book shows that history depends on historians as much as on events. McCormick has written a new history that both challenges and complements the traditional story. Once you've read *The Gathering Place*, you will never again look at Salt Lake City in quite the same way.

INTRODUCTION

The point of view informing this book is that the history of Salt Lake City is "painfully rich and diverse." By that I mean several things. First of all, Salt Lake City is no ordinary place. As historian Dale L. Morgan observed in an essay written fifty years ago, it has always been a city "with a hard-gutted individuality and a contradictory charm." For folk singer, storyteller, labor activist, and political radical Bruce "Utah" Phillips, writing in the liner notes to his compact disc, *The Telling Takes Me Home*, Salt Lake City has "a separate culture and a unique historical background which continues to affect the lives of its citizens in quite unusual ways. The twenty years I spent there had me pretty well convinced that Utah was typical of the rest of the country, which, I later discovered, it is not. When the Tourist and Publicity Department advertises in national magazines the delights of a visit to 'The Different World of Utah,' believe me, they are not just playing with words."

By "painfully rich and diverse," I mean also that the city's history is extraordinarily interesting. For the teenage daughter of friends of mine returning to Utah in 1985 after living in New York City for five years, Salt Lake City felt like the television situation-comedy of the 1950s, *Leave It To Beaver*, by which she meant something like "bland and one-dimensional." Though there is that about Salt Lake, there is much more, and there always has been. For me, filmmaker Trent Harris's characterization of Salt Lake City as "a whacked out kind of place" comes nearer the mark. "The subtext in this town is amazing," he says. "This is my favorite place in the world." On the surface placidity and complacency seem to reign, but upon probing deeper one finds "many differ-

ix

ent kinds of people cheerfully laying dynamite in the hidden cracks." In an April 19, 1999, review in *The New Yorker* magazine of the movie *SLC Punk*, Anthony Lane says, "The title's clunky, although it does contain useful information; until now, I had no idea there *were* any punks in Salt Lake City."

Third, Salt Lake City's history is complicated and ambiguous, full of paradox and irresolution. It is the story, not just of one people, but of many peoples—many voices, experiences, points of view, traditions, values, and ways of life—and of their complex interplay. Salt Lake has always been a multicultural, multiethnic, and multiracial city, and its past has belonged not to just one group, but to many. This may be the most significant aspect of the city's history, but it has not always been understood, and perhaps the single most important task historians can undertake is to make that point and explore its dimensions and implications. After all, the ancestors of contemporary Native Americans began living here at least 11,000 years ago. Since then many others have come, including Mormons seeking to build their Kingdom of God on Earth; African-American fur trappers, slaves, and soldiers; Catholic Italian laborers; Hispanic railroad section hands and farm workers; and peoples from Southeast Asia and the islands of the South Pacific. The first female state senator in the United States, Martha Hughes Cannon, was elected in Salt Lake City in 1896, and the nation's second Jewish governor, Simon Bamberger, was elected twenty years later. In the early twentieth century, Utahns voted more than a hundred socialists into office throughout the state, and the Utah State Federation of Labor was one of five state federations to officially endorse the Socialist Party of America, advising its members in 1911 to "aid in the propaganda of Socialism that we may hasten the day when the emancipation of the working class from the bonds of wage slavery shall be proclaimed in America and throughout the world." During the Great Depression of the 1930s, when Utah's unemployment rate was the nation's fourth highest at 36 percent, the Communist Party staged protest marches, rallies, and hunger strikes involving thousands of people. In the late 1940s, Fletcher Henderson, a nationally known bandleader and colleague of Duke Ellington, operated a jazz club in North Salt Lake. In 1948 the Radio City Lounge, reputedly the oldest gay bar west of the Mississippi, opened in Salt Lake City and remains under the same ownership and in the same location today. Christian Anarchist Ammon Hennacy, who served time in federal prison during World War I for his pacifism and in the 1920s and 1930s worked in New York City with Dorothy Day on her *Catholic Worker* newspaper, came to Salt Lake in 1960 and conducted his "one man revolution" until his death a decade later. During the 1960s a vibrant counterculture emerged, and in the mid-1990s the request of students at East High School to form a club for gays, lesbians, and their straight friends, that both polarized the community and gained national attention.

In the last generation or so, historians of the Utah experience have expanded their view and broadened the scope of their inquiry, producing a more nuanced account of the past than ever before. Even so, much of Utah's complexity remains relatively unknown or is too often not taken into account nor its implications explored. Many voices and stories are still missing, and it remains too easy to see Utah history as essentially the account of one people with all others secondary and marginal, peripheral to the main story. A growing number of forces and groups work to perpetuate what might be called "The Official Story." Self-destructive myths and stereotypes about Utah's past, often cultivated, both consciously and unconsciously, by the rich, the powerful, and the privileged, abound. It continues to be easy to have one kind of history and difficult to have another. Plato's words resonate: "Those who hold the power also tell the stories."

What I also mean by characterizing Salt Lake City's history as "painfully rich and diverse" is that it is not just the peaceful story of progress, if indeed it is the story of progress at all, not merely the epic tale of a brave people trying to demonstrate what the human spirit, liberated from prejudice, ignorance, and oppressive authority, could do in a remote area of the United States. Salt Lake City has emerged from the crucible of conflict—conflict based on a number of factors, including race, class, gender, and sexual orientation. This means that in order to understand its history we must go beyond merely acknowledging the presence and contributions of diverse groups and points of view, as important as that is, and examine the relationships that have existed among them, in particular among dominant and subdominant groups, the relatively powerful and the relatively less powerful, the privileged and less privileged. Though this involves many "hard to hear" stories, the goal is not to shift from "feel good" to "feel bad" history, but to comprehend more accurately the nature of the society to which we belong, the history of the groups and traditions with which we interact, and the meaning of the ideas and experiences we encounter. Failing to do so binds us—locking us into unfruitful patterns of the past and denying the possibilities of the future.

A book like this rests on the specialized research and insights of many scholars. I would particularly like to acknowledge my obligation to Thomas G. Alexander, James B. Allen, Leonard J. Arrington, Tom Carter, Ann Chambers, Howard A. Christy, Ruth Fincher, Lawrence Foster, Peter Goss, Robert Gottlieb, Dolores Hayden, Jane M. Jacobs, Leslie G. Kelen, Patricia Nelson Limerick, Kathryn L. MacKay, Helen Zeese Papanikolas, John A. Peterson, Charles Sellers, Jan Shipps, John Sillito, Linda Sillitoe, Eileen Hallet Stone, and Peter Wiley.

I am grateful to the staffs of the Utah State Historical Society Library, the LDS Church Historical Department, and the Special Collections at the University of Utah's Marriott Library for assistance in obtaining photographs and other material.

Davis Bitton kindly read an earlier version of the manuscript and offered valuable suggestions.

Nancy D. McCormick selected most of the photographs for an earlier version of this history and wrote most of the captions, and did so with considerable knowledge, skill, and insight.

John R. Sillito and Linda Sillitoe are longtime friends and collaborators. I am grateful for their friendship and support, and I admire their work, their strength, and their courage.

Lisa has challenged me to think and rethink. She has provided insight, inspiration and support, light, liveliness, and love.

The Gathering Place

Chapter 1.

THE SEARCH FOR ZION

The trail was slow and rigorous. It had been cleared only once, the year before, by the ill-fated Donner Party. Now thick scrub oak, maple, and pine impeded travel. The wayfarers followed a mountain stream, crossed it over and over, back and forth, weaving down the canyon they would later name "Emigration." They had travelled a thousand miles in three months—but now only a few miles a day.

The cool Wasatch Mountains suddenly ended. The July heat surrounded them as they moved out of the mountains and onto the valley floor. Before them lay a broad sweep of land. In his diary, one of the group, Wilford Woodruff, described a rich and fertile valley, "clothed with a heavy garment of vegetation and in the midst of which glistened the waters of the Great Salt Lake, with mountains all around towering to the skies, and streams, rivulets, and creeks of pure water running through the beautiful valley." Their leader, Brigham Young, surveyed the scene. "The spirit of light," he later wrote in his journal, "rested on us and hovered over the valley, and I felt that there the Saints would find protection and safety." This was to be the place—the place of gathering.

By colonizing standards, it was a small group. On April 14, 1847, 148 people, including three women, two children, ages six and seven, and three African-American slaves, left Winter Quarters, Nebraska, north of Omaha. They were the vanguard of those to come, the first to see the Valley of the

1

Joseph Smith inspired both fierce loyalty and irrational hatred. To some he was shiftless and cunning, a devil, a dictator, and a traitor to everything American. A onetime close associate, John C. Bennett, called him "the grossest and most infamous imposter that ever appeared upon the face of the earth." His followers, on the other hand, believed him to be a prophet through whom God had restored his ancient church to the modern world. They saw him as a dynamic and charismatic leader, "a grand example of manhood" who was "endowed with kingly faculties." According to Brigham Young, "I feel like shouting hallelu when I think that I ever knew Joseph Smith." On April 6, 1830, Smith and five other men met to organize a church. At the meeting Smith announced a revelation he had received proclaiming "the rise of the Church of Christ in these last days by the will and commandments of God" and exhorted the others to "put on the armor of God," take up "the shield of faith," and, as a small army, restore the ancient church to a world full of heresy and apostasy. Gradually members began to refer to themselves as "Saints," but others derogatorily called them "Mormons" or "Mormonites." (Private Collection.)

Great Salt Lake where the Saints would soon gather. Originally there were to have been only men, but Harriet Wheeler Young objected. "If the men of the church thought they were going out to some yonder place and pick a permanent abode for the women without even giving them the right of consultation, then they had some more guesses coming," she said. On route men and women from the sick detachment of the Mormon Battalion and a group of Mormon converts from Mississippi joined them. Soon afterward in that summer and fall of 1847 nearly 2,000 others arrived. They laid out a city; planted and harvested crops of corn, beans, and potatoes; established lumbering and salt-mining operations; and built a fort of log cabins to shelter them through the winter. A thousand miles from the nearest settlement of comparable size, Great Salt Lake City was born.

Who were these people, and why had they ventured so far into what they thought of as a wilderness? Members of the Church of Jesus Christ of Latter-day Saints, they had come to establish a religious utopia, a literal Kingdom of God on Earth—a perfect society where they would await Christ's second coming—a City of God, a New Jerusalem, the Zion of the New World.

It all began with a teenage boy named Joseph Smith. Born in Sharon, Vermont, on December 23, 1805, the son of an itinerant laborer and farmer, he moved with his family to western New York state in 1816 and four years later, when he was fourteen, claimed to have had a vision in which God the Father and Christ the Son told him the true church of God was no longer on the earth and that, in time, he would help re-establish it. Over the next ten years his visions continued. Finally, in March 1830, *The Book of Mormon, An Account Written by the Hand of Mormon Upon Plates Taken from the Plates of Nephi*, by Joseph Smith, Junior, "Author and Proprietor," appeared in bookstores. Smith said he had translated the 600-page history of pre-Columbian America from metal plates that looked like gold buried in a hillside near Palmyra, New York, to which an angel named Moroni had led him.

A month later Smith organized the Church of Christ, later renamed the Church of Jesus Christ of Latter-day Saints. As Stow S. Persons says, "It shares with Christian Science the distinction of being the most striking indigenous major American religion." Within a year membership had increased from a handful to more than 1,000. Mormonites, or Mormons, as they were soon known, exhibited a formidable talent for proselyting, and by the time of their arrival in Utah seventeen years later, their church had more than 50,000 members worldwide, 20,000 of them in the United States, and was one of the ten largest denominations in the country. By the late nineteenth century, membership had grown to nearly 300,000.

Though a detailed account of early Mormon history and theology is not necessary here, an understanding of certain points is important. Mormons were millennialists. They believed that the return of Jesus Christ and the establishment of the millennial kingdom was at hand, and they expressed those hopes with a real literalness and immediacy. For them, Joseph Smith was a latter-day prophet through whom God revealed his will, the Mormon church was God's one true church, and they were God's chosen people beleaguered on all sides by enemies of the truth. An article in the January 1, 1842, issue of the church's *Times and Seasons* made the point. Many groups, it said, were "united in unholy alliance, and combined against the saints, and one spirit seems to pervade them all." Those groups included Methodists, Presbyterians, Campbellites, Irwinites, Socialists, drunkards, gamblers, profane swearers, thieves, and robbers, but "on the other hand, we behold a handful of men, or rather of stripling youths, presenting a small but formidable front. ... In their right hand is a two-edged sword (The Word of God), and in their left the shield of faith. ... Such is the view which the two armies present at the present time. Even now we behold them rush to the battle." The enemy's arrows were "nerved up with hatred and envy, they are pointed with prejudice, & dipped in the poison of slander, falsehood, and reproach. But see! They fall harmless at the feet of the saints, being warded off by the shield of faith. Now and then an arrow of truth is hurled back upon the enemy: it pierces their hearts, and their ranks are thinned and deserted. A shout is heard th[at] will prevail—the day is ours— and so goes the battle."

As an elect people, Mormons believed that God wanted them to "gather" out of a sinful world to a place called "Zion" where they would build the Kingdom of God on Earth, live together in righteousness, and prepare for Christ's coming. As Jan Shipps says, the central fact for nineteenth-century Mormons was this sense that they were chosen, and the concept of a chosen people implied, indeed, required, the construction of a separated community, one that would be internally powerful and externally respected, a literal, and not merely a metaphorical, Kingdom of God. The Mormon church, in other words, did not just aim to teach certain doctrines or assemble people regularly to hear God's word. Its goal was the establishment of a perfect society, a model upon which all human society would ultimately be organized. As Patricia Nelson Limerick points out, "In converting to Mormonism, one converted not only to certain religious doctrines, but to a full way of life within a community of believers."

Mormons were clear about what their utopia would be like. For them it was not simply a vague notion. In the first place, they envisioned a religious society, devoted above all to discovering and following God's word, a community organized in accordance with religious principles, one integrated and controlled by religious rather than economic sanctions. As John A. Peterson says, it would be a place where "divine intelligence and spiritual power outranked business acumen on a scale of values." The goal was "to build the heavenly city on earth and to put the cause of the soul first." A religious impulse would infuse every activity, making it difficult, if not impossible, to draw a line between the religious and the secular. As Christopher Lasch notes, "The essence of Mormonism was the attempt to create a community of 'saints,' in which every 'secular' activity should be governed in accordance with a religious conception of the good society." In an insightful essay, "Making Space for the Mormons," Richard L. Bushman elaborates the point. "The Marxists tell us," he says, "that in a market society people turn themselves into commodities. We package ourselves, sell ourselves, and value people for their worth in the market of social exchange—that is, by status or position. We become in our essence what we are in our work—a professor, a stockbroker, a secretary, a car mechanic. The market invades our imaginations and takes over our ways of thinking about all of life." Mormons resisted this, seeking to fashion an entirely different society based on fundamentally different principles. Rather than a market society, they sought to create a "temple society," that is, a community with a temple as a physical feature where heaven would touch earth and where people would enter in order to "divine the meaning of existence and to put themselves in touch with the holy," but more fundamentally, a society where a particular world view dominated, and which the temple helped anchor. Rather than the market, what would define, energize, and draw people was "spiritual empowerment."

Second, the ideal society would be a theocracy. All affairs—not just religious, but also political, social, and cultural—would be under the direction of religious leaders. Only a society that God designed and closely directed could provide enduring peace and justice on the earth. Third, it would be a unified society. As Brigham Young, Joseph Smith's successor as LDS church president, said, "Except I am one with my good brethren, do not say that I am a Latter-day Saint. We must be one. Our faith must be concentrated in one great work: the building up of the Kingdom of God on earth, and our works must aim to the accomplishment of that great purpose." It followed that the Kingdom would have a strong central organization. Participants in the task of building the Kingdom would willingly submit themselves to the direction of God's leaders. Further the Mormon utopia would be based on cooperation, rather than competition. The emphasis would be on group consciousness and activity, rather than on the individual. The Mormon people would be organized as "one great family of heaven," each person working for the good of the whole rather than for individual self-interest. Finally, Mormons envisioned an essentially egalitarian society, emphasizing again and again that, "If ye are not equal in earthly things, ye cannot be equal in obtaining heavenly things."

How did Mormons propose to ensure the establishment of the Kingdom of God on Earth? For them, merely trusting the workings of God's spirit on people to limit antisocial behavior and encourage cooperation was not enough. Their earthly utopia was to be based on two practical principles: a compact pattern of settlement, and a cooperative form of economic organization.

Mormons were not to settle on individual, isolated farmsteads, as did other people. Instead, they were to live in a network of compact agricultural villages, each laid out in a grid pattern "four square with the world," with large lots and blocks and wide streets. Farmers would live in town and drive out to their fields each day for work. The idea was that if people lived close to each other and to their leaders, order, unity, and cooperation would be easier to establish and maintain. As Brigham Young's successor John Taylor said in a classic statement: "In all cases in making new settlements, the Saints should be advised to gather together in villages, ... The advantages of this plan, instead of carelessly scattering out over a wide extent of the country, are many and obvi-

SUPER HANC PETRAM ÆDIFICABO.

FOR PRESIDENT,
GEN. JOSEPH SMITH,
OF NAUVOO, ILLINOIS.
FOR VICE PRESIDENT,
SIDNEY RIGDON,
OF PENNSYLVANIA.

ous to all those who have a desire to serve the Lord. By this means, the people can retain their ecclesiastical organizations, have regular meetings of the quorums of the priesthood, and establish and maintain day and Sunday Schools, Improvement Associations, and Relief Societies. They can also cooperate for the good of all in financial and secular matters, in making ditches, fencing fields, building bridges, and other necessary improvements. Compact organization gives us many advantages of a social and civic nature that might be lost by spreading out so thinly that intercommunication is difficult, dangerous, inconvenient, and expensive." In 1833 Joseph Smith drew up a plan for such a settlement called the "Plat of the City of Zion" that God, he said, revealed to him. When one such town was filled up, he wrote, "Lay off another in the same way, and so fill up the world in these last days."

The setting up of "Mormon villages" was one concrete step to take if the Bible Commonwealth was to be established. A second necessity was the adoption of a socialistic economic system variously known as the "United Order," the "Order of Enoch," and the "Law of Consecration and Stewardship." According to Joseph Smith, God outlined the system to him in a revelation of February 1831. Under it private property would be turned over to the church and then returned to former owners in trust for their use. Members would

This lithograph appeared in The Prophet, *a Mormon church periodical published in New York City. It depicted the courts martial in early November 1838 of Joseph Smith, Sidney Rigdon, Parley P. Pratt, and other Mormon leaders following Missouri governor Boggs's "extermination order." They were sentenced to be shot in the public square in view of the Mormon people "as an example." When General Alexander W. Doniphan refused to carry out the order and denounced it as "cold-blooded murder," the prisoners were transferred to jail. Tried in a civil court and found guilty of treason, they spent five months in prison. (Private Collection.)*

(opposite) Mormons began building Nauvoo in the summer of 1839. According to Joseph Smith, the name meant "a beautiful plantation" in Hebrew. By 1843 they were confident it would be the city to which the whole world would look while kingdoms elsewhere crumbled and were calling it "the great emporium of the West." At the height of its prosperity in 1844, it was the second largest city in Illinois and boasted an impressive temple, a large hotel, sawmills, a flour mill, a tool factory, a foundry, a china factory, the beginnings of a university, an agricultural and manufacturing society, and extensive community fields where the landless could farm. By the fall of 1846, it was nearly a ghost town. (Private Collection.)

"consecrate," or deed, their property to the bishop of the church, who would then grant an "inheritance," or "stewardship," to each family out of the properties received. The amount of the stewardship would depend on the needs of the family, which the bishop and the prospective steward would jointly determine. Some people would give more to the church than they got back, and out of the surplus the bishop would grant stewardships to those who had no property to give.

What Mormons had devised was a plan for redistributing wealth and placing all families on an equal economic footing. Equality was to be maintained by requiring family heads to annually consecrate their surplus production, which would then be distributed to those who had not produced enough to provide for themselves and their families. Rejecting the highly individualistic economic order of their nineteenth-century America, Mormons stressed group interest over individual interest. Concerned not only to satisfy their religious needs, but also to provide material and social security, they tried to work out a system in which, as Mormon scholar Hugh Nibley put it, everyone got what they really needed, no one kept more than they needed, and all were equal in temporal as well as spiritual things. It was this form of economic organization that early Mormons found most appropriate to the state of spiritual perfection about to dawn. Early Mormons, in other words, were utopian socialists (though this is a term that in general their present-day counterparts are enormously uncomfortable with). They were extremely critical of their contemporary American society and viewed their immigration to Utah as an opportunity to escape deeply rooted inequities and begin anew, and their arrival in Utah was the beginning of a long-standing tradition in the state of political and cultural radicalism. Subsequent generations of Utah radicals who also challenged the basic values and structures of their society would include Godbeites of the 1860s, Populists of the 1890s, Socialists, Anarchists, and Wobblies of the early twentieth century, Communists of the 1930s, and New Leftists of the 1960s.

Though Mormons embarked on an intensely interesting experiment, their utopian and communitarian aspirations were nothing new, but were present from the earliest days of North American settlement. Jamestown and Plymouth experimented with communism in their early days. The Puritans who came to Massachusetts in the early 1600s thought of themselves as a

godly community of Saints whom God had sent on an "errand into the wilderness" to establish a "City on a Hill" that would serve as a beacon to the rest of the world. By the mid-1600s they numbered 30,000 people. Soon afterward German settlers created the "Community of the God Loving Soul" in Germantown, Pennsylvania. At the end of the eighteenth century, Mother Ann Lee and "The United Society of Believers in Christ's Second Appearing," better known simply as the "Shakers," brought communal living, as well as spiritual marriage and the doctrine of the bi-sexuality of God, to North America. By 1830, the year the Mormon church was founded, they had established eighteen separate colonies. Utopianism and communal societies, in fact, especially flourished during the period when Mormonism was taking shape. Religious

Following the destruction of the Nauvoo Expositor, Illinos governor Thomas Ford demanded the surrender of Joseph Smith and his brother Hyrum. They agreed, but with grave apprehension, Joseph reputedly saying, "I am going like a lamb to the slaughter. ... I shall die innocent, and it shall be said of me—he was murdered in cold blood." Death struck suddenly. Late on the afternoon of July 27, 1844, a mob of about 150 men attacked Carthage Jail where the Smiths were being held in an upstairs room. The guards at the jail fired at the mob, but were apparently in on the conspiracy and used blanks. A shot through the door killed Hyrum Smith instantly. With a handgun that friends had smuggled to him, Joseph wounded several men on the stairs, then tried to leap from a window to the courtyard below. As he started through the window, a number of shots hit him, and he fell to the ground mortally wounded. (Private Collection.)

faith inspired the communities of Amana in Iowa, Bethel in Missouri, Aurora in Oregon, and Adin Ballou's Christian socialist colony of Hopedale. Other communal experiments, such as Communia in Iowa, John Humphrey Noyes's Oneida Community in New York, George Ripley's Brook Farm, Bronson Alcott's Fruitlands, and Josiah Warren's Equity, differed in having a secular base, but the goal of creating a more perfect society was the same. In all, more than fifty utopian, or "intentional," communities were established in the United States in the 1830s and 1840s.

Though the Mormons were only one of many utopian movements seeking to create a new social order rather than reform the old one, they were easily the largest and most successful. Most of the mid-nineteenth-century experiments collapsed in less than twenty years and were quickly forgotten, except by historians and specialists. Seen in this context, the survival of the Mormon experiment is all the more remarkable—clear evidence of its success in creating and sustaining strong individual and group loyalties—though, of course, the Mormon church has evolved since then to become a very different organization in many ways than it once was and in particular has moved a considerable distance from its communitarian roots.

Why did Mormons seek the isolation of Utah, 1,000 miles beyond the line of non-Native American settlement, to conduct their experiment? The basic answer is simple: because for sixteen years they met with opposition, and often violence, wherever else they went.

From the moment of its founding, the Mormon church was an object of suspicion and hostility and came into conflict with its neighbors. Between 1830 and 1846, its adherents moved, more accurately, were driven, successively from New York to Ohio to Missouri to Illinois. No sanctuary lasted for more than a few years. In Hiram, Ohio, Joseph Smith was tarred and feathered. In Jackson County, Missouri, a meeting of 500 local citizens issued an ultimatum that all Mormons leave the county. Mormon leaders were harassed; the church printing plant and other businesses were wrecked; a raid on a Mormon settlement on the Big Blue River destroyed ten houses; and armed confrontation between Mormons and their enemies left people on both sides dead and injured. As can be expected, responsibility for the violence can be found on both sides.

Friction between Mormons and non-Mormons in Jackson County culminated in two events: an "extermination order" and the Haun's Mill Massacre. On October 25, 1838, Mormons and non-Mormons clashed at the "Battle of Crooked River." People on both sides were killed. Two days later, on October 27, Missouri governor Lilburn W. Boggs issued an order to the state militia that read, in part, "The Mormons must be treated as enemies, and must be exterminated or driven from the State if necessary, for the public peace." Three days later a militia unit of about 200 men attacked a small Mormon settlement at Haun's Mill, killing seventeen men and boys and wounding almost as many more. The next day the Missouri militia occupied Far West, the Mormon capital in Missouri, and made four demands: Joseph Smith and other church leaders were to surrender and stand trial; Mormon property was to be confiscated; the entire Mormon population was to leave the state; and Mormons were to give up their arms. Over the next four months some 12,000 to 15,000 Mormons left Missouri and settled in Illinois. In April 1839 Joseph Smith unexpectedly joined them. Though originally he was sentenced to be shot, the order was never carried out, and after five months' imprisonment he was allowed to escape.

During the next five years Mormons transformed Nauvoo, their main city in Illinois, from a mosquito-infested swamp on the banks of the Mississippi River into the state's second largest city, with a population of more than 15,000 people. In 1843 an English visitor described it as having "great dimen-

(opposite) *To help finance their journey west, Mormons sought federal government contracts to build forts along the Oregon Trail. President James Polk agreed instead to let 500 Mormons enlist in the U.S. Army to fight in the war against Mexico. In July 1846 the Mormon Battalion left the main body of Mormons in Iowa and began a 2,000-mile march to San Diego. They arrived after the war was over, and the only battle they fought was with a herd of wild bulls, but the $70,000 they earned helped finance the church's westward movement. This painting,* The Mormon Battalion on the Gila River, *was by George M. Ottinger, one of Utah's most significant pioneer painters. It appeared in a Mormon church periodical,* The Instructor, *June 1947. (Private Collection.)*

12

The Gathering Place

sions, laid out in beautiful order," with "handsome stores, large mansions, and fine cottages." Mormons were "a wonderfully enterprising people," he said. What impressed him most was the accomplishment of so much in such a short time.

Mormons had great expectations for Nauvoo. It would be a covenanted community—the "city upon a hill" they had long sought to establish to which the rest of the world would look for direction. Those hopes were dashed on the afternoon of June 27, 1844, when a mob of about 150 men murdered Joseph Smith and his brother Hyrum in jail while they awaited trial on charges of treason following the destruction on Smith's order of an opposition printing press. Contrary to the expectations of their enemies, however, Mormons did not scatter at the death of their prophet, and so, within a few months, a series of systematic attacks, known as "wolf hunts," began, designed to drive them from the state. According to the *Quincy Whig* newspaper, "The public sentiment of the state is against the Mormons, and it will be in vain for them to contend against it. ... It is their duty to obey the public will, and leave the state as speedily as possible." Illinois governor Thomas Ford eventually told Mormons the state could give them no protection and advised them to leave.

They had little choice. By then it was clear that if the Lord's people were to be gathered, they would have to remove themselves more completely from non-Mormons than they ever had before. Concluding that "Zion can not be gathered in the midst of Babylon," Brigham Young and other church officials reached the decision in the fall of 1845 to leave Nauvoo and lead their people west. After considering a number of possibilities, including Oregon, California, and Texas, they finally settled on the Great Basin area, thinking it would attract fewer non-Mormons in the future than would other areas. During the winter of 1845-46, Nauvoo was converted into a base camp for the great migration, which began in the spring of 1846 with a series of temporary camps in Iowa and Nebraska, and in the spring of 1847 the advance party of 148 people left for the Salt Lake Valley.

Nearly two decades of conflict increased Mormons' sense that they were a special people. Common suffering and sacrifice bound them together. They interpreted their trials as "persecution of the Saints of God for righteousness' sake," and by the time they arrived in Utah they regarded themselves more than ever as a "modern Israel," a people in flight from Egypt seeking their own

promised land. After seventeen years of travelling through "Babylon," Mormons made what they expected to be a permanent home next to the Great Salt Lake where "Zion would plant her feet to grow strong and mighty, never again to be driven by the mobs." This view still resonates for Mormons today. As a recent writer said, "This People of Utah was a chosen people who had been tried in adversity and persecution and found peace and prosperity and stability in the reaches of a desert—'freedom's last abode'—which no one else had wanted."

Why did Mormons arouse so much opposition that they were finally driven to separate themselves from the rest of American society? Why did they provoke such hatred? A number of factors were involved. Though some Mormons owned slaves, Mormons in general opposed slavery, while many of their neighbors supported it, and slavery, of course, was the most volatile issue facing the nation in the generation before the Civil War. Mormon merchants and tradesmen established stores and shops to compete with those of older settlers. Mormons tended to vote as a block and were thus seen as a political threat. Because Mormons tried to convert Native Americans to their church, some

13

non-Mormons feared a possible alliance between the two groups. The Mormon idea of themselves as a chosen people doing battle with a variety of enemies smacked of arrogance, and their doctrine that a man could have more than one wife, though not made public until 1852, outraged other Americans and stirred up public opinion against them.

None of these specific points, however, fully accounts for the depth of the antagonism. The cause was more basic. In important ways early Mormonism stood outside the mainstream of American life. As Donald Worster points out, it "represented an important exception to what was going on in the (American) culture at that time." Mormons sought to create a new kind of community, one that transcended secular society. They attempted to live against the grain of the secular world, advocating alternative ways of organizing life. They challenged, and meant to make a break with, the patterns of economic, political, and cultural life in their contemporary America. They questioned much that was well established—the separation of affairs of church from secular affairs; the independence of the individual in economic life; monogamous marriage. They were theocratic in a democratic society. They were

The first half of the Mormons' advance company's journey to Utah was relatively easy, almost leisurely and pleasant, as they followed the high grass and winding Platte River westward. Crossing the mountains, however, was more rigorous, and it often took many days to cover even a few miles. William Clayton, the group's historian, kept accurate mileage logs for future companies by counting the revolutions of the wagon wheels to figure distances traveled. After three days of such mind-boggling work, he designed a mechanical odometer. West of Fort Laramie, when Mormons left the Oregon Trail, they marked the path with ten-mile signposts to guide those to follow. In 1848 Clayton published The Latter-day Saints' Emigrant's Guide *based on his measurement of the trail.*
(Private Collection.)

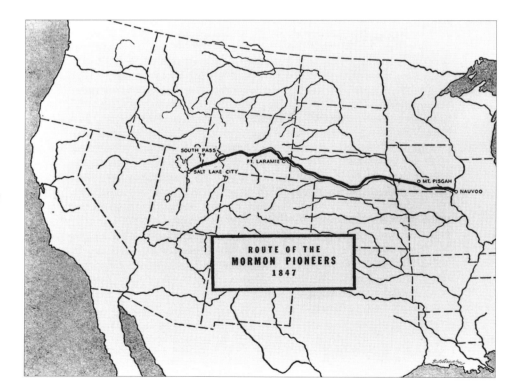

polygamous in a monogamous society. And they were utopian socialists in an emerging capitalistic order who, as Leonard J. Arrington said, "interfered with the spread of capitalist institutions." Their impulse was to reject, rather than accommodate to, the reality of the market. Theirs was a form of resistance to what Joseph Smith called a society of "bankers, lawyers, and businessmen," an opposition to what Charles Sellers terms the market revolution of Jacksonian America when "property rights won out over human rights and the nation was divided into rich and poor, city and country, commerce and farming." Mormonism was in part a movement of poor people—poor farmers, unsuccessful merchants, industrial workers, in short, the dispossessed. As William Martin says, the most important structural feature of capitalist society early Mormonism spoke to was growing class distinction and "dispossession"—the loss or lack of means of subsistence. In an essay about the Mormon church's central text, *The Book of Mormon*, Susan Curtis makes a similar point. The dramatic reordering of American life in the generation before the Civil War, as the United States evolved into a commercial society, caused considerable hardship and anxiety, she says, and while Mormons consider *The Book of Mormon* scripture, it can also be approached as a piece of nineteenth-century American literature, a vehicle Joseph Smith used to address his contemporaries, and is therefore of interest not only to the believer. Seen within the context of the 1820s and 1830s, the book was a jeremiad, a statement about and to the America of its time. It reflected the concerns of the society from which it emerged and offered advice about how to adjust to new realities and still "remain true to God's plan for the United States," and its message was a radical one.

In such circumstances conflict between Mormons and their fellow Americans was a virtual certainty. Opposition to Mormons before they came to Utah, in other words, is not mainly a study in irrationality and intolerance. Rather, conflict was caused by antagonistic economic, social, political, and cultural orders. It was thus inevitable and would not cease until one side or the other changed. Ultimately, of course, one side did. To look ahead briefly, conflict did not end after Mormons arrived in Utah but remained a constant of their experience until their decision near the end of the nineteenth century to give up many of the things that made them different, accommodate themselves to existing circumstances, and become part of the established order. As

15

The Search for Zion

Christopher Lasch says, once Mormons gave up certain distinguishing features of their faith and thus no longer posed a challenge to the ways of the larger society, conflict ceased and they became another tolerated minority. In his view, "this may well be the most important fact of Mormon history."

~

Recommended Readings

Alexander, Thomas G., and Allen, James B. *Mormons and Gentiles: A History of Salt Lake City.* Boulder, CO: Pruett Publishing Co., 1984.

Angus, Mark. *Salt Lake City Underfoot: Self-Guided Tours of Historic Neighborhoods.* Salt Lake City: Signature Books, 1996.

Arrington, Leonard J. *Great Basin Kingdom: An Economic History of the Latter-day Saints, 1830-1900.* Cambridge, MA: Harvard University Press, 1958.

Buhle, Paul, and Sullivan, Edmund. *Images of American Radicalism.* Hanover, MA: The Christopher Publishing House, 1998. Chap. 1: "Green Dreamers."

Bushman, Richard L. "Making Space for the Mormons," No. 2 in the *Leonard J. Arrington Mormon History Lecture Series.* Logan: Utah State University Press, 1998.

Curtis, Susan. "Early Nineteenth Century America and the Book of Mormon." In Vogel, Dan, ed., *The Word of God: Essays on Mormon Scripture.* Salt Lake City: Signature Books, 1996.

"Interview: Expanding Our Moral Vision Beyond the Human Community: A Conversation with Donald Worster." *Sunstone* 12 (September 1988): 30-34. Reprinted in McCormick, John S., and Sillito, John R., eds., *A World We Thought We Knew: Readings in Utah History.* Salt Lake City: University of Utah Press, 1995.

Lasch, Christopher. "The Mormon Utopia." First published in *New York Review of Books,* 26 Jan. 1967. Reprinted in his collection, *The World of Nations: Reflections on American History, Politics, and Culture.* New York: Alfred A. Knopf, 1973, 56-69.

Morgan, Dale L. "Salt Lake City: City of the Saints." In West, Ray B., ed., *Rocky Mountain Cities.* New York: W. W. Norton and Co., Inc., 1949, 179-207.

Reps, John W. *Cities of the American West: A History of Frontier Urban Planning.* Princeton, NJ: Princeton University Press, 1979, 286-311.

Sellers, Charles. *The Market Revolution: Jacksonian America, 1815-1846*. New York: Oxford University Press, 1991, esp. chap. 7.

Shipps, Jan. *Mormonism: The Story of a New Religious Tradition*. Urbana: University of Illinois Press, 1985.

Underwood, Grant. *The Millenarian World of Early Mormonism*. Urbana: University of Illinois Press, 1993.

Utah Historical Quarterly 27 (July 1959); a special issue on the history of Salt Lake City.

Chapter 2

DEFYING THE DESERT, ESTABLISHING THE KINGDOM

Great Salt Lake City, as it was first called, was the start of a vast Mormon empire. Yet in 1847 it was hard for almost anyone besides Mormons to see Utah as a "Land of Promise." Instead, it was "The Land Nobody Wanted." Nobody, that is, except Mormons and the succession of Native American peoples who had made it their home for something like 11,000 years, beginning with those whom anthropologists term Paleo-Indians, and their successors, the Great Basin and Plateau Archaic peoples; the Anasazi (or Ancient Ones, or Ancient Enemies); the Fremont; the Shoshonean, or Numic, peoples; and the Navajo. Utah history, in other words, begins, not with Mormon settlement in 1847, or the first European presence, perhaps as early as the 1500s, but at least 11,000 years ago. One way of saying this is that the first Utahns were Native Americans, and Utah history is the story of a succession of other peoples intruding on their lands.

There is no way of knowing how many Native Americans lived in what is now Utah when Mormons first arrived, though historians generally agree it was something like 20,000, and perhaps nearly twice that many. By the mid-nineteenth century there were five main groups. Each had developed viable and sophisticated belief systems and lifeways that served them well. Utah, in other words, was never a vacant wasteland waiting to be filled up by civilized

A carpenter and glazier from New England, Brigham Young joined the Mormon church in 1832 after spending two years studying church doctrine and becoming acquainted with its members to see, he said, if they had "good common sense." Fiercely loyal to Joseph Smith, he organized the Mormon migration from Missouri to Illinois and in 1846 succeeded Smith as church president and led Mormons to the Salt Lake Valley. (Private Collection.)

people. The Diné (Navajo) were in the four corners area, while four groups of Numic peoples lived in other parts of the state: Nimi (Shoshoni) in northern Utah beyond the Great Salt Lake; Nuwuvi (Southern Paiute) in southern and southwestern Utah; Newe (Goshute) west of the Great Salt Lake; and Nucia, or Nuche (Ute), who ranged over about two-thirds of present-day Utah. They were Utah's original pioneers. As Kathryn L. MacKay and Larry Cesspooch say in their introduction to a series of oral histories with Utes in Leslie Kelen's and Eileen Hallet Stone's important collection, *Missing Stories: An Oral History of Ethnic and Minority Groups in Utah*, "The Mormons ... came to actualize their own narrative of creating a literal Kingdom of God on Earth. But the earth they chose was already storied, already understood." And Native Americans in Utah today feel as deep and profound a connection to this place as do Mormons, or any other group. Their creation stories tell of human beings coming out of darkness into the light and beauty of the earth, to which they are tied by spiritual relationships that are expressed through ceremonies. "Their oral traditions connect them with this place and with all creation," David Rich Lewis says. "Southern Paiutes know how darkness rubbed against water and conceived light; how the myth-time animal beings dove down to bring up earth from the ocean floor to create land. Utes recognize how Wolf, their culture-hero, and Coyote, ordered this world, creating the tortured landscape, the seasons, death, and human beings. Navajos mark the emergence of First Man and First Woman into this fourth and final world."

Though Mormons were the first white men and women to attempt permanent settlement of Utah, they were not the first Euro-Americans to enter the area. For the previous three-quarters of a century, a variety of people and groups had crossed and recrossed the territory, and by the time Mormons arrived, a great deal was known about the area. The first to come were the Spanish. In the mid-1500s they began exploring the northern frontier of New Spain, now the southwestern United States, which included Utah, though it was not until 200 years later that the first group, led by Juan Maria Antonio Rivera, arrived in Utah, near what is now Monticello, as part of their effort to learn more about Spanish territory north of Mexico itself. It was the beginning of a significant Hispanic presence in Utah.

Rivera's group travelled as far north as the present-day Moab area and, as Thomas G. Alexander says, before turning east into Colorado erected a large cross with an inscription as a symbol of discovery, conquest, and Spanish sovereignty. Eleven years later, in July 1776, two Spanish Fathers, Francisco Atanasio Dominguez and Silvestre Velez de Escalante, set out from Santa Fe with a party of ten men in search of a route to Monterey. They spent about six weeks of their 2,000-mile, five-month journey in Utah, reaching as far west as Utah Valley before heading south and eventually giving up their quest. If they had reached California, Utah's subsequent history would have been very different. Missions and presidios would have extended northward and, as David Rich Lewis says, "Our history would have been closely tied to Spain, the Catholic Church, and the peoples of the borderlands, and Utah would not have been nearly as inviting a place for Mormons fleeing their America of the 1830s and 1840s."

The travels in Utah of Dominguez and Escalante are much better known and of greater significance than the Rivera expedition. They looked at potential sites for settlement and, according to their diary, "gave (the Indians) to understand, although they did not wholly believe it, that we were not here for what they thought, or carried goods for trading," and they made up a story

Fur trapper Louis Vasquez. The Rocky Mountain fur trade came to an end by the early 1840s. After that, Vasquez operated a fort on the South Platte and in 1843 joined Jim Bridger in building a new fort on Black's Fork, which they named Fort Bridger. It became one of the main trading posts for overland travellers and was established specifically to serve wagon trains heading to the West Coast. Among the immigrant trains it served was the ill-fated Donner-Reed Party, which followed the Hastings Cutoff through Utah, then across Nevada to California. (Private Collection.)

about a search for a lost priest, "lest they took us for scouts intending to conquer their land after we had seen it." As David Rich Lewis says, it would not be the last time Indians in Utah heard such statements. The expedition produced two important documents: a diary, which was a joint effort of Dominguez and Escalante and was the first written description of what is now Utah and western Colorado; and a map—the first based on personal observation of the area.

In the years following the Domiguez-Escalante Expedition, Spanish traders periodically pushed into Utah, and they continued to, even after the arrival of the Mormons. Still, relatively few people ventured into Utah until the 1810s, when a new group began arriving: British, French-Canadian, French, Spanish, and American fur traders, the fabled mountain men, who, over the next several decades, established temporary trading posts and thoroughly mapped and explored Utah in their search for beaver. Between 1826 and 1829, for example, Jedediah Smith led two major expeditions that covered virtually the entire state.

Historians and others have typically portrayed mountain men as colorful

Defying the Desert,
Establishing the
Kingdom

adventurers. A more fruitful way of viewing them is as representatives of the best and the worst in American life. They were profiteers—brave, resourceful, and hard working, and also violent, greedy, and racist. Part of their legacy was the image of Native Americans as savages and, thus, obstacles to progress. That view, however inaccurate and unfair, prevailed in Utah as much as it did elsewhere and justified the harsh treatment Indians received from white immigrants until the elimination of Native Americans could be rationalized as the result of the interaction of a superior group with an inferior, cultureless, and barbaric people. The fur trade, in other words, whatever else we might say about it, disrupted the lives and cultures of Native Americans in Utah and throughout North America and helped prepare the way for the ultimate dispossession of Indians from their land.

From 1843 to 1844, and again between 1845 and 1847, Captain John Charles Frémont of the United States Army Topographical Corps conducted major expeditions aimed at exploring and opening routes for overland travelers to California and Oregon. In 1845, following the first trip, he published a widely read *Report*. On a map included in it he wrote, "The Great Basin: diameter 11° of latitude, 10° of longitude: elevation above the sea between 4 and 5000 feet: surrounded by lofty mountains: contents almost unknown, but believed to be filled with rivers and lakes which have no communication with the sea, deserts and oases which have never been explored, and savage tribes, which no traveler has seen or described." In 1846 at least five separate groups of emigrants passed through Utah on their way to the West Coast. The best known was the tragic Donner-Reed Party, which became trapped in the Sierra Nevada Mountains by an early winter snow storm. Of its eighty-seven members, only forty-seven survived starvation and cannibalism.

What was Utah like, this land through which people passed for nearly a century before 1847 but did not try to colonize? It was isolated, a thousand miles from the lines of settlement at the time, and semi-arid, with average rainfall varying from between five to ten inches in much of the region to sixteen inches in the Salt Lake Valley. Dean L. May put it nicely: much of Utah "is a land that wants to be a desert." Geographers divide it into three "physiographic provinces": the Colorado Plateau and the Great Basin, both of which May characterizes as "inhospitable to plants and animals generally and man in particular," and the Rocky Mountains, near which 85 percent of Utah's popu-

lation presently lives, since they provide resources that the Great Basin and Colorado Plateau regions lack. Only about 10 percent of Utah's land surface is suitable for agriculture, and the growing season is short, as little as three months in many of the back valleys. For many who have come, it has been an uninviting land, and yet the very things keeping other people away attracted Mormons. Because it was isolated, they hoped for freedom to build their Kingdom. In the words of an observer at the time, it was a place where Mormons could "wive, thrive, work and worship." Because it was a difficult environment, survival would take extreme effort, and Mormon leaders stressed that God expected his people to be diligent. Hard work was both a practical necessity and a religious duty. Utah was a land where only a determined people could live, Brigham Young pointed out, and for that reason it was "a good place to make Saints and a good place for Saints to live."

Nearly 2,000 Mormons arrived in the Salt Lake Valley in the summer and fall of 1847. Fifty years later, during the Pioneer Jubilee of July 20-24, 1897, those who were still alive gathered on Temple Square for this photograph. (Private Collection.)

23

Defying the Desert, Establishing the Kingdom

ELLEN SANDERS KIMBALL. HARRIET DECKER YOUNG. CLARA DECKER YOUNG.
AUG-1919
B. HORNE. FIRST UTAH PIONEER WOMEN, 1847.

The advance party of Mormons that arrived in the Salt Lake Valley in July 1847 included 143 men (among them three African-American slaves), two young boys, and the three women shown here: Ellen Sanders Kimball, plural wife of Heber C. Kimball; Harriet Decker Young, plural wife of Lorenzo Dow Young; and Clara Decker Young, plural wife of Brigham Young and daughter of Harriet Decker Young. The two young boys were also sons of Harriett Young. (Private Collection.)

The Gathering Place

Before coming to Utah, the Mormons' greatest challenge was the hostility of other people. Now they faced another one. In addition to conflict with Native Americans, onto whose land they had moved uninvited, and in subsequent years with groups of non-Mormons who would come to Utah, they also faced a contest with nature. The early years were difficult, but Mormons slowly and confidently conquered their environment, and they regarded their success in meeting nature's challenge and making "the desert blossom as the rose" as among their greatest achievements, though in recent years historians, including Donald Worster and Dan L. Flores, have begun to examine the environmental costs involved in the process. According to Dale Morgan, Mormons often put it this way: "What was done was done in partnership, the Saints and the Lord working together, but the Lord wasn't getting there very fast when He was going it alone."

As Thomas Carter says in discussing early Utah architecture: "The formidable Great Basin landscape became a place where the Saints would be tested. From pulpits across the territory echoed a familiar message: A kingdom of God would be built on Earth and the desert would give way to earthly paradise." Thus, he continues, "from that first day in the summer of 1847 when the creeks of Salt Lake Valley were diverted for irrigation water, the struggle against the wilderness was joined. ... Domestication was the watchword of the day. LDS church president Brigham Young instructed his followers not to ravage and despoil the land, but rather to subdue it and make it beautiful: 'there is a great work for the Saints to do; progress and improve upon and make beautiful everything around you. Cultivate the earth and cultivate your minds. Build cities, adorn your habitations, make gardens, orchards and vineyards, and render the earth so pleasant that when you look upon your labors you may do so with pleasure, and that angels may delight to come and visit your beautiful locations.' The Edenic garden envisioned by the Utah Mormons would become the blueprint for the future. Following the Parousia, the Millennium would be ushered in according to the plan that the Saints had established in Utah. In their efforts to realize the prophecy, the kingdom builders of the Great Basin sent nature reeling before them." As Carter points out, like previous generations of Americans, Utah Mormons tended to see untamed land as "wilderness," that is, as threatening to people on several levels—in the first place, because it harbored ferocious beasts and savage men, and, on a deeper level, as an area where civil and moral laws became inoperative and behavioral restraints broke down. In building their Zion, Mormons followed a "well worked-out American tradition" of "turning nature into culture."

Given the land's aridity, any people would have had to cooperate in order to prosper. The climate forced collective behavior, as Worster says, and for that Mormons were uniquely qualified. The key to their success was what Henry Whiteside has called "guided," or "disciplined," cooperation. Salt Lake City was not settled by separate individuals, but by a group of people working together under the close direction of their church leaders. As one person put it, "The Lord spoke to Brigham, Brigham to the bishops, and the bishops to the people."

There was nothing haphazard about their efforts. The work was well planned and skillfully executed. In the first camp meeting after they entered the Salt Lake Valley, the settlers decided they would not "scatter" their labors, but would combine their efforts and work cooperatively. A kingdom built in any other way would be a fraud—not a Kingdom of God, but a kingdom of the world. Committees were established and each person was assigned a specific task. Brigham Young and other leaders selected a site for the temple and laid out the city. Their goal was to create a special kind of settlement recognizable

The "old" tabernacle on Temple Square was completed in 1851 as a public works project and was used as a meeting hall until the present tabernacle was completed in 1867. The seating capacity of the simple adobe building was 3,000 people. The carved sun on the front of the building has been preserved and may be viewed in the LDS Church Office Building. This drawing appeared in Harper's Weekly, September 18, 1858, and is from a photograph by Burr and Mogo. (Private Collection.)

26

The Gathering Place

as distinctively Mormon. Modeled loosely on Joseph Smith's "Plat of the City of Zion," it had 135 ten-acre blocks, each divided into eight 1.25-acre lots. The intention was that the lots would not be subdivided, but remain intact, with a single house in the center of each lot and set back twenty feet from the street. Houses on opposite sides of the street would not front each other. Lots were designed to be big enough for a garden, a small orchard, and sheds for poultry and livestock, but the main agricultural activity would be outside the city.

Streets were laid out 132 feet wide, with twenty-foot sidewalks on each side. All streets ran north-south or east-west, and each was named for its direction and distance from the temple site. Fourth East Street, for example, was the fourth street east of the temple and ran north and south. Third South Street was the third street south of the temple and ran east and west. Specifying all locations by their relation to the temple not only made for uniformity, but also emphasized the importance of religion in the city, and to both Mormons and others, Salt Lake became "The Temple City." The southern boundary of the original city was Ninth South Street. Beyond it was the "Big Field," laid out in larger parcels. Five-acre lots closest to the city would accommodate "mechanics and artisans." Larger lots of ten, twenty, forty, and eighty acres were for

farmers. A cooperatively built fence, seventeen miles long and eight feet high, would surround the city.

The rapid influx of new settlers soon made it necessary to survey additional streets, blocks, and lots. The original 135-block section was Plat A. In 1848 Plat B, of sixty-three blocks, was laid out to the east. Plat C, with eighty-four blocks, followed in 1849. In addition, new farm tracts were plotted west of the city beyond the Jordan River.

In laying out the original city, Mormon leaders reserved four ten-acre blocks as public squares, reasoning that they would make Salt Lake a better place to live, helping it become a true community and not merely an aggregate of individuals by providing havens from the outside world, psychological and physical resting places, shelter from noise and tension. Streets, in a sense, were thought of as rivers and public squares as natural or artificial lakes.

One of the squares was designated as the site for a temple. On a second block a committee began building a fort of log cabins where settlers would spend their first winter. In the late nineteenth century, it became Pioneer Park and included a swimming pool and a children's playground. A third block was soon known as "Union Square." Mormon immigrants often temporarily camped there before finding more permanent accommodations. Later it was the site of

Brigham Young's estate on South Temple Street included the Beehive and Lion houses, shown here in the 1860s. The Beehive House was a center of social and political activity in the growing Salt Lake Valley. There Brigham Young integrated his activities as territorial governor and president of the Mormon church, entertaining visiting dignitaries and consulting with church leaders. It was also his official residence. His family residence was the Lion House, named for the carved lion atop a front portico. It housed up to twelve of his wives and several dozen of his children. A nine-foot cobblerock wall surrounded the straw-colored adobe complex. (Courtesy Utah State Historical Society.)

The open-air, grass-covered structure in the center right of this 1855 photograph of Temple Square was the Bowery. Built in 1854 with 100 upright timbers and covered with brush and boughs, the structure afforded a place where people gathered, "in questionable comfort," according to one observer, for religious and community meetings. The 1851 adobe tabernacle is to its left. (Private Collection.)

The Council Hall was a $45,000 public works project. A two-story sandstone building located on the southwest corner of Main and South Temple streets, it was used for church, city, county, and territorial offices from 1850 until 1883, when fire destroyed it. (Private Collection.)

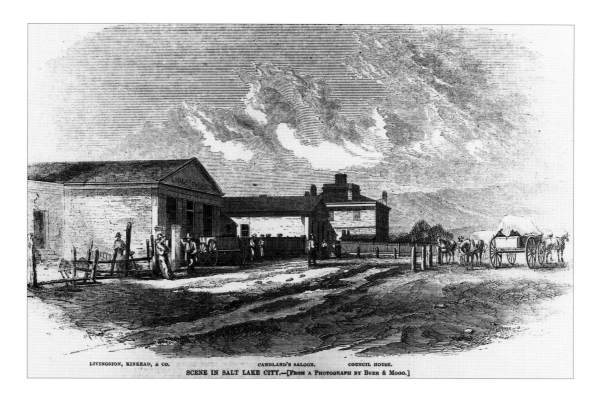

LIVINGSTON, KINKEAD, & CO.   CANDLAND'S SALOON,   COUNCIL HOUSE.
SCENE IN SALT LAKE CITY.—[FROM A PHOTOGRAPH BY BURR & MOGO.]

various educational buildings, first the University of Deseret, and since 1922 West High School. The fourth block also was a camping ground for arriving Mormon immigrants. It was commonly referred to at first as "Emigration Square," and later as "Washington Square." Between 1891 and 1894, the present Salt Lake City and County Building was constructed on it.

While one group built the fort, another planted and irrigated thirty-five acres of land. Within eight days "about three acres of corn was up two inches above ground and beans and potatoes were up and looking well." One group located timber in a nearby canyon, built a road, set up a lumbering operation, and constructed a blacksmith shop, corrals, and a community storehouse. Another group hunted, fished, and extracted salt from the Great Salt Lake. Either their luck or their aim was poor, because in eight days they netted only one rabbit, one badger, a white wolf, three sage hens, and four fish, along with 125 bushels of coarse salt and one barrel of "fine white table salt."

Even in early Salt Lake City there were stubborn individualists, and Lorenzo Dow Young was one of the earliest. He built a cabin inside the fort but before winter set in moved out and began building "a house of hewn logs, of two rooms and hallway between" on South Temple Street where the Beehive

It was not long before traveling merchants seeking to capitalize on the Mormon market began visiting Salt Lake. In 1849 James M. Livingston and Charles A. Kinkead freighted in $20,000 worth of goods and soon had five stores. Demand for their goods was so great that they initially restricted the amount of "factory cloth," sugar, and coffee that any one person could buy. The other buildings shown here in this view of the west side of Main Street between First South and South Temple streets are the post office, Globe Bakery, a barbershop and saloon, and the Council Hall. The litho-graph appeared in Harper's Weekly, *December 4, 1858. (Private Collection.)*

The first Mormons to enter the Salt Lake Valley were quick to provide themselves with shelter. Within a month of their arrival in the summer of 1847, they had built twenty-nine log cabins in the form of a stockade. By fall, when nearly 2,000 people had arrived, 450 cabins were ready. An eight-foot-thick adobe wall surrounded the fort that stood on the block that Pioneer Park now occupies. This drawing shows LDS apostle John Taylor's cabin in the fort in winter 1847. (Private Collection.)

House now is. When church authorities called him on the carpet, he explained that the fort was "low" and an unhealthy place for his pregnant wife, and they were allowed to live outside the fort the first winter. He finished his house on December 23, 1847, the first to be erected on any city lot. The rest of the nearly 2,000 people who had poured into the valley after the arrival of the advance party in July wintered in the fort or in their wagons, with lean-tos built alongside for extra room.

Early on Brigham Young announced the land policy for the new settlement. In order to eliminate land grabbing, speculation, and profiteering, there would be no buying and selling of land. "Each man must keep his lot whole," Young said, "for the Lord has given it to us without price." Land belonged to the community as a whole and would be given to people on the basis of the law of stewardship—"equal according to circumstances, wants, and needs." Unmarried men were not entitled to city lots, while polygamists had a right to separate lots for each of their families. Those who received land were to keep it only as long as they needed and used it. If not put into "productive use," it could be taken from them and given to others.

In the fall of 1847 church leaders were allowed first selection of lots. Most chose ones near the temple block. The allocation of land to the general popu-

lation took place a year later. Church members received their city lots by drawing numbers. Brigham Young and Heber C. Kimball supervised the procedure. The only cost was a surveying and recording fee of $1.50. Farm parcels were allotted in the same way.

Similar principles applied to all natural resources. "Are you not dissatisfied," Brigham Young asked, "and is there not bitterness in your feelings the moment you find a canyon, but in the possession of an individual and power given to him to control the timber, wood, rock, in short all its facilities? Does there not something start up in your breast, that causes you to feel uncomfortable?" Thus, he said, "There shall be no private ownership of the streams that come out of the canyons, nor the timber that grows on the hills. These belong to the people: all the people."

The decision regarding water was particularly crucial. Utah was the only Rocky Mountain state in which agriculture, rather than mining, was the basis of settlement, but in undertaking farming Utah settlers faced a stiff challenge. As geographer Richard H. Jackson points out, the idea that the Salt Lake Valley was a parched desert, barren and God-forsaken, when Mormons first arrived is overstated and emerged only later, in part because Mormons, both consciously and unconsciously, sought to reinforce the idea that because of their special relationship with God they were able to overcome obstacles that other people could not have. Even so, establishing permanent settlements was not easy. Early settlers, though they did not have a chemical analysis, soon dis-

3 1

Defying the Desert,
Establishing the
Kingdom

covered a practical way of assessing the fertility of a piece of land. If the only native vegetation was greasewood, shadscale, or salt grass, they knew the land was not worth farming. Rabbit brush meant better soil. If a healthy crop of sagebrush grew, they could be certain of its fertility. But water, and a lot of it, was necessary to make the soil productive. In order to produce an acre of crops in the Salt Lake Valley, land needed to receive four to five feet of water each crop year. Rainfall would not come close to providing that. Annual precipitation was only about sixteen inches, with a mere three inches of that coming during the summer season. Of necessity, then, Mormons plowed and irrigated. They were not the first to irrigate, of course. Ancient Babylon had flourished with the help of irrigated farming. Irrigation had been successfully practiced in Egypt, India, Spain, and Italy, as well as in some early societies of Central and South America. In the eighteenth century Spanish padres used it at California missions, and Spanish and Mexican settlers in the Rio Grande Valley practiced it in the 1840s. And, as Thomas G. Alexander points out, one reason Mormons understood how to dam streams and channel water in ditches was because Mormon missionaries had seen irrigation in Italy, and members of the Mormon Battalion had watched both Mexicans and Native Americans irrigate in New Mexico and California.

In developing their system of irrigation, Mormons did not rely on private enterprise or individual initiative, but on the united efforts of the entire community. When a group of people needed water, the whole group worked together to build an irrigation system. The local bishop often directed construction, announcing at Sunday meeting what work needed to be done the following week and who was to do it. After the project was finished, people were entitled to use an amount of water proportionate to the work they had put in on the project.

Ironically, the lands that Mormons so efficiently distributed, worked, and irrigated were not legally theirs. When they entered the Salt Lake Valley in 1847, it was still Mexican territory—Utah, in fact, had been a part of another country, either Spain or Mexico, longer than it had been part of the United States, and, as one historian recently pointed out in a discussion of illegal immigration in the present-day United States, the first illegal immigrants to Utah were Mormons. The United States acquired Utah the following year, in 1848, in the Treaty of Guadalupe-Hidalgo, the result of its victory in the Mexican-American War of 1846-48, when Mexico ceded to the United States nearly half of its territory, including areas that are now California, Arizona, New Mexico, Colorado, Nevada, and Utah, and more than 300 years of Spanish or Mexican control of the area ended. A United States federal land office was not established in Utah until 1869, however, and until then Mormons lived in fear that an increasingly hostile U.S. federal government might dispossess them at any time.

When they arrived in the Salt Lake Valley, Mormons intended to make their new community as self-sufficient as possible. Brigham Young stated the policy clearly in an early sermon: "The Kingdom of God cannot rise independent of the gentile nations until we produce, manufacture, and make every article of use, convenience, or necessity among our own people," and Mormons quickly moved to establish grist mills, flour mills, tanneries, and other enterprises necessary to satisfy their most urgent needs. Many were set up at the direction of church authorities. The high council asked Charles Crismon, for example, to build a gristmill on City Creek and set the amount he was to charge for grinding grain. It authorized John Neff to build "a good flour mill," directed Alanson and Ira Eldredge to "engage in the business of tanning and manufacturing leather," and asked Henry G. Sherwood to "build a glass factory as soon as circumstances will permit."

The first winter in the Salt Lake Valley was mild. The winter of 1848-49, however, was another story. It set in early and severe. Snowstorms were fre-

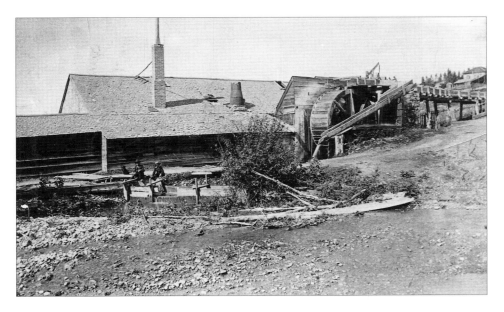

Brigham Young's gristmill was located on City Creek at North Temple and State streets. Erected in the early 1850s, it was used to grind grains and generate power for the church's blacksmith shop, located just to the east of the mill. The blacksmith shop was responsible for keeping all the tools used in the church's numerous public works projects in repair, especially during construction of the Salt Lake temple. (Courtesy Utah State Historical Society.)

Faithful Mormons brought one-tenth of their "increase" to the Deseret Store each year as tithing. Initially chickens, eggs, cattle, vegetables, cloth, and other "in kind" payments were accepted and either stored or exchanged for other goods. Early on the Tithing Office and the Deseret News both occupied this building at the northeast corner of Main and South Temple streets, where the Joseph Smith Memorial Building (formerly the Hotel Utah), now stands, across from Temple Square. (Courtesy Nelson Wadsworth.)

quent from the beginning of December through the end of February. As late as February 5, the temperature dropped to one degree below zero. No one starved, but many people were reduced to eating rawhide, sego-lily roots, and thistles. "I used to eat thistle stalks," one settler remembered, "until my stomach would be as full as a cow's." Again Mormons dealt with the situation cooperatively, rather than individually. The first step was the establishment of a community cattle and sheep herd. When some people objected that they did not want their animals included in a common herd, Brigham Young's response was characteristically blunt: "Natural feelings would say let them & their cattle go to Hell, but duty says if they will not take care of their cattle, we must do it for them. We are to be saviours of men in these last days."

In early February a committee appointed to investigate the food supply reported the availability of perhaps three-quarters of a pound of foodstuffs per person per day until harvest time, five months away. Several steps were taken to cope with the situation. Church authorities passed a regulation prohibiting the use of corn to make whiskey. Any intended for that purpose were to be "taken and given to the poor." They appointed a tax collector with power to

take from the "rich and penurious" and give to the needy. A voluntary ration-
ing and community storehouse system was set up. All those with a surplus were
asked to turn it over to their bishop so that it could be divided among those in
need. Again Brigham Young wasted no words. "If those that have do not sell to
those that have not, we will just take it and distribute it among the Poors," he
said, "and those that have and will not share willingly may be thankful that
their Heads are not found wallowing in the Snow."

In important ways, white settlement of Utah was different than that of
other areas of the United States. From the first, Utah was intended to be "a
world apart," established, as Charles S. Peterson says, "by the Children of God
who had been thrust from the Garden into the hard, cruel world and charged
to rebuild it," and in rebuilding it they worked on the assumption that people
were only stewards over their material possessions. Property rights were not
absolute, but a collective trust to be used for "the glory of God and the relief of
man's estate." Property and human effort had one purpose: the establishment
of Zion. Rejecting what some historians have called the "helter-skelter individualism" of other pioneers, Mormons sought to demonstrate to themselves,
and to the world, the virtues of a cooperative society.

～

Recommended Readings

Alley, John R., Jr. "Prelude to Dispossession: The Fur Trade's Significance for the
    Northern Utes and Southern Paiutes." *Utah Historical Quarterly* 50 (Spring
    1982): 104-23. Reprinted in McCormick and Sillito, eds., *A World We Thought
    We Knew*, 18-33.

Arrington, Leonard J. *Great Basin Kingdom*, Chap. 1: "Early Economic Experiences of
    the Latter-day Saints," and Chap. 2: "A New World."

Campbell, Eugene E. *Establishing Zion: The Mormon Church in the American West,
    1847-1869*. Salt Lake City: Signature Books, 1988.

Carter, Thomas. "Folk Design in Utah Architecture, 1849-1890." In Carter, Thomas,
    ed. *Images of an American Land: Vernacular Architecture in the Western United
    States*. Albuquerque: University of New Mexico Press, 1997.

Janetski, Joel. "150 Years of Utah Archaeology." *Utah Historical Quarterly* 65 (Spring
    1997): 100-33.

Kelen, Leslie G., and Susec, David. *Sacred Images: A Vision of Native American Rock
    Art*. Layton, UT: Gibbs Smith, Publisher, 1996.

Chapter 3

THE FIRST GENERATION

Mormons intended that Salt Lake City be a community devoted to God and organized to carrying out his will. They sought to create a self-sufficient, cooperative, egalitarian, and authoritarian society, one dedicated, as Christopher Lasch says, "not to individual enrichment but to the collective well-being of the flock." Though they never completely achieved their goal, for the first twenty years or so they came close, accomplishing, as Leonard J. Arrington points out, impressive feats of planning and development without generating the inequalities associated elsewhere with industrial progress and without even developing a money economy. Through the 1850s and 1860s, Salt Lake City was a closely woven fabric with only a few broken threads. Until the 1870s the city's population was more than 90 percent Mormon, and the Mormon church dominated every aspect of life. It directed the physical movements of its people, managed economic affairs, controlled politics, and exercised a decisive influence over marriage and family relations. As Dale Morgan says, the hand of the Mormon church was "ever active and ever present." Utah filmmaker Trent Harris says all of this in a somewhat different way. For him, Salt Lake City "was settled by a seriously radical bunch of people. They practiced polygamy, they had their own form of money, they had their own alphabet, they had their own army. They followed an early form of communism called the United Order. ... This place was wild."

From its beginnings the Mormon church had an extensive proselyting

Missionary efforts to convert people to Mormonism began as soon as the church was founded, and by 1850 Mormonism had spread throughout the United States, Canada, and Europe. Over 400 missionaries left Salt Lake between 1855 and 1864, and in large part because of their success, the city's population doubled every ten years. In 1850 approximately 6,000 people lived in the city, while by 1890 the population was officially 44,843. This photograph shows Elders A. T. Rose and G. M. Fryer in Mississippi in 1897. Their Prince Albert coats, derbies, umbrellas, and satchels were standard for missionaries at the time. (Courtesy Utah State Historical Society.)

program in both the United States and other countries, and church leaders advised new members not to live scattered around the world but instead to "gather" together in Zion where, as Richard L. Bushman says, "divine intelligence would illuminate their lives and make them into saints," and they would find refuge from the apocalyptic destruction that would precede the return of Christ. During Salt Lake's first generation, and for many years afterward, Mormon leaders brought thousands of converts to the city, drawing them from the eastern United States and Europe and then redistributing them throughout the West. "Come to the place of gathering," the church's First Presidency urged in 1852, "even in flocks, as doves fly to their windows before a storm." Salt Lake City became that gathering place, as Nauvoo, Illinois, had before it.

During the nineteenth century more than 100,000 Mormon converts from other countries arrived in Salt Lake City. Though some remained, most settled in other parts of the state. Of the 100,000, more than 50,000 were from

The First
Generation

In an attempt to unify a group that included many members who did not speak English, the Mormon church created its own phonetic Deseret Alphabet for English sounds. Brigham Young wanted a written language that everyone, no matter what language they spoke, could understand. The idea occurred to him as early as 1845, but was not seriously pursued until the 1850s, and nothing was published until 1868 when two primers appeared. The next year all of The Book of Mormon was printed in the Deseret Alphabet, but it gained little acceptance and soon fell into disuse. (Private Collection.)

the British Isles and another 30,000 from Scandinavia. Most of the others came from Canada and Western Europe, mainly Germany and Switzerland. Of those from the British Isles, the vast majority were from England, with fewer from Wales and Scotland and only a handful from Ireland. Most of the Scandinavian immigrants came from Denmark and southern Sweden.

Though they were from all walks of life, they fell mainly into three groups: farmers; artisans and craftsmen; and unskilled laborers. Mormon leaders often encouraged the immigration of people with certain skills deemed necessary at a particular time to help build the Kingdom. Thus in 1849 missionaries to the British Isles were instructed to search out "blowers, moulders and all kinds of furnace operators to immediately immigrate to the valley without delay," and in 1852 church leaders specifically asked for iron workers, potters, woolen workers, comb makers, millers, and coal miners, saying, "These are to immigrate immediately in preference to anyone else."

Most converts came, not as individuals, but as members of family groups, and they came under church sponsorship and supervision. A Perpetual Emigrating Fund provided loans to those who needed them. Liverpool, England, was the central embarkation point where converts awaited space on chartered ships. Once on board, each group had a leader who supervised every detail of their lives, from the assignment of sleeping quarters and the preparation of meals to the direction of social activities and the conduct of religious services. When immigrants reached the United States, agents of the church met them and arranged for the overland journey to Utah, providing them with teams and wagons, instructions in overland travel, and often an experienced Mormon guide. Until the early 1850s, a relief train met each company half way to Salt Lake. After that outfitting posts were established in Wyoming.

New arrivals in the city commonly camped for a few days on either Union Square, the present site of West High School, or Emigration Square, later the site of the City and County Building. The arrival of an immigrant train was often a festive event. Church authorities assigned city residents from various countries to greet their countrymen and women. Tents were set up in advance. Brass bands played. Flags waved. Children sang hymns. Brigham Young or other church leaders welcomed them. Medical aid was available to those who needed it. Food was provided. According to an 1864 *Deseret News* account, "Immediately on the arrival of the train, the bretheren and sisters came forward with soup, beef, potatoes, pies, tea, sugar, and coffee to supply the wants of those who had just come in from their long and tedious journey across the plains." One effect of this kind of reception was to confirm the sense of gathering for both new arrivals and old residents, demonstrating to every faithful Mormon that Zion was growing and soon would be delivered from its enemies.

During the years that it served as a camping ground for newly arriving Mormon immigrants, the land surrounding the present City and County Building was also a temporary camp ground for overland travellers passing through Salt Lake on their way to the West Coast. During the summer of 1862, for example, according to the *Deseret News*, "Emigration Square has presented an animated moving tableau during the past week. Trains coming and going, emigrants moving in and moving out, in large numbers, have presented a miniature of a little world with ever-changing faces and objects." Soon the square would serve other purposes. Beginning in the 1870s, it was one of the city's main athletic grounds. The primary sport was baseball, but there were also cricket, lacrosse, track and field meets, and special events, including a "Grand English and Cornish Wrestling Tournament" in July 1884. It was also Salt Lake's circus grounds beginning in 1869 when circuses began coming regularly to Utah, sometimes two or three a season, including "Montgomery's Mammoth Circus, Menagerie, and Travelling World's Fair" in 1874 and "W. W. Cole's Great Concorporation of Circus, Menagerie, Aquarium, and Congress of Living Wonders" in 1880. The square was also the location of many 4th of July celebrations until construction of the City and County Building began in 1891.

Immigrants who arrived in Salt Lake City in the fall of the year were often placed in various LDS wards for "wintering," each bishop specifying the number of families his ward could take care of and the particular skills the ward needed in its new members. Once settled, people were subject to a variety of callings from church leaders. They might be asked to help build a new meetinghouse or public building, send a wagon and supplies to aid new immigrants, fill a church position, or serve a proselyting mission. They might also be "called" to colonize a new part of Utah as, even before Salt Lake City was firmly established, Mormons began systematic exploration and colonization of the surrounding area. In order to build a commonwealth to guarantee them permanent security, they intended to settle everywhere they could as quickly as possible, and Salt Lake became the center for launching vigorous expansion into every inhabitable region of present-day Utah, as well as parts of Nevada, Arizona, Oregon, Wyoming, Colorado, New Mexico, Idaho, and California. In the first ten years, nearly 100 cities and towns were founded, and, by the end of the nineteenth century, more than 500.

"Calls" to colonize were direct and personal. Brigham Young either took people aside or announced at general conference, held twice yearly, the names of those who were requested to sell their belongings and take their families to settle a pre-selected area, according to God's direction. As Dale Morgan said, "This group from Denmark should go to the Sanpete Valley, where they would feel at home in the considerable Scandinavian colony already established there. These Swiss would go to the Rio Virgin Valley, where they too would feel at home. This brother should go to Fillmore, where good blacksmiths were

40

The Gathering Place

This portrait of two "Utah Indian Girls" was taken by Charles Ellis Johnson in his Salt Lake City studio. (Courtesy Nelson Wadsworth.)

much needed now. This sister should go to St. George, where her knowledge of cotton growing perhaps could find a field of abundant usefulness."

People might be called several times during their lives. They might have helped to make the desert blossom in one part of Zion, but if their services were needed to build the Kingdom elsewhere, Brigham Young did not hesitate to call them again, and, since the calls came from God, they were viewed as a religious duty and a test of faith, and most people accepted them, whatever the sacrifice, though, according to one observer, "Not all such calls were joyfully received." John D. Lee recalled that "I was called upon by Pres. B. Young to accompany Bro. G. A. Smith to Iron County. I replied that I was willing to help build up Zion in any way that the Lord asked. But to go to Iron County was revolting to my feelings and if I could do as much good by paying $2000 I would sooner do that than go. Pres. Young said that to make a settlement in Southern Utah was one of the most important things to be done and Brother Smith wants you to go with him, and so do I. I consented, leaving house uncovered and my business unsettled." Writing in his diary of his call in 1861 to help settle St. George, John Pulsipher said, "This news was very unexpected to me ... for I had a good home, well satisfied, and had plenty to do. But when the Apostle George A. Smith told me I was selected to go, I saw the importance of the mission to sustain Israel in the Mountains. ... We go with joy, leaving our happy home, which had cost about four years of hard work and just getting a farm into cultivation that would produce enough in one year to last us half a dozen."

For Mormons the colonization of Utah was a great success. By 1860 they numbered more than 40,000 and had founded more than 100 towns in fifteen counties in virtually every part of the territory. For Native Americans, however, it was another story. Mormon success came at their expense. For them it was a disaster, and they felt the impact immediately. As Kathryn L. MacKay and Larry Cesspooch observe, "The intruders carried childhood diseases, such as measles, whooping cough, and smallpox, which came to kill ninety percent of the peoples of the Americas—who had no immunities to these microbes. During the first winter the Mormon settlers spent in *Nuche* country, measles spread quickly among the *Nuche* who visited them. The Mormons buried thirty-six *Nuche* in one grave alone." According to Howard Christy, "The Indians, especially the Utes, declined rapidly as a result of extreme poverty brought on by usurpation of their lands, selective extermination, disease, and starvation." In 1860 one resident of Sanpete County reported that "the aborigines in this part of the Territory seem to be wasting away very fast, and the band ... has dwindled down to a mere handful of warriors," while Sanpete Indians themselves estimated that half of their children died in infancy and only one-fourth reached adulthood. In his important study, *Utah's Black Hawk War*, John A. Peterson estimates that by 1865, less than twenty years after the Mormon settlement of Utah began, "the Indians of Utah were probably outnumbered at a ratio of at least ten to one." According to the 1900 U.S. Census, the Native American population of Utah was 2,623—a decline of at least 90 percent during the preceding fifty years since white settlement of Utah began.

It could hardly have been otherwise. According to John A. Peterson, Brigham Young's policy was "to establish settlements on all rivers and streams throughout a tremendously large area and, by thus gaining control of important water resources in a semiarid region, he hoped to keep gentiles out and establish a huge empire where his people could practice their religion in peace. Unfortunately for the Indians, however, the very spots where Young placed settlements, often rich alluvial plains where rivers exited canyons, were the most productive components of the ecosystems upon which they depended for subsistence." As David Madsen points out, "All of Utah's towns sit on archaeological sites. This means that almost every town in Utah today is in a place where Indian people were living when the new settlers came." And, correspondingly, almost every present-day Utah town is a site from which Native Americans were displaced.

When Mormons first arrived in the Salt Lake Valley, both Utes and Shoshonis claimed it, but neither held it securely, and Mormons were thus able to begin their first settlement with little impact on Native Americans and little opposition from them. Once Mormons began expanding beyond the Salt Lake Valley, however, that changed. Their move south into Utah Valley in 1849 put them in the midst of the single most important Northern Ute settlement, a major trade crossroads, and an annual gathering place for all of the Ute bands for 200 miles to the east and south. Displaced from their lands, Utes fought back. Brigham Young countered with an iron fist, ordering a "selective extermination campaign" against Utah Valley Indians. As Linda Sillitoe says, it was "an eerie echo of a Missouri governor's extermination order against Mormons." The men were all to be killed, while the women and children would be spared if they "behaved" themselves. In February 1850 a militia force rode from Salt Lake and laid siege to a group of about seventy Utes led by Old Elk and Stick-in-Head. After two days of fighting, the Indians retreated. Some of them fled up Rock Canyon, where most of them died of wounds, exposure, or their old enemy, measles. The main group travelled south and, with their families, surrendered to the militia.

The next morning twenty-nine Ute men were killed in a confrontation on the ice at the south end of Utah Lake, and the remaining women and children were taken prisoner. The best estimates are that only thirteen of the seventy or eighty male Utes who had engaged in the Utah Valley battle survived. One Ute warrior, An-kar-tewets, and several dozen women and children were temporarily confined at Fort Utah until the following spring when they were taken to Salt Lake City to learn the "arts of civilization." According to John A. Peterson, "Some of them soon died, however, only intensifying native torment.

Charles R. Savage took this photograph in July 1866 on the day these men returned from fighting in the Black Hawk War. They were identified, from left to right, beginning at the back, as Alma Pratt, Conrad Wilkinson, William B. Dougall, William Goforth, Solomon F. Kimball, Jasper Conrad, Henry Snell, and Edward D. Woolley, Jr. The photograph appeared in the Mormon church's Improvement Era, *September 1908.* (Private Collection.)

44

The Gathering Place

Within months, most of the survivors had slipped away one by one to carry their bitterness to their people." The extermination policy continued for another year, when, as Peterson says, "a final and gruesome indignity occurred." Dr. James Blake, a non-Mormon army surgeon who was in Utah with Captain Howard Stansbury's expedition, commissioned several Mormons to return to the battlefields to decapitate the corpses that still lay frozen in the snow. Abner Blackburn wrote an account of the affair: "A few days after the last batle with the Indians, a government surgeon wanted James Or and me to take a sley [and] cross over on the ice and secure the Indians heads, for he wanted to send them to Washington to a medical institution. [We] hired a sley [and] crost over the ice. The weather was bitter cold. The surgeon to[o]k out his box of instruments and comenced. It took him a quarter of an hour to cut off one head. The sun was getting low and [it was] frezing cold. Jim and me took the job in our own hands. We were not going to wait on the surgeons slow motion. Jerked our knives out and had them all off in a few minutes. They were frozen and come off easy in our fassion. The surgeon stood back and watched us finish the job." According to Peterson, forty or fifty heads "were boxed up and taken to the fort, where they were openly viewed as curiosities by the settlers. Before the grisly contents of the boxes could be delivered to the doctor in Salt Lake City, however, 'the weather turned warm' and 'the indian heads smelt loud' and turned 'green with rot.'"

The situation was essentially repeated wherever Mormons expanded, in the process turning Indian lands into townsites, grazing fields, farm land, and graveyards, and Utah during the 1850s and 1860s might be characterized as a "dark and bloody ground." The major conflicts were the Walker War of 1853-54, the Tintic War of 1856, the Black Hawk War of 1865-72, which took place mainly in Sanpete and Sevier counties and revolved around Indian subsistence raiding to avoid starvation, and the Battle of Bear River, also known as the Bear River Massacre, where, on a cold January day in 1863, Colonel Patrick Connor's U.S. Army force attacked and destroyed a Shoshoni village and killed over 240 men, women, and children—more than died in any other single white/Indian confrontation in the United States in the last half of the nineteenth century.

For Native Americans in Utah, the result by the late nineteenth century, as Mormon leader Jacob Hamblin said in 1880, was that "the watering places are all occupied by the white man. The grass that produc[es] mutch seed is all et out. The sunflowere seed is destroyed in fact thare is nothing for them to depend upon but beg or starve." Sowiette was the head chief of the Northern Utes. His name meant "Man That Picks Fish From the Water," but by 1865 he was telling whites that it meant "Nearly Starved." The history of the white/Indian experience in Utah, in other words, was much the same as it was elsewhere in the United States. Like other Americans, Mormons were so confident of their own way of life that they felt comfortable in imposing it on others. Several points Jill Lepore makes about the Puritan settlers of New England apply to early Mormon settlers of Utah as well: they paid little attention to the reasons Indians had for fighting back, and one of the most disheartening experiences for them following their arrival in Utah was that Indians did not immediately recognize their presumed superiority. Like the Puritans who declared

Massachusetts legally a vacuum, even though thousands of Algonquians, Abnakis, Wampanoags, and Pawtuckets lived there, Mormon settlers were intruders who encroached on Native American lands. Indians, once they realized the extent and impact of the white presence, resisted. Conflict ensued, and Native Americans were ultimately defeated. In part the story was one of "contact, conflict, and conquest." As Eugene E. Campbell says, "On the frontier Mormons acted much like other Americans in the east and south: they occupied Indian land, killed resisters, and called upon the federal government to remove Indians to another part of the region."

The last half of the nineteenth century, then, was a time of dramatic change in the lives of Utah's Native Americans. Much of the world they inhabited changed before their eyes as they encountered a people who arrived with a formula for civilizing them and who felt they had a perfect right to invade their land because they saw Indians as savage, primitive, backward people and, as such, obstacles to progress who would either become civilized by adopting Mormon ways or die. According to Apostle John Taylor, who would become the church's third president, when Mormons came to Utah, they settled "among the red savages of the forest. We had no fields to go to and no houses built; when we went there it was a desert—a howling wilderness, and the natives with which we were surrounded were as savage as the country itself." Given such attitudes, faced with an unending flood of people to their lands, and under the onslaught of war and disease, Native American numbers dwindled. Their old ways of life were destroyed, new ways were imposed, and their lands passed into non-Indian hands. One people's expansion entailed another's dispossession. Extending one way of life meant destroying another.

The full story is a complex one, and historians are just beginning to tell it. It is central to Utah's history, however, and not merely a subplot in a larger epic, marginal to the main story—though it is often thought of in that way, with the actions and experiences of Native Americans receiving minimal attention. Yet, as John A. Peterson suggests, writing specifically about the Black Hawk War, Black Hawk (Antonga), Mountain, Sanpitch, Tamaritz, Tabby, Kanosh, and Sowiette influenced the flow of events in early Utah as profoundly as did Brigham Young, Daniel H. Wells, and Patrick E. Connor, and are as deserving of our attention. It is a story in which Native Americans were not merely passive victims, but agents in their own behalf, responding in the range of ways available to them. They made their own history, though, as with all people, as Karl Marx pointed out, they did so under circumstances not of their own choosing. As Patricia Nelson Limerick says, rather than only victims, it is more helpful for historians to see Native Americans as actors in a complex world of narrowing circumstances and then to ask certain questions: What were the challenges facing them as other people moved onto their land? What did they try to do to get the best they could out of a bad bargain? What strategies did they adopt and why? What were the results? Those who lived through and participated in the changes saw things in their own way. Their views were sometimes different from those of white Americans at the time and from what white Americans today might expect them to be. They varied according to time, circumstance, tribe, place, gender, and individual experiences and character, but taken together their views give us an idea of what it meant to live on the other side of the frontier and be subject to "civilization."

During Salt Lake City's first generation, Mormons clearly exhibited an extraordinary willingness to do whatever church leaders directed. In addition to the process of immigration and colonization, that willingness was clearly evident in one of the most dramatic episodes in Salt Lake City's history, the Utah War. On July 24, 1857, while celebrating the tenth anniversary of the city's founding, Brigham Young received word that president of the United States James Buchanan had ordered the largest peacetime army in the nation's history to put down what he took to be a Mormon "rebellion" in Utah and replace Young with a non-Mormon governor. Eventually a peaceful compromise was reached, but not before Mormon leaders had mobilized their people in far-reaching ways. Church leaders called all missionaries back to Utah; directed settlers in outlying areas to leave their houses and move to the central valleys of Utah; and sent a force of men eastward to delay the approaching army by raiding its supply trains, driving off its livestock, and burning the grass before it. Finally, while peace negotiations were still in progress, Brigham Young ordered the "Move South," directing that the entire northern part of the state, including Salt Lake City, be abandoned. Everyone living north of Utah Valley was to retreat to one of several areas in southern Utah. Whether or not they returned would depend on what the army did.

The Move South began in March 1858 and took about two months to complete. According to one report, an average of 600 wagons passed through

Salt Lake City each day during the first two weeks of May. In all, 30,000 people joined the rush, packing their belongings, loading their wagons, and leaving dried straw and kindling in the doorways of their houses. According to Brigham Young, "There shall not be one building, nor one foot of lumber, nor a stick, nor a tree, nor a particle of grass and hay that will burn, left in reach of our enemies." When the army marched through Salt Lake on June 26, 1858, the city was almost entirely deserted. Only a few men were left, with orders to "fire" the city in case the army went back on its pledge not to occupy it. According to one officer, "every man, woman, and child had, under the direction of the prophet departed—fled! ... It was substantially a city of the dead, and might have been depopulated by a pest or famine."

The Utah War ended without bloodshed. President Buchanan granted Mormons a "free and full pardon." Troops occupied no Utah towns, but instead established Camp Floyd, forty miles to the southwest of Salt Lake, and on June 30 Brigham Young declared, "All who wish to return to their homes in Great Salt Lake City are at liberty to do so."

The Mormon church took the lead in economic as well as political affairs in Salt Lake City, organizing the economy so that all activities contributed to the goal of building the Kingdom. Church leaders saw to it that every business or industry established was one that the community needed and that would work in the interest of the whole, not just of private individuals. As J. Kenneth Davies says, the goal was "the establishment of a self-sufficient, highly diversified, centrally directed economy separate from that of the nation ... not based on private ownership and direction but on a combination of private, state, and Church ownership—with Church direction. The distribution of the goods produced was to be more or less on the basis of equality and need. ... Profits, if any, were to be used to build up the Kingdom, not to enhance personal worth. ... There was to be no accommodation to the economic system of the world." Thus, four months after arriving in the valley, church authorities appointed a committee "to regulate the price of grinding and all things worthy of note." In 1849 the prices mill owners charged were made "subject to the order of the bishops." Beginning in 1859 church leaders discouraged the importation of "luxury" goods, including tea, coffee, tobacco, and liquor, and encouraged local production of all items. "We can produce them or do without them," Brigham Young said. As part of the effort toward self-sufficiency, a program of

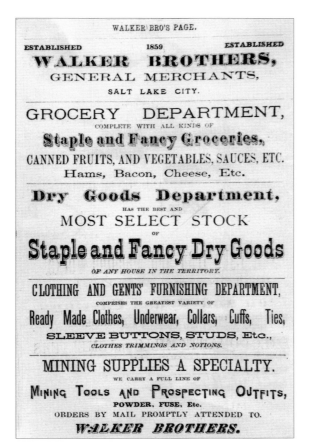

The four Walker brothers—Samuel Sharp, Joseph Robinson, David Frederick, and Mathew Henry ("Sharp," "Rob," "Fred," and "Matt")—opened a general store in 1859 in Fairfield, Utah, where the U.S. Army had established Camp Floyd during the 1857-58 Utah War. They soon added a banking section. Both did so well that they opened a store in Salt Lake City the next year where it quickly became one of the city's most successful, and the brothers were soon among Salt Lake's prominent residents. This advertisement is from the late nineteenth century. (Private Collection.)

industrial development was undertaken. In Salt Lake City the Deseret Pottery Factory was established, paper mills were set up to produce paper for the *Deseret News*, a sugar factory was begun, after which the Sugarhouse area took its name, and a cotton factory and a woolen mill were established. An effort was even made to produce silk. In 1864 the church fixed prices of agricultural products to prevent Mormon farmers from undercutting each other when they sold to mining and military camps, and in 1866 church leaders called for a boycott of non-Mormon merchants. Two years later it formed Zion's Cooperative Mercantile Institution (ZCMI) as a way of lowering prices and driving non-Mormons out of business.

Salt Lake City also had an extensive public works program. Organized in 1850, with Daniel H. Wells as superintendent, it was established to construct public and church buildings and to initiate enterprises not profitable for pri-

Jenkins and Sons' Saddle and Harness shop, 78 East 200 South, was one of Salt Lake's earliest businesses. Founded in 1855, it made harnesses, whips, saddles, and other leather goods, helping to supply the Salt Lake Valley with necessities that otherwise would have had to be freighted in. (Courtesy Utah State Historical Society.)

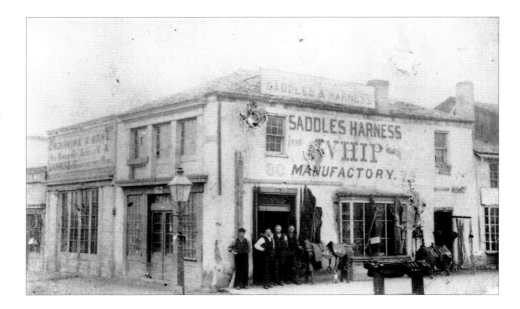

Some people travelled more than 100 miles to witness the dedication of the Mormon tabernacle on Temple Square in August 1867. For two years as many as fifty men worked on the exterior for salaries of $2.00 to $3.50 a day. The 80-foot high, 250-foot long wooden roof was self-supporting. A bridgework of arches was held together with wooden pegs, split open at the ends with a permanent wedge driven into them. Wherever timbers cracked from stress, they were wrapped with green rawhide, since it contracted when it dried. (Private Collection.)

vate individuals to undertake. Its headquarters, on the northeast corner of the temple block, contained carpenter, paint, stonecutting, and blacksmith shops. An adobe yard was nearby, and a lime kiln was established at the mouth of one of the nearby canyons. Within a few years, a machine shop, foundry, and nail factory were also in operation.

The public works program usually employed between 200 and 500 people and on occasion more than 1,000. A wide variety of projects was undertaken, including construction of the Council House, completed in 1855 on the southwest corner of Main and South Temple streets and used for a variety of purposes, such as Mormon church services and sessions of the territorial legislature; the Old Tabernacle, 1851; the Endowment House, 1855; a public bath house near the northern limits of the city on the site where the city- owned Wasatch Springs later was and the Children's Museum now is; the General Tithing Office and Bishop's Storehouse, site of what is now the Joseph Smith Memorial Building, formerly the Hotel Utah; the Salt Lake Theatre; a store for Livingston and Kinkead, the first merchants in Salt Lake; a wall around the temple block and the beginning of a wall around the entire city; an official resi-

The east side of Main Street remained a residential area longer than the west side, but by the 1860s businesses began springing up on it. Extending south of Daniel H. Wells's house on the southeast corner of South Temple and Main, at the far left of this photograph, were a millinery shop, telegraph office, liquor store, and two dry goods and grocery stores. In 1876 the ZCMI building, with its impressive brick and iron façade, was erected in their place. (Private Collection.)

The Salt Lake Theatre opened in March 1862 on the northwest corner of State Street and First South. It was razed in 1928. Though the exterior was relatively plain, the interior, particularly after an 1873 renovation, strove for the elegance of a European opera house and seated an estimated 1,500 people. The painting at the rear of the stage in this photograph was by Alfred Lambourne. (Courtesy Utah State Historical Society.)

dence for Brigham Young; private houses for other church leaders; and several schoolhouses.

The Mormon church dominated political affairs in Salt Lake City during its first generation even more than it did economic matters. As one observer said, what existed was "the politics of unanimity." Until 1870 neither local nor national political parties existed in Utah. Only one set of candidates appeared on the ballot. Church authorities had often selected them, and no candidates were elected in Salt Lake without church approval until 1890 when, for the first time in the city's history, non-Mormons were elected as mayor and city councilmen. Voting was limited to "yes" or "no." The "marked ballot" system was used—each ballot was numbered and the number was recorded in the registry next to the voter's name. A *Deseret News* editorial on January 29, 1878, while denying that marked ballots had been used to identify or ostracize

Brigham Young encouraged the development of iron manufacturing. The Silver Brothers Iron Works Co. began in 1866 and was Salt Lake's earliest pioneer foundry. Specializing in castings, they did the iron work for the McCornick block, still standing at 74 South Main Street, the Templeton Hotel, and the bronze oxen, shown here, for the Salt Lake LDS temple. (Courtesy Utah State Historical Society.)

those who voted against church candidates, went on to say that "while no one should be injured in consequence of his breaking loose from his associates and joining with those who oppose them, it cannot be expected that the dissenter will receive as much cordial friendship, countenance and support from his former fellow-partisans as those who remain in accord with them." In effect, the electoral process was seen as the equivalent of the Mormon church practice of regularly "sustaining" its general authorities. Brigham Young made this clear in 1847, saying, "It is the right of the Twelve to nominate the officers and the people to receive them." The theory behind such political practices was that civil government was an arm of the church with specific functions to perform, and the rights of voters were limited to consent. As Parley P. Pratt said in 1844, before Mormons arrived in Utah, "The voice of the people is rather a sanction, a strength, and support to that which God chooses. They do not confer the authority in the first place, nor can they take it away." George A. Smith said he supported a political system in which "the voice of the people consent to the voice of God." Opposition was a tool of the devil that would destroy orderly government. Political parties brought discord, self-interest, and corruption.

During Salt Lake City's early years, the Mormon church directed not only immigration and colonization, as well as economic, political, and social

The First
Generation

affairs, but through its advocacy of plural marriage, or polygamy, as the ideal marital arrangement also influenced the most intimate of personal relationships. ("Polygamy" is an umbrella term, embracing both "polygyny"—one husband with multiple wives—and "polyandry"—one wife with multiple husbands. Mormons practiced polygyny, but most people then and since have referred to it as polygamy.) The practice outraged nineteenth-century Americans, and criticism was widespread and intense. Virtually everyone was opposed to it. As Patricia Nelson Limerick says, "The idea of one man in possession of more than one woman would strike most non-Mormon Americans as deviant, licentious, and *very* interesting—a shocking matter of sexual excess." Government officials, politicians of both major political parties, private citizens, journalists, ministers, women's groups, and people scattered across the political, social, and religious spectrum denounced it as an immoral and corrupt institution. In 1856 the newly formed Republican Party described black slavery and polygamy as "the twin relics of barbarism" and promised to abolish each of them. Utah had both, and after the Civil War, when the first relic had been destroyed, at least officially, attacks on Mormon polygamy intensified, and it came to be characterized as a menace to everything Americans held sacred. Much of the criticism was lurid and sensational, written by journalists out to produce stories that would sell, but many critics were sincere reformers seeking to expose what they regarded as a great moral evil. Whether sincere or opportunistic, however, the thrust of the criticism was that polygamy was an oppressive and dehumanizing system that both victimized women and posed a grave threat to American society. It was based on neither romantic love nor tender sentiment, but on lust. Under it women were treated as sexual objects subject to a man's bidding. Moreover, they were physically exploited, just as African-American slaves had been. One motive for taking a plural wife, it was asserted, was to reduce one's own workload. Each time a man married he was in effect hiring another laborer to work for him. Plural wives were thus seen as essentially slaves, and the parallel was explicitly drawn between black slaves in the South and Mormon women. But, it was argued, unlike blacks, Mormon women were complicit in their own enslavement because they could have chosen not to enter into plural marriages. Thus, as Sarah Barringer Gordon points out, for antipolygamists of all kinds, polygamy was dangerous because it

54

The Gathering Place

was fundamentally at odds with liberty—a clear illustration that freedom to choose could be negated by wrong choices.

Mormons responded to these criticisms in a number of ways, pointing out that Old Testament prophets practiced polygamy; that a man could love more than one woman just as he could love more than one child; that polygamy allowed women who might not otherwise marry the chance to be wives and mothers; that it led to a reduction in prostitution and other forms of immorality; and that it meant fewer divorces. This latter claim was undercut by the fact that in 1852 the Utah territorial legislature passed the most permissive divorce statute in the country, allowing a judge to grant a divorce "when it shall be made to appear to the satisfaction and conviction of the court, that the parties cannot live in peace and union together, and that their welfare requires a separation." As Sarah Barringer Gordon says, "Indeed, divorce was more common among nineteenth-century Mormons in Utah than among residents of other jurisdictions in the United States. ... the rate of divorce in Utah was extraordinarily high." In 1870 Utah had the second highest divorce rate in the United States at one divorce for every 185 marriages, while the national average was one divorce per 664 marriages. In 1880 Utah's divorce rate was the tenth highest in the country and twice the national average.

Whatever else they said, however, Mormons' essential point in defending polygamy was that it was a commandment from God. It was not just something they had chosen to do, but something God, in a revelation to Joseph Smith recorded in July 1843, had ordered them to practice (though it was not publicly acknowledged until August 1852), and for that reason, Mormons had little doubt as to its future. According to Brigham Young in 1852, polygamy "will sail over and ride triumphantly above all the prejudice and priestcraft of the day; it will be fostered and believed in by the more intelligent portions of the world, as one of the best doctrines ever proclaimed to any people."

Among polygamy's strongest defenders were Mormon women. As Patricia Nelson Limerick says, "From time to time, Mormon women held meetings to declare their loyalty to the institution of polygamy. At one such meeting, 'for nearly three hours one speaker after another defended polygamy, all believing it to be an important doctrine, given by God to aid in redeeming a sinful world from a condition of sin and pollution to one of holiness and purity.'" According to Sarah D. Rich, "Many may think it very strange that I would consent for my dear husband, whom I loved as I did my own life, and lived with him for many years, to take more wives. This I could not have done if I had not believed it to be right in the sight of God, and believed it to be one principle of His gospel once again restored to earth, that those holding the priesthood of heaven might by obeying this order attain to a higher glory in the eternal world." In 1884 Helen Mar Kimball Whitney, a daughter of Mormon apostle Heber C. Kimball, and a plural wife first of Joseph Smith and later of Apostle Horace K. Whitney, published a pamphlet entitled *Why We Practice Plural Marriage*. Polygamy, she said, had allowed her to be a mother, and she extolled the rewards of motherhood. She also attacked the sinfulness of the world, in particular birth control, adultery, and prostitution, saying that polygamy was a way to avoid such evils, and she maintained that the sacrifice polygamy required had made her a better person. Even so, polygamy was clearly difficult for her, as it was for others, and it seems fair to say that, in general, Mormon women did not so much embrace, as put up with, it. As Whitney frankly admitted, she accepted polygamy because, though "I am afraid of no man, I feared to rebel against the Almighty."

Contemporary Americans widely assumed that all Mormons married on a grand scale. Some did. Brigham Young, for example, had what one historian termed an "overabundance" of more than fifty wives, and he fathered fifty-seven children. His counsellor in the First Presidency, Heber C. Kimball, married forty-five women and was the father of sixty-five children. John D. Lee was husband to eighteen wives, and Orson Pratt, who delivered the first public address on plural marriage, to ten. They were exceptions, however. The best estimates are that at the peak in the late nineteenth century, between 20 and 30 percent of Mormon families were polygamous, while for the period as a whole, 10 percent of families were polygamous, 5 percent of married men had more than one wife, and 12 percent of married women were plural wives. The majority of Mormon polygamists, perhaps two-thirds, had only two wives, and only one in twenty had more than four.

Though polygamy was a minority practice, it nonetheless was of great consequence. While only a small percentage of rank-and-file Mormons practiced polygamy, virtually all church leaders did, from general authorities down to bishops' counselors. In addition, only church leaders could authorize and perform plural marriages. Usually a man did not simply decide to take an addi-

tional wife. His church superiors asked him to; he was expected to agree; and church leaders often refused to ordain men to church callings unless they practiced polygamy, or agreed to, while plural wives had a greater chance of holding church positions than those who were not. Finally, because Mormons saw polygamy as the ideal marriage system and an essential part of their faith, and because it clashed so directly with prevailing moral assumptions in the United States and aroused such intense criticism, it served as a device for measuring loyalty to the church. Adopting it was, in effect, a declaration of an overriding commitment to Mormonism, while rejecting it, even in theory, was equivalent to rejecting Zion.

What all of this amounts to is that during its first generation Salt Lake was no ordinary city. Its most striking characteristic was the degree of unity

Brigham Young had more than fifty wives and over fifty children. This photograph of some of his daughters, known as "the big ten," was taken in the early 1860s by Edward Martin. (Courtesy Nelson Wadsworth.)

and cohesion. The emphasis was on the life of the community as opposed to private satisfactions. Almost a closed society, it offered a life orderly and harmonious for the believer, but difficult for the skeptic. The city's singularity can be overstated. Even so, its single-mindedness, unity of purpose, and willingness to submerge individualism for the good of society were found in few other places.

~

Recommended Readings

Campbell Eugene E. *Establishing Zion*, Chap. 6: "The Mormons and the Indians—Ideals versus Realities."

Christy, Howard A. "Open Hand and Mailed Fist: Mormon-Indian Relations in Utah, 1847-52." *Utah Historical Quarterly* 46 (Summer 1978): 216-35.

_____. "'What Virtue There is in Stone,' and Other Pungent Talk on the Early Utah Frontier." *Utah Historical Quarterly* 59 (Summer 1991): 300-19.

Crum, Steven J. "The 'White Pine War' of 1875: A Case of White Hysteria." *Utah Historical Quarterly* 59 (Summer 1991): 286-99.

Davies, J. Kenneth. "The Accommodation of Mormonism and Politico-Economic Reality." *Dialogue: A Journal of Mormon Thought* 3 (Spring 1968): 42-54.

Foster, Lawrence. *Women, Family, and Utopia: Communal Experiments of the Shakers, the Oneida Community, and the Mormons.* Syracuse, NY: Syracuse University Press, 1991.

Gordon, Sarah Barringer. "'The Liberty of Self-Degradation': Polygamy, Women Suffrage, and Consent in Nineteenth-Century America." *Journal of American History* 83 (Dec. 1996): 815-47.

Limerick, Patricia Nelson. *The Legacy of Conquest: The Unbroken Past of the American West.* New York: W. W. Norton and Co., Inc., 1987. Esp. Chap. 8: "Racialism on the Run," 259-92.

MacKay, Kathryn L., and Cesspooch, Larry. "Preface: Book One: Ute Community." In Kelen, Leslie G., and Stone, Eileen Hallet, *Missing Stories: An Oral History of Ethnic and Minority Groups in Utah.* Salt Lake City: University of Utah Press, 1996, 12-18.

Madsen, Carol Cornwall. "'At Their Peril': Utah Law and the Case of Plural Wives, 1850-1900." *Western Historical Quarterly* 21 (Nov. 1990): 425-43. Reprinted in McCormick and Sillito, *A World We Thought We Knew*, 68-84.

Pascoe, Peggy. *Relations of Rescue: The Search for Female Moral Authority in the American West, 1874-1939.* New York: Oxford University Press, 1990.

Peterson, John A. *Utah's Black Hawk War.* Salt Lake City: University of Utah Press, 1998.

Tanner, Annie Clark. *A Mormon Mother: The Autobiography of Annie Clark Tanner.* Salt Lake City: Tanner Trust Fund and the University of Utah Library, 1969.

Topping, Gary R. *Glen Canyon and the San Juan Country.* Moscow: University of Idaho Press, 1997, chap. 2: "Indians of the San Juan Country."

Van Wagoner, Richard S. *Mormon Polygamy: A History.* Salt Lake City: Signature Books, 1986.

Winkler, Albert. "The Circleville Massacre: A Brutal Incident in Utah's Black Hawk War." *Utah Historical Quarterly* 55 (Winter 1987): 4-21.

_____. "The Ute Mode of War in the Conflict of 1865-68." *Utah Historical Quarterly* 60 (Fall 1992): 300-18.

Chapter 4.

CONFLICT AND CONCESSION

(opposite) The completion of the transcontinental railroad at Promontory Summit, Utah, on May 10, 1869, had an immediate economic impact on Utah. During their first year of operation after the coming of the railroad, Utah mines shipped ten tons of ore out of the state, ranchers sent beef to San Francisco where it sold for 12¢ a pound, and farmers sold 60,000 pounds of dried peaches to eastern markets. This photograph, entitled "East Shaking Hands With West," was taken moments after the golden spike was driven and shows the Union Pacific's Grenville M. Dodge shaking hands with the Central Pacific's chief engineer, Samuel S. Montague. The photograph was taken by A. J. Russell. (Courtesy Nelson Wadsworth.)

As historian Charles S. Peterson says, Salt Lake City initially represented an attempt to construct a bulwark against time and intrusion. Gradually at first, however, and then more rapidly, Salt Lake moved away from its founders' ideals as competing economic, political, and cultural systems penetrated the city, and it became increasingly clear that, for better of worse, it would not be the kind of place its founders envisioned. Instead it would find increasing comfort, and eventually assimilate irreparably, with the outside, gentile, and capitalistic worlds. Two factors were particularly crucial in that evolution: the coming of the railroad in 1869 and the formal decision of the Mormon church in 1890 to give up much of what had made it different and integrate itself into the mainstream of American life.

The completion of the transcontinental railroad on May 10, 1869, at Promontory, Utah, and the spread of a network of rails throughout the territory in the next decades brought far-reaching changes to Salt Lake. It worked a profound transformation on the face of the city; stimulated the immigration of non-Mormons—including businessmen seeking profits and federal officials who arrived to fill territory offices; made possible the large-scale development of mining; and helped promote the diversification of Utah's economy and its integration into the economy of the United States.

When the railroad was extended to Salt Lake City in early 1870, Mor-

mons were ambivalent. On the one hand, they welcomed the railroad because it would speed the gathering of Zion by making travel quicker and easier. On the other hand, they were apprehensive about the changes they knew it would bring. By 1900 the tracks of a dozen railroads extended north, south, east, and west within the city, and a railroad-terminal district was well established. The pattern of land use near the railroad depots and along the railroad tracks changed dramatically, and a "westside" split off from the rest of the city. The transition was gradual, but inexorable. What eventually became identified as the westside was originally undifferentiated from the rest of the city. It was a low density area of large lots and blocks, wide streets, irrigation ditches, and small one- and two-story adobe houses set well back from the street. Virtually

61

Conflict and Concession

62

The Gathering Place

all of its residents were Mormons, most of them farmers who drove to their fields each day for work, craftsmen, or small businessmen serving the needs of the immediate neighborhood. After 1870 the area became increasingly commercialized and industrialized. A growing number of wholesale and light manufacturing enterprises, small stores, rooming houses, hotels, "commission houses," and saloons dotted the area. By 1890 a stockyard, two breweries, and two tanneries were located at the north end of the area near 300 West Street and 500 North Street, while at the south end, at about 900 South Street and 500 West Street, were a brickyard, a brewery, a biscuit factory, a salt works, and a soup factory. Scattered in between were similar establishments, including two lumberyards, several foundries, and an ice factory.

The evolution of the two blocks north of the Old Fort, now Pioneer Park, where the original settlers spent their first winter, illustrates the railroad's impact. As part of the first plat of the city, the two blocks were each originally di-

vided into eight 1.25-acre lots. In 1855 twenty private residences were located
on them. In 1870 there were twenty-nine, a 45 percent increase that paralleled
the 50 percent increase in the city's population during the same period. According to the 1867 *Salt Lake City Directory*, all the residents of both blocks
were working-class Mormons. Their occupations included clerk, cabinet-
maker, saddler, tanner, teamster, policeman, mason, and stonecutter. In the
1880s the blocks began to change. New residential construction ended. Commercial structures began to replace existing houses. Behind them ran railroad
spurs. By the mid-1880s two warehouses, a lumberyard, and a coal yard existed
in the midst of what were still mainly residential blocks. In the 1890s five more
warehouses were built. The first decade of the twentieth century saw a new
street, Eccles Avenue—now Pierpont Avenue—bisect one of the blocks. On
it a small warehouse and a larger produce warehouse were built. In the next
dozen years, five additional warehouses were built on the two blocks, and the
transformation of the area from residential to commercial and industrial was
complete.

The isolation of the westside also led to the sections that remained residential becoming working-class neighborhoods, many of whose residents
worked for the railroads and associated enterprises. In comparison, the North
Bench, or Avenues as it came to be called, attracted a growing middle- and up-
per-middle-class population. The factors at work were its elevation, which
provided a view of the valley, as well as clean air above the valley's smelter
haze; its proximity to the city center; and an extensive and moderately priced
public transit system connecting it both with the downtown and with other
parts of the city. At the same time, South Temple Street, running along the
Avenues's south edge, was lined with the mansions of non-Mormon mining
millionaires, while areas east and south of the city center attracted middle-class residents. This trend toward the development of distinct sections of
the city grew stronger in the twentieth century. In 1894, for example, the federal government donated sixty acres of Fort Douglas to the Territory of Utah to
establish the University of Utah, and within a decade developers were laying
out prestigious new neighborhoods along the east bench to the north and
south of the campus—including Federal Heights, on former Fort Douglas land
between the Avenues and the campus, Gilmer Park, southwest of the university, and the "Ivy League" streets several blocks south.

As the westside evolved into a mixed commercial/industrial/working-class residential section following the expansion of the railroad, it became increasingly blighted. The large lots were subdivided, and new streets and courts were cut through the original blocks. The new streets were subject to little regulation, however, and easily degenerated into crowded back alleys of squalor. City services were extended to the westside much slower than to other parts of the city. Disagreeable industries and enterprises were increasingly located there, including, by the 1890s, the city dump, estray pound, and crematory. While streets began to be paved, curbs and gutters installed, and sewers placed in some sections of the city beginning in the 1890s, parts of the westside were without them until the 1920s.

With the coming of the railroad, the city's non-Mormon population increased rapidly, and Salt Lake quickly became the focus of non-Mormon activity in Utah. Non-Mormons had lived in Salt Lake almost from the beginning, but during the city's first quarter century, they remained relatively few in number. In 1867, three years before the arrival of the railroad, the city's population was about 93 percent Mormon. Of more than 11,000 residents, perhaps 750 did not belong to the Mormon church. In general they fell into three groups: federal government officials, soldiers, and merchants. By 1874 the "gentile" population had more than tripled to about 2,500 and was continuing to grow. In the twenty years after the railroad's arrival, Salt Lake's non-Mormon population grew more than twice as fast as the Mormon population, increasing from fewer than 1,000 before the railroad to about 23,000 twenty years later, and by 1891 Mormon and non-Mormon populations in the city were roughly equal.

One of the most significant groups in Salt Lake City's population in the late nineteenth century was a small, but steadily growing African-American community. Three African-Americans slaves—Green Flake, Oscar Crosby, and Hark Lay—were members of the first group of Mormons to enter the Salt Lake Valley in July 1847, but blacks had been part of Utah's history even before that. They hunted and trapped for beaver in the 1820s—James P. Beckwourth is the best known—and Jacob Dodson was a member of John C. Frémont's 1843 expedition. In 1850 the official African-American population of Utah, all of whom lived in the Salt Lake Valley, was fifty, nearly equally divided between slaves and free men and women. One of them was Biddy Ma-

Green Flake was one of three black slaves who accompanied the first group of Mormon settlers to enter the Salt Lake Valley in the summer of 1847. According to some accounts, he drove Brigham Young's wagon. Shown here are four generations of Flake's descendants (left to right): Martha J. Perkins Howell (granddaughter), Mary Lucille Perkins Bankhead (great-granddaughter), Juanita Spillman (great-great-great-granddaughter), and Ruth Jackson (great-great-grand-daughter). (Courtesy Utah State Historical Society.)

son. She was born a slave on August 15, 1818, probably in Georgia. Like all slaves, she was forbidden by law to learn to read and write, but she managed to gain a good knowledge of livestock, herbal medicine, nursing, and midwifery, skills, as Dolores Hayden says, "that were useful to her owners and ones that would later enable her to earn her living." She became the property of Robert Marion Smith and his wife, Rebecca Crosby Smith, owners of a plantation in Mississippi. The Smiths had six children, whose births she probably attended, and Rebecca Smith often needed nursing care, which Mason later told relatives and friends she provided. In addition, she was required to work in the cotton fields and with livestock, and she added to her master's wealth by bearing three children who became slaves.

In the spring of 1848 the Smiths, having converted to Mormonism the year before, joined a group of Mississippi Mormons who planned to travel

Conflict and Concession

overland to the Salt Lake Valley. According to John Brown, who recorded the trip in his autobiography, fifty-six whites and thirty-four slaves, including Mason, were in the party. They arrived in late 1848 and rushed to complete log shelters so they could move into them as December snows began to fall. On the journey Mason was in charge of herding the livestock behind the wagons. With a ten-year-old daughter, a four-year-old daughter, and a baby daughter at her breast, she walked the several thousand miles of the trip in seven months. A single parent and a nursing mother, she was also a slave and was thus expected to work for her keep and walk behind the animals when others rode. The Smiths stayed in the Salt Lake Valley for only three years and then travelled to California to help establish San Bernardino. Robert Smith took his slaves, who now included Mason, a woman named Hannah, and their eight children, with him, but Mason won her freedom in 1856 by successfully challenging in court her master's effort to take her and her children to Texas, and she lived in California the rest of her life. She became a successful midwife and nurse, between 1856 and her death in 1891, delivering hundreds of babies; practiced herbal medicine and became a well-known healer; and in the mid-1860s, after ten years of hard work and savings, bought a small house and became one of the first African-American women to own property in her own right in Los Angeles. In 1872 she was one of the organizers of the First African Methodist Episcopal Church in Los Angeles.

As part of the Compromise of 1850, the U.S. Congress left it to the people of each territory to decide whether slavery would be permitted. In 1852 the Utah Territorial Legislature formally legalized slavery, though it had existed since 1847 even before it was legally sanctioned, and exchanges and sales of black slaves and payment of them as tithing to the Mormon church, and in general treating them as chattel, continued until Congress abolished slavery in the territories a decade later. On September 7, 1859, for example, the Salt Lake City clerk recorded the sale of a twenty-six-year-old "negro boy" for $800 to William H. Hooper, who had been elected the previous month as Utah's delegate to the U.S. Congress. The 1852 Utah law allowed the buying and selling of slaves of African descent and prohibited miscegenation. It required slave owners to provide sufficient food, shelter, clothing, and recreation, as well as eighteen months of schooling to slaves between the ages of six and twenty, and specified that a slave was "to labor faithfully all reasonable hours, and do such

Amanda Leggroan Chambers and her husband, Samuel D. Chambers, arrived in Salt Lake City in April 1870 with their son, Peter. Samuel initially worked in a sawmill in Little Cottonwood Canyon and later became a successful farmer.

service with fidelity as may be required by his or her master or mistress." The majority of slaves labored on small farms scattered throughout the valley, though some worked in small businesses in the city. A few escaped and joined wagon trains travelling through the territory, but most remained in slavery until it ended with the Civil War. Thirty years later Mr. and Mrs. Alex Bankhead described for *The Broad Ax*, a black community newspaper in Salt Lake City, "The joyful expressions which were upon the faces of all the slaves when they ascertained they had acquired their freedom through the fortunes of war."

After the Civil War, Utah's black population grew slowly but steadily. Some were members of the Mormon church who came to Utah to join their fellow Saints in building the Kingdom, but most were not Mormons and came for other reasons. According to the 1870 census, Utah's African-American population was 118, while by 1900 it had increased to 678, most of them in Salt Lake and Uintah counties. As Ronald G. Coleman says, "Black males found employment as cooks, waiters, and porters on the railroads, and in hotels. Although few blacks actually worked in the mines, the wealth derived

67

Conflict and Concession

*Detective Paul Cephas Howell
was a member of Salt Lake
City's police force in the 1890s.
He was Salt Lake's first African-American police officer.*

from mining and other commercial enterprises led to the employment of many black women as domestics in the homes of white Utahns." In addition, companies of black soldiers were stationed at Fort Duchesne in Uintah County from 1886 to 1901 and at Fort Douglas in Salt Lake City from 1896 to 1899. Two of only three African Americans to graduate from the U.S. Military Academy at West Point in the nineteenth century, lieutenants John Alexander and Charles Young served at Fort Duchesne, as did Benjamin O. Davis, Sr., who later became the army's first black general.

From the first, free African Americans met the same kind of prejudice and discrimination in Utah as they did elsewhere in the United States. On December 11, 1866, for example, Brigham Young, Jr., recorded in his diary that "a nigger" was found dead in Salt Lake City with a note pinned to his corpse that read: "Let this be a warning to all niggers that they meddle not with white women." More common, though, were restrictions in employment, housing, and public accommodations. As Ronald G. Coleman says, "African Americans were routinely denied access to public accommodations. J. Gordon McPherson, a veteran of the Spanish American War, was prevented from serving on a jury after complaints from several white jurors. State law prohibited interracial couples from obtaining a marriage license." Black Utahns, he concludes, "were in a position similar to that of other African Americans throughout the United

States—they were a numerical minority residing in the midst of a majority who believed in the notions of white superiority and black inferiority." In part, they responded to their exclusion in the way new immigrants during the same period did, by speaking out in their own behalf. Thus in October 1896 Private Thomas A. Ernest wrote in a letter to *The Salt Lake Tribune* that the men of the 24th Infantry had enlisted in the military "to uphold the honor and dignity of their country as their fathers enlisted to found and preserve it," and, he said, "We object to being classed as lawless barbarians. We were men before we were soldiers, we are men now, and will continue to be men after we are through soldiering. We ask the people of Salt Lake to treat us as such."

Over time African Americans also developed a rich social and cultural life, with their own clubs, community centers, fraternal organizations, newspapers, and churches. In the 1890s, for example, three black newspapers were founded: *The Democratic Headlight*, edited by J. Gordon McPherson; *The Broad Ax*, edited by Julius F. Taylor; and *The Plain Dealer*, whose editor was William W. Taylor. Churches were especially important. The first predominantly black church in Utah was Salt Lake's Trinity African Methodist Episcopal Church, founded in 1890. Salt Lake's Calvary Baptist Church soon followed. Both have continued to the present to address the spiritual and secular needs of the city's African-American community.

If the railroad provided the means for large numbers of non-Mormons to come to Salt Lake, mining provided an important motive. Utah was rich in mineral resources, in particular gold, silver, lead, zinc, coal, and copper. The development of the mining industry began in the early 1860s with the arrival of the Third California Infantry, under the command of Colonel Patrick E. Connor, which had been sent to Utah in 1862 to guard the overland mail routes during the Civil War and keep an eye on Mormons as well, since the federal government questioned their loyalty. A staunch anti-Mormon, Connor reported on one occasion that Mormons were "a community of traitors, murderers, fanatics, and whores," and he quickly set about to reduce Mormon church influence in the territory by exploring and developing its mineral wealth. If gold, silver, and other precious metals were found, he reasoned, the resulting flood of miners into the territory would overwhelm the Mormons and gentiles would soon predominate, so he sent the men under his command out to prospect. By locating deposits, staking claims, and establishing mining districts, they almost single-handedly opened Utah's mining industry.

Until it became possible to transport large quantities of ore to distant markets, however, mining would not really grow, and the industry did not become of great importance until the completion of the transcontinental railroad in 1869 and the subsequent spread of rails throughout the territory. After that mining developed on a large scale and Utah's economy took on a new dimension, with rich mines flourishing in the Wasatch and Oquirrh mountains east and west of Salt Lake City, at Park City in Summit County, at Rush Valley in Tooele County, in the Tintic Mountains, in the coal fields of Carbon County, and at numerous central and southern Utah sites. By the early twentieth century, mining was a major industry second only to agriculture, and Utah was one of the leading mining states in the country. According to the 1860 census, four people listed their occupation as miner. In 1870 there were more than 500, and by World War I over 10,000. The value of minerals mined increased from $190,000 in 1869 to $10 million in 1882, and to over $100 million by the middle of World War I. In 1916 Utah was second in the nation in silver production, third in lead, and fourth in copper. With the exception of the coal mines of Carbon County, the richest mines were in the canyons surrounding Salt Lake City, and the valley soon became a major mining and smelting center, with six copper and lead smelters in operation in 1910, and by some calculations the Salt Lake Valley was the most important smeltering area in the world. A visiting journalist put it nicely: Utah was one large mining camp and Salt Lake City was its Main Street.

At first mining was primarily a non-Mormon undertaking. The lure of riches from the earth was not nearly as strong for Mormons as it was for others, and non-Mormons thus predominated among both owners and workers. From the early days of settlement, Mormons had mined on a small scale as part of their effort to develop a self-sufficient economy. Every community needed stone for building, lime for mortar, coal for heating, lead for ammunition, and iron for tools, but Mormons had little desire to develop mineral resources on a large scale. Church leaders believed mining had a disintegrating moral influence on a society. More importantly, they agreed with Colonel Connor that a rush of non-Mormons into Utah would follow a successful discovery of precious metals, undermining the isolation and unity within a religious community that they sought. Moreover, they said, a permanent society could not be

70

The Gathering Place

built on mining. Mines became exhausted; ghost towns developed; people moved away. The foundation of permanence and stability was agriculture. Mormon apostle Erastus Snow spoke for many in saying, "It is better for us to live in peace and good order, and to raise wheat, corn, potatoes, and fruit than to suffer the evils of a mining life."

Mining helped give birth to two groups, a small wealthy class and a large working class. It formed the basis of huge personal fortunes, spawned extensive financial empires, and gave rise to a new economic and social elite. Park City, for example, was the most important mining district in Utah in the nineteenth century and produced twenty-three millionaires by the early 1890s. One of them, David Keith, came from Virginia City, Nevada, to supervise installation of a 500-ton Cornish pump with a working capacity of 4 million gallons a day to remove water from the Ontario Mine. Thomas Kearns also built his fortune in Park City. Legend has it that he arrived in town in the late 1880s with only a pack on his back and a dime in his pocket. A decade later he was a multi-millionaire, owner with Keith of *The Salt Lake Tribune*, and one of Utah's U.S. senators. A third Park City millionaire was Susanna Bransford Emery Holmes Delitch Engalitcheff, Utah's famed and flamboyant "Silver Queen," whose worldwide travels and lavish entertainments outlasted her four marriages and her $100 million fortune. As much as anyone, she represented the quick fortunes and luxury living that mining sometimes produced in Utah.

Kearns, Keith, Engalitcheff, and others were by far the exceptions, however. While mining society was theoretically upwardly mobile, and the industrious would become wealthy, in fact only a relatively few did. "Mining is Nature's great lottery scheme," a contemporary observer said, and as with any lottery, only a few people held winning tickets. One person might work hard and yet lose everything but his shirt, while another would make thousands of dollars in a few hours. Of course the age of individual entrepreneurs did not last long. Individuals and partnerships with little backing made most of the initial discoveries, but by the late 1870s or so the easily accessible surface ores were exhausted. After that large corporations with substantial capital, including the Guggenheim interests, took over the development of mining, employing a larger and larger workforce. After that most people involved in mining were wage workers, and there was nothing romantic about their work. They received about $3.00 a day until well past the turn of the century and, as Dean L.

71

May says, deserved more. Until 1896, when the first Utah State Legislature passed a law limiting work in the mines to eight hours a day, miners typically worked ten or twelve hours a day, six days a week. Accidents were common. As one worker said, "There are all sorts of ways to get yourself killed or maimed in a mine." Hoists were dangerous. So were falling rocks and runaway ore cars. Falls down mine shafts were one of the most common causes of fatalities. The air was often so bad that the candles miners carried burned at only one-fifth of their normal intensity. Miners became ill and died from lead poisoning. Methane gas was a serious hazard. A frightening number of miners developed lung diseases. Job insecurity plagued them. Few could count on full-time work year round. The periodic recessions and depressions that affected the American economy as a whole and the mining industry in particular resulted in long periods of unemployment and often wiped out the savings of even the most frugal families, and once out of work, miners were left adrift. Public relief was nonexistent and private charity insufficient. The situation would not improve much until the 1930s when, after decades of struggle, as labor unrest, unionization, and conflict between capital and labor became more and more a part of the state's history, Utah's mines were finally unionized.

As Philip F. Notarianni says, mining sparked both population growth and population diversity in Utah. Most mine workers were newcomers, many of them "new immigrants" from eastern and southern Europe and Asia. By the early twentieth century, the residents of Park City, which a generation earlier had been the home of a few Mormon farmers, included several dozen national groups, among them Chinese, who had initially come to build the transcontinental railroad, Japanese, Greeks, Italians, Slavs, and Serbs. The situation was similar in Murray. Located eight miles south of Salt Lake City, and initially an agricultural village with a largely Mormon, native-born, and old immigrant population, it had changed considerably by the early twentieth century. The population increased from under 1,000 in 1870 to more than 4,000 in 1910 and included many more ethnic and national groups. By 1910 the lead smelter of the American Smelting and Refining Company was the largest in the world and employed 43 percent of Murray's workforce. More than half of the population—54 percent—were new immigrants, mainly Greeks, along with what were at the time commonly referred to as Austrians, but in fact were Slavs, Serbs, and Croats, as well as a smaller number of Italians.

One effect of mining on Salt Lake City was to alter its landscape. Many of the mansions on South Temple Street, known as Brigham Street until the early twentieth century, were built with the mining money of people who engaged in public acts of what Thorstein Veblen called "conspicuous consumption" as easily as did their counterparts elsewhere in the United States. A number of these mansions have been demolished over the years, but some remain, including David Keith's and Thomas Kearns's, now the governor's official residence. Mining money also built St. Ann's Orphanage, now a private school; Judge Memorial High School, originally a miners' hospital that Mary Judge intended as a tribute to her husband, John, who died of lung disease at the age of forty-two after long years of working in the mines; and a number of skyscrapers and commercial buildings, including the McIntyre Building, the McCornick Block, the Kearns Building, the Keith Building, the Judge Building, and the 1905 public library building that now houses the Hansen Planetarium. Mining also paid for the buildings that make up the Exchange Place Historic District at the south end of Main Street near 400 South, all of which were built around 1910 by non-Mormon mining men, in particular Samuel Newhouse, in an effort to construct a gentile business district at the south end of the commercial area to balance the Mormon businesses at the north end. Mining helped to finance the Alta Club, too, as a symbol of gentile, and genteel, prosperity. Founded in 1883, its original eighty-one members were all non-Mormons, mainly mining men. Mormons were initially excluded from membership. After the turn of the century, though, they were gradually admitted—but no women until 1987—and for the next several decades the club served as an important instrument of accommodation between Utah's elite Mormon and non-Mormon communities.

The rapid increase in the late nineteenth century in Salt Lake City's non-Mormon population, in combination with the continuing efforts of Mormons to establish the Kingdom of God, served to drive people into increasingly hostile camps. It was perhaps the city's most striking feature. The population was sharply divided into two groups—those inside the Kingdom and those outside. Virtually every aspect of the city's life became entangled in that division, both reflecting it and becoming an occasion for its expression. Two school systems existed, and while most teachers and students in the public schools were Mormon, those in the growing number of private schools were not. The emer-

73

Conflict and
Concession

Don't Be a "Bastard"

Election, Monday, Aug. 3, 1891.

Let Honest Men TAKE CARE
How They Vote.

The LIBERALS have unjustly raised our taxes.
The LIBERALS have piled up houses of ill fame.
The LIBERALS have poisoned the earth and air.
The LIBERALS have open saloons all day Sunday.
The LIBERALS have heaped up unnecessary offices.
The LIBERAL "four boodlers" should be voted down.
The LIBERALS have ruined the fair name of our city.
The LIBERALS have given the gamblers a carte blanche.
The LIBERALS have recklessly squandered the people's money
The LIBERALS have made our citizens politically dishonest
The LIBERALS have given Salt Lake work to Omaha workmen
The LIBERALS have given Salt Lake work to Denver workmen
The LIBERALS have not given Salt Lake work to Salt
    Lake workmen.
The LIBERALS have caused property values to decrease
    since they have been in the city government.

A Democrat Votes the Democratic Ticket;
A Republican Votes the Republican Ticket;
What is he who VOTES A "BASTARD" TICKET?

Judging from this campaign poster, Salt Lake City's 1891 municipal election was a rough-and-tumble affair. The Mormon church had disbanded its People's Party two months earlier. The Liberal Party, however, was not dissolved until 1893, and until then elections were still essentially contests between Mormons and non-Mormons. (Private Collection.)

gence of fraternal organizations, such as the Independent Order of Odd Fellows and the Ancient Order of United Workmen, coincided with the growth of the territory's non-Mormon population, and Mormons, through either formal policy or custom and practice, were typically excluded from membership. Mormons and non-Mormons sometimes held their own separate celebrations of the 4th of July and other national holidays, and, as D. Michael Quinn says, it was not until 1888 that Mormons and non-Mormons held a joint Independence Day celebration. Distinct Mormon and non-Mormon residential neighborhoods developed. In general, non-Mormons lived in the southern and western portion of the city, near the downtown area, while Mormons tended to live to the north and east. Salt Lake's first concentration of non-Mormons was in the nine-block area bounded by 300 South, Main Street, 600 South, and 300 West. In the late 1860s one-third of its residents were non-Mormons.

Local politics did not revolve around national political parties or national issues. Instead there was the Mormon church's People's Party and an anti-church Liberal Party, and elections were contests, not between Democrats and Republicans, but between Mormons and non-Mormons, with people essentially voting for or against the Mormon church. Non-Mormons founded the Liberal Party on February 9, 1870, at a meeting that a group of Mormons led by Presiding Bishopric counselor Jesse C. Little sought to disrupt. It was Utah's first political party. *The Salt Lake Tribune* soon became its voice. In the view of party organizers, only a façade of democracy existed in Utah. In the absence of political parties, people simply went through the motions when voting, and real political power rested with Mormon leaders. Non-Mormons were effectively disenfranchised, with no voice in government, and they would not have one until they formed their own party to represent themselves, their interests, and their position. As Henry W. Lawrence, and the others who joined him in founding the Liberal Party, saw it, Utah was essentially a theocracy. In their view, the Mormon church dominated political affairs to such an extent that a virtual union of church and state existed, with the state subservient to the church and the rights of Utah citizens subordinate to the wishes of a politically irresponsible priesthood. As a remedy, Liberals called for separation of church and state, the right of people to vote without direction from Mormon authorities, and the election of officials responsible to the people as a whole, not to a particular church or its officers. Their intention, according to Robert N. Baskin, a party founder, was to "establish republican American rule in the place of the usurped rule of the priesthood of the Mormon church."

In response, the Mormon church formed its own People's Party, with the church-owned *Deseret News* as its organ. Church leaders determined party policies and named its candidates. In 1876 *The Salt Lake Tribune* labeled People's Party nominees for city offices "a Priesthood city ticket." It was made up, the paper said, of "1 President of the Church, 1 Apostle, 2 Bishops, 3 Bishops' Counselors, 2 sons-in-law of Brigham Young, and Brigham's private secretary." In reply the *Deseret News* characterized the Liberal Party platform as simply, "D—n the Mormons."

In its early years Liberal Party candidates had no real expectation of actually winning office. In the 1870 Salt Lake City election, the Liberal mayoral candidate, Henry W. Lawrence, received only 302 of 2,301 votes cast. A former Mormon bishop's counsellor who had been expelled from the church in 1869 with other "Godbeites" for calling into question certain of its theological beliefs as well as its economic practices, Lawrence would go on to be a founder

Conflict and
Concession

Bishop Daniel S. Tuttle arrived in Utah in 1867 and began organizing Episcopal church activities, even though his first congregation only included three people—all women. Under his direction, Salt Lake City's St. Mark's Cathedral was completed in 1871, St. Mark's Hospital was established in 1874, and Rowland Hall-St. Mark's School opened in 1880. By the 1890s nearly 500 Episcopalians lived in Salt Lake City. This photograph was taken in 1918 when Tuttle was 81 years old. (Courtesy Utah State Historical Society.)

of two radical political parties in Utah, the Populist Party of the 1890s and the Socialist Party of America in the first decade of the twentieth century, and would be elected to the Salt Lake City Commission in 1911 as a Socialist. The People's Party candidate in the 1870 election, Daniel H. Wells, a member of the Mormon church's First Presidency, received 1,999 votes—a margin of more than 7 to 1 over Lawrence. In the 1872 election the margin increased to 8 to 1. While they did not initially expect to win, Liberals did hope to provide an organization through which Salt Lake's non-Mormon population could focus their discontents and energies and lay a foundation for their eventual full participation in political affairs. Indeed, they became an increasingly significant force, particularly in the largest cities and in mining communities, and by the late 1880s began to win political office. In Ogden in 1889 and in Salt Lake City in 1890 Liberals elected the mayor and a majority of city council members and in 1891 elected one-third of the territorial legislature.

The Liberal Party was but one source of organized opposition to the Mormon church. By the mid-1870s a variety of non-Mormon churches was firmly established in the city. The policy of Episcopalians, Catholics, and Jews was one of peaceful coexistence with Mormons. Protestant churches, on the other hand, were more combative. They generally sought both to convert "deluded" Mormons and to alert the American people and the federal government to the "Mormon problem," and a major thrust of Protestant efforts was speaking

tours throughout the United States to keep the American public informed about conditions in Utah and to raise money for Protestant activities there. They campaigned specifically for the establishment of a tax-supported public school system free of Mormon control; the abolition of plural marriage; the establishment of the secret ballot; a guarantee of separation of church and state; and a denial of statehood for Utah as long as Mormons remained dominant.

Another organization opposed to the Mormon church was the Anti-Polygamy Society, a group of some 200 non-Mormon women, founded in 1878. Dedicated to the abolition of polygamy, they published a monthly magazine, *The Anti-Polygamy Standard*, and conducted a regular series of lectures and meetings where non-Mormon women attacked polygamy and former plural wives discussed their experiences. At one meeting, *The Anti-Polygamy Standard* reported, "Mrs. Hunt, a member of the Society, and one who has drunk the bitter cup of polygamy to the very dregs ... drew a ghastly, but accurate picture of the foul demon that desolates happy homes; ... the pathos and infinite sadness of Mrs. Hunt's impassioned word painting could only have emanated from the depths of a woman's heart, whose noblest instincts and most sacred feelings had been immolated upon the altar of a false God."

Conflict and
Concession

This floor plan of the Lion House was published in 1866 in a book entitled, The Mormon Prophet and His Harem, by Catherine V. Waite. The text provided a detailed description of each room. For example, in describing "Parlor No. 1" on the main floor, it said, in part: "You enter the parlor from the left, and find a long, narrow room, with a large window in front, and four on the side, all heavily curtained. A beautiful Brussels carpet ... covers the floor. Two centre-tables, of solid mahogany, are placed at equal distances form the ends of the room. An elegant rose-wood piano sits at the lower end of the room."

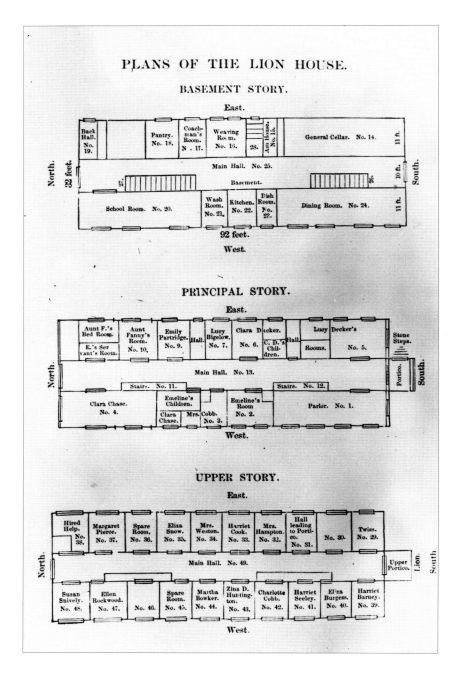

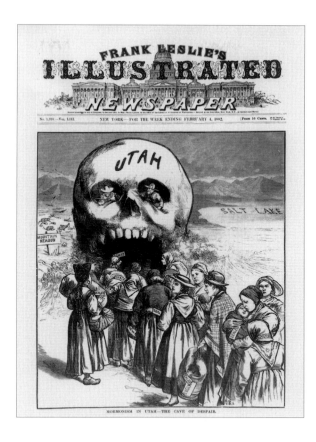

The Mormon system of plural marriage profoundly disturbed most nineteenth-century Americans, and Mormon "slavery" became the subject of a vast and sensational literature purporting to reveal polygamy's true nature. Typically, polygamy was seen as a thinly disguised system of prostitution and economic exploitation. Mormon men were portrayed as villainous lechers and Mormon women their pitiful victims. This cartoon was from Frank Leslie's Illustrated Newspaper, *February 4, 1882, published in New York City.*

The Anti-Polygamy Society not only attacked polygamy, but also called for the repeal of women's suffrage in Utah as a way of reducing the Mormon vote and thus the power of the Mormon church. In its view the franchise only tightened women's bonds, "increasing the spread of polygamy and the consequent degradation of woman, to make them, if possible, greater slaves than before, and enhancing the power of the Mormon priesthood." Non-Mormon women in Utah, in other words, were willing to lose their right to vote if Mormon women, who out-numbered them, also lost theirs. Women throughout the nation supported that position. In 1884 a petition that had been circulated among women attending Methodist home missionary society meetings was submitted to Congress calling for the revocation of women's suffrage in Utah. It contained 250,000 signatures.

The beginning of the end of the Mormon Kingdom of God came when the U.S. Congress passed the Edmunds Act in 1882. It outlawed plural marriage; denied polygamists the right to vote, hold office, or serve on juries; vacated all elective offices in Utah; and placed much of Utah's government in

79

Conflict and
Concession

In the 1880s federal marshals pursued Mormon men wanted for polygamy. Circulars such as this one offered rewards for their arrest. Always on the move, the men often went by cover of night from ingenious hideouts in their own houses to retreats up nearby canyons or to the houses of friends. They circulated around the territory, going even as far as Canada and Mexico. A highly effective communication system warned them of approaching "federals" and kept leaders in touch with each other.

80

the hands of a five-man presidential commission. Within a year the Utah Commission had excluded more than 12,000 people from registering and voting by administering a test oath to men asking them to "solemnly swear" that "I do not live or cohabit with more than one woman in the marriage relation." Following a test case in which the U.S. Supreme Court found the Edmunds Act to be constitutional, federal authorities began systematic prosecution of Mormons. Ultimately, more than 1,200 men were convicted of either polygamy or "unlawful cohabitation," fined an average of $300, and sent to prison, typically for six months. Rudger Clawson, who had two wives, served the longest term—three years and one month. Some plural wives served time in prison as well, having been sentenced for refusing to testify against their husbands. According to D. Michael Quinn, in October 1882 Annie Gallifant Connelly, who was then pregnant, was the first Mormon woman sentenced to the penitentiary for refusing to answer questions about her polygamous husband. For a similar refusal, Belle Harris served a three-month prison term and kept a diary of the experience. Her infant daughter stayed in prison with her.

The July 15, 1885, issue of the *Salt Lake City Woman's Exponent* listed six other women charged with contempt of court for refusing to testify against their husbands.

Because the Edmunds Act required them to give up a religious principle that they believed came from God, many Mormons decided to evade arrest by going into hiding, or "on the underground." Mormon president John Taylor set the example. On March 31, 1885, he gave what turned out to be the last public address of his life. In his view, the United States was "no longer a land of liberty." Under such conditions, he said, "We must take care of ourselves as best we may, and avoid being caught in any of their snares." He would die for the truth, Taylor proclaimed, but would "Never! No Never! ... disobey my God or forsake my wives and children." After his speech, he disappeared from public view. He died, still in hiding, two and a half years later—two months after taking still another plural wife.

Taylor's counsellors followed his example. Joseph F. Smith was sent on a

Convicted polygamists posed with George Q. Cannon in this 1888 photograph at the Utah Territorial Penitentiary, located in what is now Sugarhouse Park. Cannon, a member of the church's First Presidency, and the husband of five wives and father of thirty-two children, was elected as Utah's delegate to Congress for five terms beginning in 1870. In 1880 Congress denied him a seat on the grounds that polygamists were not eligible for public office—even though he received 18,567 votes and Allen G. Campbell, his opponent, only 1,357. (Private Collection.)

church mission to Hawaii and did not return until 1889. U.S. marshals chased George Q. Cannon all over the western United States before finally capturing him in February 1886 on his way to Mexico. He escaped during the return to Salt Lake, but was recaptured. Released on $45,000 bail pending trial, he forfeited bail and escaped to Arizona. Later he surrendered to federal officials, was tried and convicted, and spent nine months in prison. Going to prison had at least one good effect, he said. "It proves our leading men are willing to suffer, but not to concede."

In Salt Lake City in 1885 one group of Mormons hoped to decrease pressure on church members by catching federal officials and other non-Mormons in houses of prostitution. Brigham Young Hampton, who directed the effort, recounted the story in his diary. A "citizen's committee" of twenty-five policemen and "home missionaries" worked for five or six months, he said, gathering evidence against "the Government Office Holders that are prosicuting and persicuting the Servants of God for keeping his law of Marriage." The committee hired two prostitutes and set them up in houses on West Temple Street with apertures in the doors and walls, where committee members could view "the bestial conduct within." According to Hampton, he conducted the operation by the authority of the church's First Presidency. A *Deseret News* editorial on December 14, 1885, argued in support of the undertaking: "It was the only way by which their guilt could be proven beyond question. It was disgusting business, no doubt. But which was the most disgusting, the detestation of their bestiality, or the acts which were witnessed?" The first of a number of people arrested was the deputy U.S. marshal who had led the search resulting in the arrest of Mormon apostle Lorenzo Snow. Ultimately, however, the strategy backfired. After the U.S. District Court dismissed all prosecutions, a grand jury indicted Hampton for conspiracy and for operating a brothel. He was found guilty and served one year in the county jail. After his release from prison, Hampton asked church officials to reimburse him for expenses incurred during the brothel operation and for income lost during his imprisonment. They initially balked, but in June 1900, according to D. Michael Quinn, the First Presidency agreed to pay him $3,600 for his "detective work" in 1885, and George Q. Cannon referred to Hampton's brothel operation as "services rendered the Church" and "work in behalf of the Church."

In 1887 Congress brought more pressure to bear on the Mormon church

with the passage of the Edmunds-Tucker Act. It dissolved the Corporation of the Church of Jesus Christ of Latter-day Saints; provided for the confiscation of all church property in excess of $50,000; did away with the Nauvoo Legion (a territorial militia) and the Perpetual Emigrating Fund; transferred control of public schools to a federal appointee; and abolished the right of all Utah women, Mormon and non-Mormon, to vote. By the summer of 1888 a government receiver had taken possession of about $1 million worth of church property, including the Temple Block, the Tithing Yard and Tithing Office, the Church Historian's Office, the Gardo House, the Church Farm, the church's stock in the Deseret Telegraph Company, the Salt Lake Gas Company and other businesses, 50,000 head of cattle, and $239,000 in cash.

In 1890 the U.S. Supreme Court, in a 5-4 decision, found the Edmunds-Tucker Act constitutional, saying in part, "Looking at the case as the finding of the facts presents it, we have before us a contumacious organization, wielding by its resources an immense power in the Territory of Utah, and employing those resources and that power in constantly attempting to oppose, thwart, and subvert the legislation of Congress and the will of the government of the United States. Under these circumstances we have no doubt of the power of the Congress to do as it did. ... The tale is one of patience on the part of the

Three- to five-ton boulders from Big Cottonwood Canyon were cut into blocks for the Salt Lake LDS temple. People remembered "the curious spectacle of six or eight toiling oxen drawing a cart, underneath which was suspended by chains a monster rock from the mountains." It often took four days to bring a single rock from the quarry to the temple block, and the road was strewn with the wreckage of wagons and carts unable to bear the strain. (Private Collection.)

Workers on the Salt Lake LDS temple posed for this photograph in the 1880s. (Private Collection.)

American government and people, and of contempt and resistance to law on the part of the Mormons. Whatever persecutions they may have suffered in the early part of their history in Missouri and Illinois, they have no excuse for their persistent defiance of law under the government of the United States."

Threatened with extinction or, at the very least, reduction to a small and insignificant sect, Mormon leaders, after lengthy and agonizing discussions, decided at last to undertake a process of rapprochement with the United States and bring the church into the mainstream of American life. In the face of enormous pressure, the church consciously embarked on what it hoped would be the road to prosperity and security: cooperation with the nation's dominant political and economic forces. From posing a radical challenge to the American way of life, Mormonism would deliberately seek to be incorporated into it. Leonard J. Arrington has called the decision "the great capitulation."

In 1890 Mormon president Wilford Woodruff, stating that he was "acting for the temporal salvation of the Church," issued a "Manifesto" proclaiming an end to the further performance of plural marriage. As Jan Shipps says, it signaled the beginning of the end of a world that not only tolerated, but celebrated, polygamy. More importantly, it was part of an unstated bargain involving a fundamental alteration in the way political and economic power was exercised. A year later, in June 1891, the church dissolved its People's Party and attempted to evenly divide the Mormon population between the Democratic and Republican parties. Eighteen months after that, following much debate occasioned by fear, such measures were only temporary expedients designed to gain statehood for Utah and would be abandoned thereafter, the Liberal Party also disbanded, and for the first time in its history, Salt Lake City's population followed national party lines.

Just as its politics changed, so did its economic philosophy and practices, and during the decade of the 1890s the Mormon church abandoned its efforts to establish a self-sufficient, communitarian economy and began a process of participation in, and accommodation to, the national economy. As Leonard J. Arrington points out, it sold most church-owned businesses to private individuals, including non-Mormons; operated those businesses it kept as income-producing ventures, rather than shared community cooperatives; and no longer insisted that its members "take counsel" about their economic affairs.

ZCMI, for example, became just another company, with no social obligations; it operated on the basis of profit, not social welfare; the group of Mormon businessmen who bought it no longer paid 10 percent of its profits to the church as a tithe; and non-Mormons were no longer prohibited from owning stock.

The 1890s were a turning point in Salt Lake City's history. After fifty years of seeking to withdraw from the world, the city began a process of coming together with it. As competing systems—the outside, the gentile, and, most crucially, the capitalistic worlds—penetrated Mormon country, it was increasingly integrated into the national economy and became more and more, but never completely, a secular American city of the late nineteenth and early twentieth centuries. The commercial ideal increasingly replaced the communal, just as in Puritan Massachusetts 250 years earlier the Bible commonwealth evolved into a commercial commonwealth. Salt Lake made its peace with contemporary capitalism and began to serve as an appendage to it, and as it did, the Mormon church evolved from being the dominant force to become one of many vested interests, though an enormously important one. Religious division between Mormons and non-Mormons was still evident, but so, increasingly, were ethnic, class, and gender divisions as new groups sought to establish their authority and their place. Clearly, by the end of the nineteenth century, the original dream was at an end.

~

Recommended Readings

Arrington. *Great Basin Kingdom*, Chap. 12: "The Raid," and Chap. 13: "Aftermath."

Campbell, Eugene E., and Campbell, Bruce L. "Divorce Among Mormon Polygamists: Extent and Explanations." *Utah Historical Quarterly* 46 (Winter 1978): 4-23.

Coleman, Ronald G. "Blacks in Utah History: An Unknown Legacy." In Papanikolas, Helen Z., ed., *The Peoples of Utah*. Salt Lake City: Utah State Historical Society, 1976.

_____. "A History of Blacks in Utah, 1825-1910." University of Utah. Ph.d. dissertation, 1980.

_____. "African Americans in Utah." In Powell, Allan Kent, ed., *Utah History Encyclopedia*. Salt Lake City: University of Utah Press, 1994, 2-5

Davis, France. *Light in the Midst of Zion: A History of Black Baptists in Utah, 1892-1996*. Salt Lake City: University Publishing, 1997.

Dwyer, Robert J. *The Gentile Comes to Utah: A Study in Religious and Social Conflict, 1867-1890*. Salt Lake City: Western Epics, 1971.

McCormick, John S. *The Historic Buildings of Downtown Salt Lake City*. Salt Lake City: Utah State Historical Society, 1982.

Quinn, D. Michael. "LDS Church Authority and New Plural Marriages, 1890-1904." *Dialogue, A Journal of Mormon Thought* 18 (Spring 1985): 9-105.

Utah Historical Quarterly 31 (Summer 1963); a special issue on mining in Utah.

Walker, Ronald W. *Wayward Saints: The Godbeites and Brigham Young*. Urbana: University of Illinois Press, 1998.

(opposite) Saltair dazzled tourists and Utahns alike. Beginning in 1893, the elaborate "pleasure palace" that the Mormon church built on pilings over the Great Salt Lake offered swimming, dancing, and a variety of amusements. The church intended that it be both a "wholesome place of recreation," especially for Mormon families, and a "Coney Island of the West." Fresh water, brought in by rail and stored in the pavilion's four onion-shaped domes, washed away the glistening salt from bathers. The hippodrome featured Wild West shows, bullfights, and boxing matches. The dance floor, one of several in the United States to advertise itself as the nation's largest, often attracted more than 5,000 people on a weekend. (Private Collection.)

87

Conflict and
Concession

Chapter 5.

THE NINETEENTH-CENTURY CITY

In 1850 Great Salt Lake City—as it was officially known until 1868—was little more than an overgrown agricultural village. By the beginning of the twentieth century, it had become a city. The population had essentially doubled every twenty years and in 1900 was more than 50,000. By 1920 it would more than double again to nearly 120,000. In 1880 Salt Lake had an eight-person police force. By 1920 it had grown to 125, including two female officers. In 1880 Salt Lake and Lawrence, Kansas, were the only cities in the western United States without a board of health, while in 1920 Salt Lake officials proudly proclaimed the city's board of health to be the best in the nation. In 1880 Salt Lake had no large public parks. In 1920 there were thirteen, and the city operated an extensive year-round park recreation program because, according to city officials, "Free recreation must follow free education if America is to be truly great."

City streets and businesses began to be lighted with electricity in the spring of 1881 following the founding of the Salt Lake Power, Light, and Heating Company, and by the turn of the century the downtown was a maze of wires and poles. A streetcar system, established in 1872 with horse- and mule-drawn cars, was electrified in 1889 and served 10,000 people a day. By 1900 there were four daily newspapers and a dozen weeklies, ten cigar factories, the Keeley Institute "for the cure of Drunkenness, Opium, Cocaine, Ciga-

This view of Temple Square was taken in 1893 when the capstone was laid on the Salt Lake Mormon temple. The ceremonies attracted an estimated 30,000-50,000 people. A 12.5-foot Angel Moroni, made of hammered bronze, was added the following year. (Courtesy Nelson Wadsworth.)

rette and Tobacco Habits," two museums, ten pawnbrokers, sixty-eight realtors, and a well-established red-light district. Dale L. Morgan's description of Salt Lake in 1949 fit the city in 1900 just about as well: "glass show windows which parade up and down Main Street; ... theaters with their anxious chromium and neon; the pool halls, third-rate cafes, and four-rate hotels hanging on grimly to the lateral streets; the smoke-grimed colors of all the business establishments, warring one with another for attention. ... a plentitude of politicians to run the town, and a still greater supply of those wanting their turn."

The growth of Salt Lake City's population in the nineteenth century was steady but not spectacular. During the first winter of 1847-48, nearly 2,000 people lived in the valley. Ten years later the population was a little over 8,000, and by the turn of the century it was officially 53,531. The period of most rapid growth was the decade of the 1880s, when the population grew from 20,000 to nearly 45,000—an increase of 125 percent.

Throughout the nineteenth century a majority of Salt Lake's residents was native-born. As in most other U.S. cities, however, a significant minority was foreign-born. In 1880, 37 percent of the population had been born in other countries, and Salt Lake was almost as much of an "immigrant city" as New York, whose population was 40 percent immigrant. As in the rest of the

An 1880 view of First South, looking east. The old City Hall, now relocated across from the State Capitol Building, is on the right and the Salt Lake Theatre is on the left. In the foreground are some of the city's more than three dozen saloons and liquor dealers. Twenty years later, in 1900, the number of saloons had nearly tripled, to 97. (Private Collection.)

country, most of the immigrants who arrived before 1880 came from the British Isles and western and northern Europe. Unlike most other western U.S. cities, however, Salt Lake did not have a significant number of black residents—in 1880, only 86. On the other hand, women outnumbered men 52 percent to 48 percent, the highest percentage of women in any city in the West.

No provision existed in the original plan of Salt Lake City for a business district, but within a few years one began to develop. It was centered on the west side of Main Street between South Temple and 100 South streets. James A. Livingston and Charles A. Kinkead opened the first store there in 1850, a short distance south of the Council House then being built on the southwest corner of Main and South Temple streets. The previous year they had opened the first retail store in Salt Lake City near Union Square, the present site of

Wires and poles created a confusing jumble in downtown Salt Lake in the early twentieth century, as this photograph of Main Street, looking north from near Third South, makes clear. Poles were erected down the center and both sides of the streets. To add to the chaos, a variety of electric, trolley, and telephone companies used their own poles and lines. The David Keith Building, 242 South Main, constructed in 1902, is at the far left. (Private Collection.)

West High School, where many immigrants stopped temporarily upon their arrival in the valley. In rapid succession other businesses, large and small, began to fill both sides of the street. In 1854 eight stores were built on Main Street and six others opened in other parts of the city. Among the earliest businesses were several saloons, and for a period in the late 1850s Main Street was unofficially known as "Whiskey Street." By 1880 the core of the business district extended south along Main Street and one block on either side to about 200 South; by 1890 it stretched to 300 South, and by the early twentieth century to 400 South.

The city's early commercial buildings were one or two stories high, from one to three bays wide, of wood or adobe construction. A few had flat roofs, but most were gabled, though an extended false façade often concealed the gabling. In 1855 the Council House, the Valley House Hotel, and the Mormon church's Tithing Office were the only multi-story buildings. In the early 1860s more elaborate buildings began to appear. William Jennings, Utah's first millionaire, built his Eagle Emporium on the southwest corner of Main and 100

91

South in 1863. It became the first home of ZCMI five years later. The building still stands but has twice undergone extensive remodeling. Across the street William Godbe built his three-story Exchange Building. In 1866 *Harper's Weekly* described it as "palatial in appearance" and remarked that the buildings housing two other prominent business—Kimball and Lawrence and the Walker Brothers—were "equal to many in the Eastern States."

Few buildings are left from Salt Lake's early commercial period. With the demolition of the Amussen Jewelry Building in the 1970s to make way for the Crossroads Mall, the only remaining commercial building constructed before the coming of the railroad is the Eagle Emporium, now Zions Bank. The First National Bank (161 South Main), the adjoining Hepworth-Carthey Building, and a portion of the ZCMI storefront were erected before 1880. A handful of the remaining older commercial buildings dates from the late 1880s and early 1890s, when Salt Lake experienced a building boom cut short by the depression of 1893-97, but most are from the twentieth century.

As Salt Lake City's population grew, the face of the city changed. In the late 1850s the area known as the Avenues—originally called both the North Bench and the Dry Bench—was platted. In general the dimensions of the Avenues were half those of the rest of the city. Blocks and lots were smaller, houses closer to the street and to each other, and streets and sidewalks narrower. The Avenues were not set up for farmers and agricultural pursuits, but for artisans, tradesmen, and workers who wanted to be close to the business district and did not need farmland. With the coming of the railroad, the Avenues became an area where many railroad workers lived.

The Avenues were the first major departure from the original plan of Salt Lake City, but others soon followed as the city's population outgrew the original platted area. The establishment of the streetcar system in 1872 made it possible for people to live outside the city and commute to and from downtown. Beginning in the 1880s new residential sections were carved out of what had been farmland south of 900 South Street, the original southern limit of the city. Reflecting the evolution away from the self-sufficient Mormon village its founders had originally planned, these new "streetcar suburbs" were laid out on an entirely different plan from that of the original city. The blocks were smaller and rectangular in shape, rather than square, lots were smaller and more numerous, and streets narrower. The Perkins subdivision near 900 East

The Gathering Place

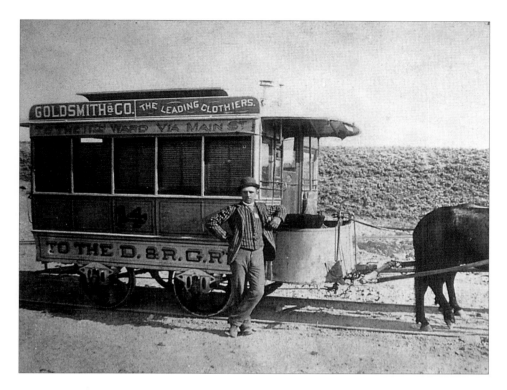

*Mule-drawn trolley cars, such
as this one, provided Salt Lake's
first public transportation. The
Salt Lake City Street Railway
Company began operation in
1872 and soon had twenty-one
mule- and horse-drawn cars and
fourteen miles of track. In 1889
the first electric streetcar took
its maiden run. According to
The Deseret News, "People
along the line stared as though
an apparition were flying by."
By 1914 approximately half of
the city's adult population rode
streetcars every day, and a record 38.9 million fares were
collected. (Private Collection.)*

and 1700 South, about which historian Roger Roper has written, is one example.

At the same time changes were taking place in the city's older sections. Large lots were subdivided, and new streets and courts were cut through the original blocks. The idea was to enable more people to live closer to town. The new streets were subject to little regulation, however, and instead of becoming quiet retreats from the noise and dirt of the city, they often degenerated into crowded back alleys of squalor. The Mormon church, which had planned so carefully in the early years, gradually lost influence. City government would not begin to establish zoning and building regulations until the 1920s, and until then planning was effectively in the hands of individual private promoters whose main concern was profit rather than community well being.

By the turn of the century, then, Salt Lake was no longer the uniform city its founders had intended. There were now three types of street patterns: the original large square blocks of ten acres, with new streets and courts crisscrossing most of them; the small square blocks of 2.5 acres on the steep ground of the Avenues; and the newer rectangular blocks of the southern extension.

As in most nineteenth-century American cities, the "good old days" in

93

The Nineteenth-
Century City

Salt Lake were not always so good. Filth clogged the streets. Dead animals decayed at intersections. Garbage piled up in yards. Household wastes ran onto the ground or into open gutters. Privy vaults and cesspools overflowed and leaked. Human wastes and industrial by-products contaminated drinking water. Construction of a sewer system did not begin until the 1890s, and parts of the city were without one until the 1920s.

Work animals were an important part of Salt Lake City's life before the turn of the century. In 1880 an estimated 6,000 work animals left behind sixty tons of manure and 3,000 gallons of urine during a normal working day, yet, like most cities at the time, Salt Lake had no program of regular street cleaning and maintenance. City workers cleaned the streets only occasionally, and when "street dirt" was collected, it was typically used to fill holes in vacant lots and low spots in city streets.

Dead animals were of special concern. Horses in particular had a way of dying at inopportune moments. If no one was around, people often left their carcasses lying in the street rather than pay removal costs. While some cities left it up to individuals to dispose of dead animals, in Salt Lake it was the responsibility of the city marshall to see that they were quickly removed from city streets and buried outside the city limits. Even so, dead animals were a

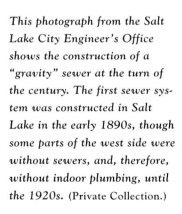

This photograph from the Salt Lake City Engineer's Office shows the construction of a "gravity" sewer at the turn of the century. The first sewer system was constructed in Salt Lake in the early 1890s, though some parts of the west side were without sewers, and, therefore, without indoor plumbing, until the 1920s. (Private Collection.)

Until they began to be paved around the turn of the century, streets in downtown Salt Lake City were a mess. During the dry season, the dust was often several inches deep, and during wet weather the mud was even deeper, as this view of South Temple, looking east from Main Street, shows. It was taken in March 1902. (Private Collection.)

constant problem, and Salt Lake newspapers described decaying horses lying by curbs for several days, and since before the coming of the automobile streets often served as playgrounds for children, the sight of them playing near dead animals was common.

Salt Lake streets were not only filthy, they were dusty in summer and muddy in winter. In 1880 no streets in the entire city were paved; by 1904 only 4.05 miles had been. Garbage collection was haphazard. City workers collected garbage periodically and took it to vacant ground outside the west city limits. People often chose not to use garbage collection, however, and simply burned, buried, or dumped their household wastes. In 1880 only six cities in the western United States had sewer systems, and Salt Lake was not one of them. Instead, it relied on open ditches, cesspools, and privy vaults, none of which worked very well.

Soon after Salt Lake City's founding, residents began a program of digging ditches along both sides of streets to convey water diverted from the valley's streams. Ultimately the ditches fed into the Jordan River. The water in them was to be used for irrigation, drinking, and carrying away human, animal, and household wastes and was supposed to flow fast enough to prevent the accumulation of filth. In fact, however, the effluence often moved slowly, and ditches became overloaded and stagnant. This was particularly true in the

95

The Nineteenth-
Century City

downtown area, where the amount of waste was greatest, and foul odors plagued the business district.

Cesspools and privy vaults worked no better. According to contemporary estimates, most of them leaked. Some cities regulated their construction and cleaning, but Salt Lake did not, and in 1880 the city officially reported the water in many of the wells in the city was contaminated and "rendered unfit for use," with "zymotic," or contagious, diseases rampant. When privy vaults and cesspools were emptied, their contents were buried in vacant lots within the city, hauled outside the west city limits, or sold to farmers as manure.

Prostitution, once nearly unknown in Salt Lake, emerged as the city grew. While at first glance it may seem an interesting, but ultimately trivial, subject, and a peripheral aspect of the city's history, just the opposite is true. Because prostitution is deeply rooted in the fabric of communities, its study can provide valuable insight into social structures and cultural values and practices, functioning as a lens through which to focus on a range of issues, including politics, women's economic and social status, and aspects of race, class, gender, and sexual orientation.

In 1871 Mormon church general authority Seymour B. Young wrote that "Salt Lake City has for the first time in its history houses of ill fame almost on

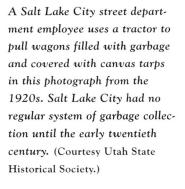

A Salt Lake City street department employee uses a tractor to pull wagons filled with garbage and covered with canvas tarps in this photograph from the 1920s. Salt Lake City had no regular system of garbage collection until the early twentieth century. (Courtesy Utah State Historical Society.)

every corner." While Young overstated the situation, presumably to make a point, by the early 1870s prostitution was both prevalent and easily visible, and city officials were dealing with it in much the way other cities did. Laws prohibiting it were on the books, but city officials essentially saw them as politically expedient concessions to middle-class morality. Prostitution could not be eliminated, they believed, but only confined to particular parts of town where it might be watched and regulated. As Salt Lake City chief of police Arthur Pratt said in 1895, "I think the best plan is to put prostitutes in one locality as much as possible and keep them under surveillance. The evil cannot be suppressed. It must be restrained and kept under a strict police control. It is a more difficult problem to handle when the women are scattered out than when they are kept together."

From the early 1870s until the 1930s, Salt Lake's primary red-light district was located in the downtown area on what is now Regent Street—then named, appropriately enough, Commercial Street. In 1903 *The Salt Lake Tribune* described it as "a resort of gamblers and fast women." According to the *Deseret News* half a dozen years later, the occupants of Commercial Street included "the demi-monde, the male parasite, the dope fiend, the gambler, and the beggar."

Owners of buildings that housed brothels were typically citizens and businesses of "eminent respectability." In the 1890s they included police chief Pratt; Gustave Holmes, owner of the fashionable Knutsford Hotel, a director of the National Bank of the Republic, and in 1909 the fifth largest taxpayer in Salt Lake County; and the Brigham Young Trust Company, whose officers included prominent Mormon church officials. According to D. Michael Quinn, in January 1897 Mormon apostle Brigham Young, Jr., temporarily resigned as vice-president of the company because, he said, George Q. Cannon, its president and a member of the church's First Presidency, allowed its property on Commercial Street to become "a first class brothel." It was operated by Ada Wilson and known as "The Palace." Apostle Heber J. Grant and other high-ranking LDS officials were invited to Wilson's "opening ball," and, according to Anthon H. Lund, were later "astonished to find that they had been in a regular whore-house." According to Jeffrey Nichols, the Brigham Young Trust Company and its successor owned properties in Salt Lake City that were used for prostitution into the 1930s. Today only one building of the several dozen that once served as "houses of ill fame" remains on Regent Street. Built

Commercial Street (renamed Regent Street in the 1920s), looking north from Second South, in 1916, was the center of Salt Lake City's first red-light district beginning in the 1870s. (Private Collection.)

in 1893 for Gustave Holmes, a "parlor house," so named because prostitutes ordinarily received their customers in a common parlor or sitting room, was upstairs, while Nic Schmeider's Leader Cigar Factory, one of ten in the city at the time, was located on the first floor. The cigar factory remained in the building through the 1920s. After that a tailor shop and a series of other small businesses occupied it. The Felt Electric Company was located there in the 1980s and 1990s. At the end of the 1990s, the tenant was a martial arts studio.

As in other American cities, an unofficial licensing system for prostitutes existed in Salt Lake. The way it operated varied over time. In 1886 prostitutes

Socialist Henry W. Lawrence, a prominent businessman who had previously been active in the Liberal Party, was elected to the Salt Lake City Commission in 1911. The Socialist Party of America was active throughout Utah between 1900 and the early 1920s, electing more than 100 socialists to office in fourteen cities and towns throughout the state and to the state legislature. (Private Collection.)

and their madams were periodically arrested, fined a maximum of $50 each, given physical examinations, and released. Between arrests, *The Salt Lake Tribune* said, they were "allowed to go along without fear of molestation as long as they did not ply their trade so openly and brazenly as to offend the public eye." That was not always the case, however. According to *The Tribune*, in September 1901 "Mary Belvun, the landlady of one of the Commercial Street shacks, was up on the old charge. She has been told to leave the city, but refused to do so. Mary based her refusal on the grounds that she had as much right here as any others of her class. She had paid the monthly fine exacted by the city for two months past." By 1908 a registration system existed. Police kept track of names and addresses of madams and their houses. The madams, in turn, gave lists of the women who worked for them to police. Every month each woman was expected to pay a "fine" of $10. After examining the books in which the names of prostitutes were recorded, the *Deseret News* reported that during the summer of 1908 an average of 148 women had been arrested and fined each month. The more than $1,500 collected monthly went into the city's general fund. In the mid-1910s city policy was to license brothels as "rooming houses" and require prostitutes to live and work only in them. Thus, in 1916, the upper floor of one Commercial Street building was the "Svea Rooming House," and

The Nineteenth-Century City

William Thurston Brown was minister of Salt Lake City's Unitarian church during his three-year stay in Utah, 1907-10. During that time he was one of the state's most articulate and widely read Socialists. A prolific writer, he contributed to a range of radical journals, from anarchist publications to Socialist ones, and wrote a number of lengthy pamphlets, including How Capitalism Has Hypnotized Society. *(Private Collection.)*

Cora Thompson, whose arrest on charges of prostitution was reported several times in the *Deseret News,* was listed in the *Salt Lake City Directory* as its "manager."

During these years the south end of Commercial Street became "soap box corner" where Socialists, Anarchists, Wobblies, and other political "undesirables" whom city officials hoped to marginalize by confining to the periphery of respectable society were allowed to speak. The mayor and city commission also allowed them to speak farther north on Commercial Street at Orpheum Avenue and on 200 South near Franklin Avenue, which was also a red light district. Others were routinely given permits to speak on Main Street. This represented something of a backlash against political radicalism in Utah in the late nineteenth and especially early twentieth centuries: the Industrial Workers of the World (IWW) was active throughout Utah, particularly in mining towns; more than a hundred socialists had been elected to office throughout the state by the early 1920s, including Henry W. Lawrence, whom Salt Lake City voters elected as city commissioner in 1911; and on three occa-

A Christian Socialist, and known nationwide as "Utah's Socialist Bishop," the Right Reverend Franklin Spencer Spalding was Episcopal bishop of Utah from 1905 until his accidental death in 1914. During those years he guided Episcopal affairs in Utah while at the same time actively participating in the growing Socialist movement. In 1911 he was one of the founders of the Church Socialist League and served as its first president. (Private Collection.)

sions the Utah State Federation of Labor officially endorsed the Socialist Party, resolving in 1912 "that as a state organization, we aid in the propaganda of Socialism, that we may hasten the day when the emancipation of the working class from the bonds of wage slavery shall be proclaimed in America and throughout the world."

A fuller account of the subject would embrace not only electoral politics, but a range of aspects of what might be termed Salt Lake City's "radical culture," including the Populist Party's People's Church, which invited "all those interested in rational religion, ethical culture, and social progress" to join; the Workingmen's Club which met regularly on "Industrial Square" to discuss topics such as "Reform or Revoltuion: Which Shall We Have" and "Millionaires and Paupers"; the Independent Free Thought Spiritualistic Church; the Modern School, a private elementary and secondary school based on the educational theories of Spanish anarchist Francisco Ferrer and the second of more than thirty to be founded in the United States; occasions such as "New Year's Eve With the Socialists"; "Julia Gilbert's Ladies Working Class Orchestra";

Handbill advertising a Socialist Party rally, sometime between 1914 and 1917. J. Alex Bevan was elected to the Utah State Legislature from Tooele County in 1914 as a socialist and was re-elected in 1916. Brigham H. Rowberry was a longtime Socialist Party activist from Tooele. (Courtesy Mrs. Cleone Hogevoll.)

"Red Sunday" celebrations and "Socialist Day" at Wandamere Resort, which attracted 1,000 people; parades such as one on October 15, 1911, in support of striking railroad workers across the United States that proceeded from Federation of Labor Hall to Main Street, up Main and around the Brigham Young monument, and ended at the Salt Lake Theatre, where a "benefit entertainment" was held for strikers; free speech fights in Liberty Park, where Socialists, anarchists, and Wobblies joined together in the right to stand on soap boxes and deliver their revolutionary speeches without interference or the threat of violence against them; the Socialist Social Club; the Political Refugee Defense League; the Union Socialist Labor and Propaganda League; and publications like *The Intermountain Worker* and *The Crisis*, which advertised itself as "A Socialist Paper for Non-Socialists. All the News of the World of Labor. Largest Circulation of Any Weekly in Utah."

A fuller account would also include a range of people. Utah's Episcopal bishop from 1905 until 1914, Franklin Spalding, was a Christian Socialist widely known throughout the United States as "Utah's Socialist Bishop." William Thurston Brown was minister of Salt Lake's Unitarian church from 1907 until 1910. In addition to preaching regular sermons and giving weekly lectures that, the *Herald Independent* newspaper said, were "startling in tone, socialistic in aspect, and decidely revolutionary in character," he was a socialist organizer who, as Paul Avrich noted, travelled throughout the country "denouncing the evils of capitalism and upholding the rights of labor, free speech, and free love." In a 1909 sermon on "Marriage As It Has Been and Is, and Marriage As It Ought To Be," he argued: "The idea of a wife is one of two things. She, if she be the wife of a working man, is a slave, or better, the slave of a slave; if she be the wife of a man of money, she is a toy. Never, however, is she re-

Newspaper boys in front of the Deseret News *building at the turn of the century. At the time, an estimated 20 percent of children in the U.S. between the ages of ten and fourteen held full-time jobs, as did a smaller, but still significant, number of children younger than ten. (Courtesy Utah State Historical Society.)*

garded by man to be his equal. She is an attachment, a cook, a housekeeper, or a toy." Virginia Snow Stephen was an art instructor at the University of Utah and daughter of Lorenzo Snow, fifth president of the Mormon church. "Do you believe there is justice for the poor working factory girl, or for the ill-paid person in other employment?" she wrote to a friend. "If you knew and had seen right here in Salt Lake City what I have seen with my own eyes, you might change your view." Emma Goldman, the most important anarchist in the United States, called her "a very courageous and able woman." In 1914 Stephen became involved in the struggle to save Joe Hill, a songwriter and organizer for the IWW. After he was executed in 1915 and the University of Utah fired her for her involvement in the case, she married another Wobbly and moved to California.

~

Recommended Readings

Haglund, Karl T., and Notarianni, Philip F. *The Avenues of Salt Lake City.* Salt Lake City: Utah State Historical Society, 1980.

McCormick, John S. "Red Lights in Zion: Salt Lake City's Stockade, 1908-1911." *Utah Historical Quarterly* 50 (Spring 1982): 168-81. Reprinted in McCormick and Sillito, *A World We Thought We Knew,* 173-83.

McCormick, John S., and Sillito, John R. "Respectable Reformers: Utah Socialists in Power, 1900-1925." In McCormick and Sillito, *A World We Thought We Knew,* 115-29.

Nichols, Jeffrey. "Prostitution and Polygamy: The Contest Over Morality in Salt Lake City, 1847-1918." Ph.D. diss., University of Utah, 1998.

The Gathering Place

Chapter 6.

A CITY OF IMMIGRANTS

Throughout the nineteenth century Salt Lake was a city of immigrants. In 1880 more than one-third of the population was foreign-born, while two-thirds had either been born in other countries or their parents had. Most were Mormon converts from the British Isles, Western Europe, and Scandinavia. Toward the end of the nineteenth century, that began to change as new groups, part of a stream of 25 million people who reached the shores of the United States between 1880 and 1910, mainly from eastern and southern Europe, Asia, the Middle East, and Mexico, arrived in increasing numbers. The 1910 census counted more than 2,000 Japanese in Utah, 3,100 Italians, 4,000 Greeks, and 3,500 Serbs and Austrians—and those figures were low, census takers having missed many people who moved from place to place in search of work. In 1900 only about 100 Hispanics resided permanently in Utah, most of them in the southeastern corner of the state where they worked mainly as ranch hands and sheepherders. In 1920 there were nearly 2,000, most of them in the Salt Lake Valley, and by 1930 the number had doubled to over 4,000.

Visible signs of Salt Lake's changing population were everywhere. According to *The Salt Lake Tribune*, in 1897, "A prominent feature of nearly all New Year's parades was a huge Chinese dragon two hundred feet long which progressed along the street like a gigantic centipede. The dragon itself, which swayed from side to side, had a head six feet tall spitting fire from its red mouth." There were new churches, including the Cathedral of the Madeleine and Our Lady of Guadalupe Catholic Mission, and a Spanish-speaking branch of the Mormon church, *La Rama Mexicana*; three Jewish synagogues; a Japanese Buddhist temple and a Japanese Church of Christ; the Holy Trinity Greek Orthodox Church; the Trinity African Methodist Episcopal Church; and the Calvary Baptist Church. New organizations appeared, including *Comision Honorifica Mexicana* and *La Cruz Azul,* both of which helped Mexicans immigrating to Utah and sponsored Mexican celebrations on *Cinco de Mayo* and *Dieciseis de Septiembre.* There were new wedding and funeral ceremonies and new festivals and celebrations. The Salt Lake City cemetery included Japanese, Chinese, Jewish, and Catholic sections. New faces appeared on city streets and on the job. By the early 1920s, 20 percent of section crew members on the Los Angeles and Salt Lake Railroad were Hispanic. New foreign language newspapers were sold on street corners, including the Greek *To Fos* and *O Ergatis*, the Italian *Il Minatore*, and the Japanese *Utah Nippo.* Kuniko Teresawa and her husband, Uneo, began publishing the latter soon after their arrival in Salt Lake in 1914. When he died, she continued it until she was more than ninety years old. At first the paper came out every day, then every other day, then every week, and finally once a month, but she did not change its name, she said, because she still worked on it every day, no matter how often it was published. New restaurants were everywhere, as well as new musical instruments and new music. Yugoslavians brought the tambura, Greeks the lyra and the laouto. There were new games, like "Boccie," an Italian game similar to lawn bowling.

The experience of new immigrants in Utah was much the same as it was in the rest of the United States, including the concern their presence occasioned and the prejudice and discrimination they met—except that in some ways in Utah they were outsiders even more than elsewhere. Not only had they come from different parts of the world than had earlier groups, but most were not Mormons. The vast majority were young, single men who came by chance, not design. Utah was where they happened to get a job, or had friends or relatives, or decided to get off a freight train after a long and exhausting ride. For at least the first generation, they mainly worked at "pick and shovel" jobs, primarily on the railroads and in the mines. Most intended to stay only

temporarily, until they could save enough money to re-establish themselves in their homeland.

Strangers in a strange land, every new immigrant group fought against the Anglo-American community's dominance as they struggled to make both a living and a life, nurturing community and family ties, and in that struggle they met as much prejudice and discrimination in Utah as they did elsewhere in the United States, and its legacy persists to the present. Ethnic divisions ran deep. Utahns have always been highly ambivalent about how much they value people from other cultures, about whether diversity is a strength or a weakness, something to be embraced or feared; they have been as susceptible as people anywhere in the United States to periodic irrational fears that the barbarians

Participants in Salt Lake City's first Mexican-American celebration, early 1930s. (Private Collection.)

A City of
Immigrants

are at the gates, that we are being overrun with immigrants who take jobs from American citizens, are a drain on society's resources, refuse to assimilate, or, more seriously, are incapable of assimilating and threaten cultural and political unity. Thus the threat of being dispossessed in one way or another that various groups have regularly faced and their often heroic efforts to make a place for themselves are constantly recurring themes in Salt Lake's history.

Suspicion of foreign-born residents was particularly high in the early twentieth century. A push for "100% Americanization" emerged, and politicians were quick to exploit the sentiment. The feeling was widespread that only the Anglo-Saxon race had the qualities necessary for American society to survive and that the future of the country depended on having a relatively homogeneous population. A headline in the June 27, 1907, *Deseret News*, "Vicious Dago Scoundrel Murders Inoffensive White Railroad Worker," and an editorial in the November 6, 1913, *Carbon County News*, "The 'Japs' are all right in their place, but that place is not beside Anglo-Saxon women, and the sooner the latter find it out the better for them," expressed sentiments all too common. In 1904 Mayor Joseph Stratton of Murray called a series of public meetings to consider requiring that all new immigrants leave the city. As he saw it, "[H]eterogeneous elements ... do not fit into the scheme of American society or community." Murray was "going steadily downhill because of the presence of this low element," he said. "We want to see our town go ahead. It will continue to get worse so long as these foreigners stay here and work for cheap wages. We must get rid of them now." According to Helen Ong Louie, "When I came over, the United States discriminated against Oriental people. They looked down at you. They really looked down." Racial slurs were nothing out of the ordinary. "Chink, Chink, Chinaman" was a common expression. Segregation was widespread. "Discrimination was absolutely public in Salt Lake," Helen Kuramada recalled. "We couldn't go to city swimming pools. Our parents paid taxes, but we couldn't swim in the Liberty Park pool. When we went to a movie at one of the better theatres, we couldn't sit downstairs. We had to go upstairs—to the balconies." Job opportunities for Chinese immigrants were limited to working in "a restaurant, a laundry, maybe a small grocery," Bob Louie said. "That's about all. They didn't have any other opportunities. They couldn't go out and walk into an office and get a job."

108

The Gathering Place

Hostility peaked during strikes and periods of labor unrest, when it was easy to characterize immigrants as disruptive agitators who did not understand American ways and values. The Carbon County coal strike of 1903-1904 and the Bingham and Murray strikes of 1912 failed because in each case the company was able to exploit ethnic divisions, effectively playing on the widespread nativist sentiment of the time and portraying the striking miners, who were mainly new immigrants from eastern and southern Europe, as un-American, radical, and dangerous. World War I brought added distrust. Hostility intensified in the mid-1920s with the organization of the Ku Klux Klan in Utah as part of the Klan's resurgence across the United States in the years following World War I. The Klan's slogan stated its goal in no uncertain terms: "Native, White, Protestant Supremacy." Active throughout the country, particularly in the Midwest, it had a nationwide membership of 5 million by 1920.

In Utah the Klan was strongest in Salt Lake, Utah, and Carbon counties, where its members burned crosses, staged parades along Main streets, threatened immigrant men who were seen with American women, and vandalized immigrant-owned businesses. The Utah Klan held its first state convention on Ensign Peak north of Salt Lake City, with burning crosses visible throughout the valley. As Helen Zeese Papanikolas says, "Immigrants and their children saw white-robed Klan members march down Salt Lake City, Helper, and Magna streets and watched crosses burning on Salt Lake's Ensign Peak, on Bingham and Helper mountainsides, and near the Magna graveyard. Stories of Klan attacks bombarded the children's ears. Immigrants who had married American women were most vulnerable—crosses burned in front of their businesses, women clerks and waitresses working for immigrants were threatened. In Helper, the Klan invaded stores, rampaged through them, and forced American women employees to their houses. A child watching a cross burning at night was forever wounded in spirit."

To help them deal with the problems they faced, immigrants gathered together, forming small colonies within the larger community, and ethnic neighborhoods became a feature of cities and towns in Utah, as they did throughout the United States. It was not so much that immigrants chose to cluster together as that they were forced to. Salt Lake's Greeks and Italians could not cross State Street without someone asking, "A little far east, aren't you?" and running the risk of being referred to as "God damned Greeks" and "Dirty

A City of
Immigrants

Japanese immigrants began coming to Utah in the late 1880s to work on the railroads. According to the 1910 census, 2,110 Japanese men and women lived in Utah; in 1920 this rose to more than 3,000, most of them residing in the Salt Lake Valley. They faced the same problems that other new immigrants did: a sense of displacement, ridicule, discrimination, and employment handicaps. To meet these problems, they developed agencies of their own to provide mutual support. Churches were particularly important, as were newspapers. Shiro Iida founded The Rocky Mountain Times *in 1907. The* Utah Nippo *followed seven years later and was published until the early 1990s.* (Private Collection.)

The Gathering Place

Dagoes." Residents of Chinatown could not venture far beyond Plum Alley without the risk of being beaten up, and illegally lived in the back of their cafes and laundries because they could not rent apartments. As Elaine Kim explains in a recent discussion of the Korean-American experience in the United States, ethnic neighborhoods functioned as a kind of home, or anchor, a potential refuge, a place where people could go without being asked, "Who are you and what are you doing here? Where did you come from and when are you going back?" They were "safe zones" where marginalized groups could retreat for healing and mutual recognition and to construct shared relationships, knowledge, meaning, and claims to bring with them in their interaction with dominant groups.

In Salt Lake "Little Tokyo" sprang up around a two-block area of 100 South Street between West Temple and 300 West, an area the Salt Palace Convention Center now largely occupies. Restaurants, dry-cleaning establishments, fish markets, a tofu bean-cake factory, barbershops, hotels, rooming houses, a Japanese Church of Christ and a Buddhist temple, a Japanese school, and the fraternal society Hiroshima Ken Jin Kai met many of the needs of the

Japanese community, "strengthened their traditional cultural values," as Nancy J. Taniguchi says, "and enhanced community ties."

Italian-owned grocery stores, saloons, restaurants, and other shops were part of "Little Italy" that emerged along Salt Lake's 200 South Street between the Union Pacific and Denver and Rio Grande Western railroad depots. Around Plum Alley, which ran north and south dividing the block between Main and State streets and 100 and 200 South, the Chinese developed a compact community of their own, with grocery and merchandise stores, laundries, and restaurants. According to Anand A. Yang, "At its height in the late nineteenth and early twentieth centuries, as many as one thousand people may have resided in this area of less than a city block."

Little Syria grew up around the area of 300 South and 500 West. In the late 1920s a two-story Victorian Italianate residence at 126 South 200 West, originally built in the 1880s for Mormon businessman Lewis S. Hills, became the Hogar Hotel, a boarding house and community center for Basque immigrants making their way to ranches throughout the Intermountain West. Nearby, on West 200 South between 400 and 600 West streets, was Greek-

A City of
Immigrants

Chin Sig, pictured here, was one of 271 Chinese men and women who officially lived in Salt Lake in 1890. Chinese immigrants first came to Utah in the late 1860s as laborers on the transcontinental railroad. In the 1870s most of Utah's Chinese population lived in Box Elder County, where almost all worked as section hands on the railroad. Gradually they moved into other occupations, including mining. Many opened small businesses in Ogden, Salt Lake City, Park City, and other Utah towns. (Private Collection.)

Since the turn of the century, the largest Chinese population in Utah has been in Salt Lake City. Like many other immigrants, they tended to congregate together in sections of the city. Salt Lake's Chinatown was located in the downtown area on Plum Alley, shown here, where there were Chinese groceries, merchants, laundries, and restaurants. (Private Collection.)

Many of Utah's first generation of Greek immigrants intended to stay only temporarily, long enough to accumulate a nest egg before returning to their homeland. As the years passed, however, more and more settled permanently. Often they sent to Greece for "picture brides" whom friends and relatives had selected for them. Weddings, such as this one, were performed on Sundays. A wedding feast followed. Rice and Jordan almonds were thrown at the couple as symbols of fertility. (Private Collection.)

town, the most extensive of Salt Lake's ethnic neighborhoods and, thanks to the work of Helen Zeese Papanikolas, the best known. Along its two-block area were small hotels and boardinghouses, coffeehouses, saloons, grocery stores, bakeries, and import stores selling octopus, Turkish tobacco, olive oil, goat cheese, liqueurs, figs, dates, and Greek-language newspapers. In 1911 nearly sixty Greek businesses occupied the two blocks.

The coffeehouse in particular was an important institution. As Papaikolas says, it was the true home of many Greeks. In its gregariousness they found a refuge from the prejudice they faced and the sense of displacement and malaise they felt. It was a community center often providing their only social life. There they gathered to drink, smoke, play cards, and talk. Political meetings were held there, as well as musical events and English language classes. At the same time, native-born Americans peering into a coffeehouse at men reading newspapers in a foreign language, drinking, gambling, talking, laughing, and arguing took it as proof that Greeks could never become part of American society.

Thirty or so buildings were once part of Greektown. All were constructed between about 1900 and 1910. With one exception Anglo businessmen built them as investment properties and in turn rented them to Greeks. They were mostly what might be called "anonymous" buildings: relatively small, plain

113

A City of
Immigrants

Interior of the Open Heart
Coffeehouse in Salt Lake City's
Greektown in the mid-1920s.
The owner, Emmanuel
Katsanevas, stands at the left.
(Private Collection.)

brick structures of one or two stories, with little detailing and few ornamental elements, except perhaps some decorative brickwork. Only a dozen buildings remain today. Most of the others were demolished in the 1980s, and those left are not likely to survive much longer. Even a little information about their origin helps convey a sense of the immigrant experience in Salt Lake during the early part of this century.

The building at 537 West 200 South was built in 1905 for a local real estate speculator named F. B. Huggerman. For the next fifteen years he leased it to a succession of Greek businesses—a coffeehouse until 1908 and then a series of bakeries. A Greek bakery occupied 537 (rear) West 200 South from 1912 to 1942, while 543 West 200 South was in turn a Greek grocery, restaurant, saloon, and coffeehouse from 1911, when it was built, until the mid-1920s. The only Greektown building not constructed by Anglo businessmen, it was built as income property for Nicholas Stathakos, a native of Athens who came to Utah in 1905 and became a prominent businessman with extensive real estate holdings. The building at 561 West 200 South was built in 1910 for

114

John J. Corum, a Salt Lake real estate speculator. Following its construction, he rented it to Panagiotes Fotis, George Roussos, Chris Regas, and Tom Koulias, who operated a saloon on a ground floor and a boarding house for Greek immigrants on the second. By 1914 the building's tenants were Anast Koulis's saloon and coffeehouse; Frank Manos's boarding house; and Peter Zaharias's barbershop. Similar businesses occupied the building through the 1930s. Corum also owned a building across the street at 540 West 200 South that he built in 1908. He first leased it to Greek businessman Louis Kourmalis, who operated a saloon there. A succession of other Greek businesses followed, including John Econome's cigar shop in 1910, Christian Chronopoulis's confectionery in 1912, and Louis Peran's restaurant from 1925 to 1946.

Alex Rizos, a graduate of the University of Athens who came to the United States in 1904 and received a degree in pharmacy from the University of Minnesota in 1907, operated a drugstore for many years in the building, now demolished, at 480 West 200 South. In addition to conventional medicines, he dispensed such Greek remedies as *manjouni*, "a tonic made of quinine sulphate, powdered Peruvian bark, honey, nux vomica, rhubarb herb, cinnamon, and other ingredients." *To Fos (The Light)*, a newspaper printed in Greek, was published for several years at 460 West 200 South. Its founder and editor was Dr. Peter Kassinkos, a Greek physician, whose stated goal was to educate Greeks about U.S. laws and customs so they might become informed citizens. From 1916 to 1919, another Greek-language paper, *O Evzone*, which viewed itself as a voice of the working class and advocated the rights of Greek laborers, occupied the same building. The structure, now demolished, at 592-598 West 200 South was built about 1900 by James Hegney and was occupied until 1904 by the H. Alma Reiser Grocery and Dry Goods Company. Hegney owned it until the 1920s, but from 1907 to 1912 it was the headquarters of Leonidas G. Skliris and his Italian-Greek Mercantile Company. Known as the "Czar of the Greeks," Skliris became a leading labor agent in Utah and the Intermountain West, recruiting immigrants mainly for mining and railroad jobs, and charging them a large initial fee and a sum to be deducted from their wages each month. Those who arrived on their own also often went to him for work. For Utah Copper Company operations at Bingham, he imported all Greek and Slavic workers. (Edward Daigoro Hashimota provided Japanese workers, while Mo-

A City of
Immigrants

ses Paggi supplied Italians.) In addition to providing cheap labor for industry, Skliris and other labor agents brought in strikebreakers, as in the 1912 Bingham strike, who were easily recruited from among immigrants desperate for work.

Greek immigrants built their first church in Salt Lake in 1905. A small yellow brick building with a central dome, located just to the south of the present Denver and Rio Grande Depot, it served not only Greeks but also Serbians and Russians for almost twenty years. In the mid-1920s a much larger structure, the present Holy Trinity Greek Orthodox Church, at 279 South 300 West, was built. A fine example of Byzantine design, its first service was held on the Day of the Dormition of the Virgin, August 13, 1924. Trains and stages brought Greeks from surrounding mining, mill, and smelting towns. The congregation met at the old church and walked to the new one with the priest, the chanter, and small boys holding banners leading the way. It was consecrated the next summer, on August 2, 1925.

Ethnic neighborhoods were clearly places imbued with bitter memories as well as more positive stories. They functioned on many levels: as neighborhoods with a rich community life; as places of shelter and protection; as political territories—segregated, or "bounded" spaces, as Dolores Hayden says, with some form of enforcement of the boundaries; and as what French sociologist Henri Lefebvre calls "counter-space" standing in opposition to and challenging existing political structures and relations of power, offering an oppositional vision. They attested to the power of one cultural landscape to contradict another and set up a political dialogue with the surrounding city and its political, social, and cultural traditions. Like other city spaces, they can be understood in terms of power or authority, as architectural historian Camille Wells says, "as efforts to assume, extend, resist, or accommodate" power. This was in part what Lefebvre meant when he said that "space is permeated with social relations; it is not only supported by social relations but it is also producing and produced by social relations." In other words, people make spaces, and spaces in turn make people.

Several years after Greektown was well established, the area also became Salt Lake's primary quasi-legal red-light district. Its story underscores the hostility that existed toward ethnic communities at the time and also provides a clear example of the extent to which Salt Lake City had moved away from its

MRS. DORA B. TOPHAM,
Under the name of Belle London, She Is the Queen of the Ogden Underworld, and, in Company With Various Respectable Citizens of Salt Lake, Who Compose the Citizens' Investment Company, Is Owner of the West Side Stockade, and Is Active Manager of That Walled City of Sin.

The Intermountain Republican ran this photograph of Belle London in its May 20, 1909, edition with the following explanation: "Mrs. Dora B. Topham. Under the name of Belle London, she is the queen of the Ogden underworld, and, in company with various respectable citizens of Salt Lake, who compose the Citizens' Investment Company, is owner of the West Side Stockade, and is active manager of that walled city of sin." (Private Collection.)

initial status as a "Mormon commonwealth." Early in the twentieth century Salt Lake businessmen began lobbying city officials to move the city's red-light district from Commercial Street in the central business district to a more isolated location. Within a few years, their efforts were successful. In his annual report for 1907, Salt Lake police chief Thomas Pitt recommended the creation of a separate district, or "stockade," surrounded by a high fence, where prostitutes could be confined, licensed, regulated by the police, and inspected on a regular basis by medical doctors. Soon afterward, Mayor John Bransford, with the approval of the city council, contacted Belle London, Ogden's best-known madam. Under the guise of a newly formed real estate firm, the Citizens' Investment Company, she bought most of the interior of Block 64, Plat A, in the center of Salt Lake's Greek community, built a "stockade" of about 100 "cribs" and several parlor houses, and enclosed the entire complex with a brick wall. She also constructed two buildings on the outside of the wall on 100 South. One of them provided living quarters on its upper floors for women of the stockade and housed a cafe on the ground level; the other served as a bar and saloon. The architect of one of the buildings was Lewis D. Martin, a member of

117

A City of
Immigrants

the city council. He also designed the stockade itself and a two-story business building and hotel across the street on 200 South that Mayor Bransford owned.

On December 18, 1908, Salt Lake City police announced that all prostitutes on Commercial Street and nearby Victoria Alley had until 4:00 a.m. to vacate the area. They could leave town, go to jail, or move to the stockade. Most of the women, perhaps 100 in all, chose the stockade where, according to city councilman Martin Mulvey, the police would leave them alone. Only if they worked elsewhere in the city would they be arrested.

Why had city officials decided to locate the stockade in Greektown? According to Mayor Bransford, it was in part because the "foreign element" had moved there, thus destroying what had once been a respectable residential area. "We found that most of the better class of residents were leaving the area anyway," he said, "because of the influx of Italians and Greeks who live in that neighborhood." In addition, Bransford, though he did not mention it, owned property across the street from the stockade, and following its construction he built a two-story building, renting out the ground floor to Greek businesses and the upper floor as living quarters to women working in the stockade.

The stockade operated for nearly three years until, on September 28, 1911, Belle London made an unexpected announcement: "The stockade will be closed on Thursday and the same will not be opened again. So soon as I can arrange my business I shall advertize the property for sale." Reaction to her announcement was mixed. A *Salt Lake Telegram* editorial expressed regret. Because prostitution was inevitable, the paper said, a "segregated district" was the best way to control it, and the stockade's closure would make regulation harder. Police chief Samuel Barlow agreed, contending that control of prostitution would now be "infinitely more difficult." The *Deseret News* and the *Salt Lake Herald* were skeptical that London really intended to close the stockade permanently. As the *Herald* saw it, her intent was "merely to embarrass the good citizens of the community by turning a flood of scarlet women into the streets, thus creating a condition more horrible, if possible, than the stockade itself." That accomplished, the paper predicted, the stockade would soon reopen. The *Deseret News* agreed, pointing out that "this turning loose of 300 prostitutes in Salt Lake where they will infiltrate the business district, flaunt themselves on the streets, and offend the public morals" would occur during the weekend of the Mormon church's general conference when the city would be filled with out-of-town visitors. London meant what she said, however, and the stockade soon closed and was demolished. The ground remained vacant for a number of years until the early 1950s when the Rio Grande Lumberyard took it over and operated there for nearly forty years.

London's reasons for closing the stockade remain unclear. A factor may have been that less than a month earlier she had been convicted of pandering and faced the possibility of a twenty-year sentence—though following her subsequent appeal, the conviction was overturned. The important point, though, is that its closure brought no substantial changes. It did not mean the end of prostitution in the city nor of segregated vice districts. Prostitution continued to exist, and everyone knew it, though, as before, the subject was excluded from polite conversation. Women of the former stockade either remained near West Second South, returned to Commercial Street, or worked in other areas of the city. Laws prohibiting prostitution remained on the books but continued to be selectively enforced. The continued goal of public officials was not the

A City of
Immigrants

elimination of prostitution, but its de facto licensing and attempted confinement to certain areas. Commercial Street remained a red-light district until the late 1930s and West Second South until the late 1970s.

Soon after the stockade closed, the Women's Welfare Committee asked William N. Knerr, who was running for the Salt Lake City Commission on the Socialist Party ticket, and in 1917 would be appointed the first head of the Utah State Industrial Commission, his views as a prospective city official on prostitution. In the first place, he said, though the police pretend to be against prostitution, they were "grafters" and wanted to see it continue so they would continue to receive payoffs. More than that, "Gambling, intemperance, and prostitution are alike products of the capitalistic system, which gambles on life, is based upon the sale of the bodies and minds of men and women and compels the majority of the people to prostitute the best that is in them for bare existence. There will always be women prostitutes as long as the majority of men are bodily and mental prostitutes for a wage, and as long as the woman has not the right and the opporunity of independent self-employment and has to look to some man for support. It is utterly foolish to attempt to abolish prostitution while employers are permitted to hire girls to work in stores and factories at a wage actually lower than what is necessary for bare essentials of food and clothing."

Although there are areas today in Salt Lake City where African Americans, Hispanics, and members of other ethnic groups predominate, Little Italy, Chinatown, Greek, "Bohunk," and "Jap" towns are gone. They began to disappear, and city officials sometimes forcibly broke them up, as in the case of Chinatown, during the 1940s. By that time the U.S. Congress had passed the National Origins Act of 1929 and other legislation aimed at not only limiting the total number of immigrants to this country in any one year, but, more to the point, those deemed "undesirable" because of their ethnic background. Since then most of the buildings in the old ethnic neighborhoods have been torn down. Large parking terraces have completely replaced Chinatown. Other than the Bertolini Block (147 West 200 South), little remains of the Italian section. Nearly the entire Japanese section was demolished in the late 1960s when the Salt Palace, a sports and convention center, was built. Only the 1924 Japanese Church of Christ remains to document the early Japanese experience in Salt Lake, and its future is uncertain.

~

Recommended Readings

Gerlach, Larry. *Blazing Crosses in Zion: The Ku Klux Klan in Utah*. Logan: Utah State University Press, 1982.

Hayden, Dolores. *The Power of Place: Urban Landscapes as Public History*. Cambridge, MA: MIT Press, 1995.

Kelen, Leslie G., and Fuller, Sandra T. *The Other Utahns: A Photographic Portfolio*. Salt Lake City: University of Utah Press, 1988.

_____ and Stone. *Missing Stories*.

Nagata, Ted, ed. *Japanese Americans in Utah*. [Salt Lake City:] JA Centennial Committee, 1997.

Papanikolas, Helen Z. *The Apple Falls from the Tree: Stories*. Athens: Swallow Press/Ohio University Press, 1996.

_____, ed. *The Peoples of Utah*. Salt Lake City: Utah State Historical Society, 1976.

_____. *Small Bird Tell Me: Stories of Greek Immigrants in Utah*. Athens: Swallow Press/Ohio University Press, 1993.

_____. *Toil and Rage in a New Land: The Greek Immigrants in Utah*. A special issue of *Utah Historical Quarterly* 38 (Spring 1970).

Takaki, Ronald. *A Different Mirror: A History of Multicultural America*. New York: Little Brown and Co., 1993.

Utah Historical Quarterly 40 (Summer 1972); a special issue on ethnic minority groups in Utah.

Chapter 7.

THE BUILT ENVIRONMENT

(opposite) This homecoming arch at Second South and Main streets, shown here on August 19, 1899, was erected to celebrate the return of Utah veterans from the Spanish-American War. In 1898, when U.S. president McKinley asked Utah for a quota of 500 troops, 700 men volunteered within a few days. Most Utah regiments served in the Philippines, fighting with Filipinos against the Spanish. Some then stayed on to fight against the same Filipino people who, once free of Spanish control, wanted to be independent rather than become a protectorate of the United States. (Courtesy Utah State Historical Society.)

Buildings are deeply woven into the fabric of a community. Individual buildings—those of the rich, the famous, the influential, and the privileged, and the more modest, even mundane, houses, union halls, and small work places of ordinary people of limited means—as well as public spaces and the layout of an entire city—render history visible. Most of Salt Lake City's built environment from the turn of the century has been lost, but that which remains is central to understanding the kind of place it was. It articulates how Salt Lake organized itself, what its interests and aspirations were, what it thought and what it valued, how power operated and what efforts there were to assume, extend, resist, or accommodate it, and the ways particular groups sought to represent themselves and establish their authority and their place. Discussion in previous chapters of Salt Lake City's red-light districts and its ethnic neighborhoods illustrates the point. So does a consideration of many of the city's older buildings that still remain today.

Any number of old buildings could be discussed as a way of indicating the kind of place Salt Lake City was in the early twentieth century. The Promised Valley Playhouse, at 132 South State, was built in 1905 as the Orpheum Vaudeville Theatre and opened on Christmas Day, promising "at all times the best obtainable of European and American Vaudeville Attractions." The exterior featured a twelve-foot statue of Venus, symbol of the Orpheum vaudeville circuit, atop the building, and two large stone busts of Zeus flanking the en-

trance. More than 1,300 people attended its opening. The first program was a
varied one. According to *The Salt Lake Tribune*:

> Lucy and Lucifer provoked the first amusement on the program in a
> comedy skit which they designated "The Fool's Errand." Then Nelle Florede,
> winsome, pretty and chic, captivated the audience in a number of catchy
> songs and made it clear that she will be one of the week's favorites. The
> Henlier Sisters, advertised as being late from Daly's Theatre, New York,
> reeled off a series of songs and dancing specialties that won warm applause.
> Lewis McCord and Company perpetrated "The Night Before," a dress re-
> hearsal of "Romeo and Juliet," in a manner that caused the audience to ex-
> press the thought that this particular number should always be given the night

123

The Built
Environment

before if it is kept on the bill. The Kinodrome, a new moving picture device, gave a marvelously realistic representation of the operations of a train robbing crew, after which the LeBrun Grand Opera trio stepped onto the stage in breathless haste, on a run from their train, to give a scene from "Il Trovatore," which they did in commendable style and finish. The Three Jacksons gave a scientific boxing bout and engaged in other athletic exercises that stamped them as artists in their class.

A second Orpheum Theatre opened in Salt Lake City in 1913, now the Capitol Theatre, at 68 West 200 South. The architect, Albert Langsburgh, was Italian-trained and San Francisco-based, and his work signaled the importation of out-of-state architects and new design styles to the city. An example of what was described at the time as the "Italian Renaissance" style, it featured a profusion of ornate Renaissance Revival detailing then unknown in Salt Lake, including exquisite terra-cotta figurines, cherubs, musical instruments, drama masks, moldings, and brackets. The interior was as extravagant as the exterior. According to the *Deseret News*, at the theatre's opening on August 2, 1913, the lobby was "lined with marble flags, domed by a striking ground ceiling in Caen stone and flanked by supporting pillars." The staircases to the balconies were marble and the original color scheme French gray and gold, "the gold being subdued with French lacquers in blue and mulberry which go well with the gold orsini velvet draperies, in turn relieved by mulberry and rose-colored silk underdrapes."

During the first quarter of the twentieth century, a new architectural form appeared in the United States—the "skyscraper"—and it quickly became the hallmark of the modern city. Not only great cities such as New York and Chicago, but small and middle-sized ones as well soon sprouted structures that soared ten, twenty, or more stories above the low commercial blocks of the traditional city. Skyscrapers burst upon the scene in Salt Lake City in the early twentieth century, beginning with the construction of the *Deseret News* Building in 1902, transforming the downtown and providing further evidence that Salt Lake no longer sought to hold itself aloof from the American mainstream, as it had in the nineteenth century, but was seeking to be forward-looking and "great" in the same sense that other American cities were.

The six-story *Deseret News* Building, located across the street south from Temple Square, marked the northern boundary of the central business district. Its German-born architect, Richard K. A. Kletting, had worked on several major

European projects, including the Bon Marche, Credit de Lyonais, and the Sacre Coeur at Monmarte before coming to Utah in the mid-1880s. Following his arrival he embarked on a long and distinguished career, designing some of the best-known buildings in Utah, including the State Capitol, the Saltair Pavilion, and the original Salt Palace. His *Deseret News* Building had a highly decorative façade with both classical and modern elements. "Modernized" with a sheathing of metal and glass in the 1950s, and demolished in the mid-1990s, the eighteen-story Gateway Tower West rose in its place in the summer of 1998.

Between 1906 and 1907 a group of Mormon and non-Mormon businessmen, partners in a way they would not have been a generation earlier, built another skyscraper, the Utah Savings and Trust Building at 235 South Main. A narrow seven-story building with a stone façade, it was one of the earliest reinforced concrete buildings in Utah. It was demolished in the mid-1990s. In 1909 the eight-story McIntyre Building, 68 South Main, was completed. It is one of the Intermountain West's best examples of the Sullivanesque style of architecture, developed by Louis Sullivan, father of the skyscraper. Although modern in their verticality, Sullivan's works were based on the classicist principle that every work of art should be a finite object with a beginning, a middle, and an end. Designed by Richard Kletting, the McIntyre Building closely resembled Sullivan's Gage Building in Chicago. Its soaring vertical effect was created by unbroken piers that terminated under the cornice. From a technological standpoint, it was the prototype for later reinforced concrete skyscrapers in Utah and was built for William H. McIntyre, a prominent non-Mormon rancher and mining entrepreneur who made his initial fortune when he and his brother bought 7,000 head of Mexican longhorn cattle in Texas for $3.75 a head and drove them to Salt Lake, where they sold for $24.00 a head. In the 1880s he invested in the undeveloped Mammoth Mine in the Tintic Mining District, and it soon became one of the most productive mines in the state.

Two years later, in 1911, another excellent example of the Sullivanesque style, the ten-story Kearns Building, rose on Main Street. Out-of-state architects were responsible for more and more of Salt Lake's buildings, and the Los Angeles firm of Parkinson and Bergstrom, architects of the Hotel Utah, designed the Kearns Building for Thomas Kearns, who had made a fortune in mining in Park City in the late nineteenth century. Kearns served as U.S. senator from Utah from 1901 to 1905 and was part owner of *The Salt Lake Tribune*

125

The Built
Environment

from 1901 until his death in 1918. The story of his senate career illustrates much about the political situation in Utah at the time. In the early twentieth century no candidate for national political office in Utah could be elected without the support of the Mormon church. To avoid antagonizing local non-Mormons, however, and to prevent national politicians from asserting that the Mormon church still controlled politics in Utah, it was understood that one of Utah's U.S. senators would always be a Mormon and the other a non-Mormon. As a Catholic, Kearns was a member of a church that had stood aloof from the bitter crusade against Mormonism that had characterized the latter part of the nineteenth century, and he had never personally been conspicuous as an anti-Mormon, and with the support of Mormon authorities the Utah State Legislature was comfortable electing him to the U.S. Senate in 1901. In return for church support, he agreed to back Reed Smoot, a Mormon apostle, for the other senate seat in 1903. Kearns changed his mind, however, and in 1903 refused to endorse Smoot. As a result, when Kearns came up for reelection in 1905, Mormon authorities refused to support him. Rather than enter a race he knew he could not win, Kearns declined to run for re-election and returned to Utah, where he helped found the anti-Mormon American Party and purchased *The Salt Lake Tribune* and continued its anti-Mormon policies.

Between 1908 and 1910, the twin eleven-story Boston and Newhouse buildings were constructed on the corners of Exchange Place near 400 South and Main. Non-Mormon mining millionaire Samuel Newhouse financed them and named them after himself and his Boston Consolidated Mine. The designer of both was Henry Ives Cobb, a well-known New York and Chicago architect. His intention was to design buildings appropriate for New York's financial district, and they effectively contributed to Newhouse's dream of creating a miniature "Wall Street of the West" in Salt Lake City. Stone-faced and classically detailed, they are visually divided into three horizontal sections equivalent to the base, shaft, and capital of a classical column. The first two floors form the base, the third through ninth floors the shaft, and the upper two floors an elaborately decorated capital. They were intended to complement two similar buildings to be situated at the east entrance of Exchange Place on State Street. Due to Newhouse's subsequent bankruptcy, however, the State Street buildings were never constructed.

Cobb also designed the nearby eleven-story Newhouse Hotel. It officially opened for business on March 27, 1915, and was designed to compete with the Mormon church-owned Hotel Utah. Several weeks earlier, in its March 4 issue, *The Salt Lake Tribune* provided a lengthy description. According to the newspaper, it was "a palatial hostelry, ... one of the finest in the entire country. ... The hotel will contain 400 rooms, every one an outside room, and connected with a bathroom. On the main floor the lobby will be finished in Caen stone, counters and desks in marble. A large imposing marble stairway leads from the lobby to the mezzanine in two directions. On the southeast corner will be the Louis XIV cafe, distinctive in beauty. Connecting with this room will be the Georgian garden, which, without doubt, will be the most beautiful cafe in the west. ... The barber shop might fittingly be called the marble barber shop. This room will be finished entirely in marble."

The Walker Bank Building, at 200 South and Main, was completed in 1912. Eighteen stories high, and the tallest building west of the Missouri River, it was featured in several national magazines. *The Salt Lake Tribune* hailed it as "but another step typifying the new Salt Lake City, a metropolis which is destined to be unrivaled between Chicago and San Francisco," and testimony "of the strides this city is taking," a "monument to the progress and future of Salt Lake."

During World War I construction on Main Street came to a virtual halt. Only the fourteen-story Deseret National Bank (1918-19), at 100 South and Main, similar in design to the Walker Bank Building, was built during the war years. A depression followed the war, and commercial construction was slow in resuming. Finally in 1924 two more skyscrapers were erected: the thirteen-story Continental Bank Building, at 200 South and Main, and the ten-story Ezra Thompson/*Tribune* Building, at 143 South Main. The latter has been home of *The Salt Lake Tribune* since 1937, but was originally built for Ezra Thompson, a prominent businessman and politician who had made his fortune in mining. Thompson was twice elected mayor of Salt Lake City—once as a Republican and once as a member of the anti-Mormon American Party. The building is Salt Lake's best example of the art deco style popular throughout the United States in the 1920s and 1930s. It never really caught on in Utah, however, and few examples survive.

In addition to skyscrapers, other downtown buildings from the early twentieth century also reflect Salt Lake City's changing social, cultural, and economic patterns. The McCornick Block, 74 South Main, was built between 1890 and 1893 as a bank for William S. McCornick and Company. A native of Canada, McCornick made his initial fortune in Nevada with a lumber company that supplied the needs of mines in the Comstock Lode. After moving to Salt Lake City in 1873, he established a small banking house that eventually became the largest private bank between the Missouri River and the Pacific Coast. In the 1880s he participated in some of Utah's largest and most successful mining ventures, including the Silver King, the Daly and the Daly-West in Park City, and several Mercur and Eureka mines. Later he became president of the Raft River Land and Cattle Company, promoter of the San Pedro, Los Angeles, and Salt Lake Railroad, and was an organizer of the Rocky Mountain Bell Telephone Company. He was also president of the Board of Trustees of the Utah State Agricultural College and the first president of the Salt Lake City Chamber of Commerce.

This U.S. Army enlistment brochure circulated in Salt Lake City during World War I asking "men to be men" and join the army. There was little trouble in getting volunteers. After facing hostility and suspicion for years, Utahns were anxious to demonstrate their patriotism and overwhelmingly supported the war, contributing more than their quota of men, money, and materials.

Read This!   Think It Over!

A–for AMERICA. Are you fit to attend her?
R–is for Right.   Our Republic o'er all.
M–is for MEN well trained to defend her.
Y–is for YOU–will you answer her call?

For three years you have seen your country oppressed with numerous wrongs. Your Government, although above all other, devoted to peace, has been forced to draw the sword to rely for redress of injuries on your valor.

Will you stand with your arms folded and look on this interesting struggle? Are you not related to the men who FOUGHT FOR THE STARS AND STRIPES IN 1776?

Men of Utah and Idaho.

Has your race degenerated? Or are you under the influence of contending factions, forgotten your country.

Have you not a wish for fame? YES! You desire your share. Then seize the present moment and advance to your country's aid.

GIRLS.

Don't let the men hide behind your skirts. A man who won't support his country won't support his wife.

MILLION MEN NEEDED AT ONCE:
              BETWEEN AGE 18 AND 40

Come in companies, half companies, pairs or single. But come. Organize for a short tour in your country's service.

You can be accepted for enlistment by your Postmaster or at

U. S. Army Recruiting Station,

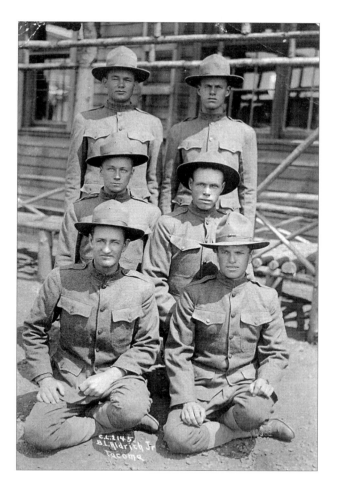

The Daft Block, 128 South Main, was built between 1887 and 1889 for Sarah A. Daft. She came to Utah from England in 1856 with her husband and after his death in 1881 continued to develop the family's financial interests. She held large amounts of stock in the Independent Telephone Company, managed extensive mining properties, and owned considerable real estate in Salt Lake. The building's architect was E. L. T. Harrison, a Mormon convert from England. Soon after his arrival in Salt Lake City in 1861, he designed the interior of the Salt Lake Theatre. Later commissions included the William S. Godbe house, a flamboyant Gothic Revival residence, the Grand Opera House, and numerous other residential and commercial buildings, but he was as well known for his literary and religious activities as for his architecture. In 1864 he joined with Edward Tullidge to found the *Peep O'Day*, perhaps the first literary magazine in the Intermountain West, and in 1869 he and other members of the dissident Godbeites were excommunicated from the Mormon

The Built Environment

Salt Lakers were encouraged to "sow the seeds of victory" and conserve food and fuel as their contribution to the World War I home front effort, and "victory gardens" were common. This photograph shows the garden of University of Utah professor David R. Allen at 263 Elizabeth Street. It was taken on June 21, 1918. (Courtesy Utah State Historical Society.)

church for their disagreement with various points of Mormon theology and economic and political practice.

The Tracy Loan and Trust Company Building, 151 South Main, was built in 1916 for the bank Russell Lord Tracy founded. A native of Ohio, he was quartermaster at the Cheyenne, Wyoming, army depot in the late 1870s, established a banking business in Cheyenne in 1884, and in 1892 moved the firm to Salt Lake City. In addition to his business activities, he was widely known in Utah for his establishment of the Tracy Wigwam Boy Scout Camp in Millcreek Canyon and the Tracy Aviary at Liberty Park.

The First National Bank Building, 161 South Main, was built in 1871-72 to house Warren Hussey's First National Bank of Utah. Its designer, Richard M. Upjohn of New York City, was one of the United States' most distinguished nineteenth-century architects. Home of the first bank to be chartered in Utah, its upper floors were also one of the earliest meeting places for Masonic lodges in Salt Lake City. Over time it also housed the Wells Fargo Company, the Atlantic and Pacific Telegraph Company, the Masonic Library, the Utah Territorial Library, and the law offices of Simon Bamberger, a businessman and politician. Governor of Utah from 1917 to 1921, he was the first non-Mormon elected as governor following statehood in 1896.

The *Salt Lake Herald* Building, 165 South Main, was constructed in 1905 as headquarters for one of Salt Lake's four daily newspapers, the *Salt Lake Herald*. Following its founding in 1870, editor E. L. Sloan announced that it would

The Gathering Place

be a staunch defender of the Mormon church. "Deeming it better to represent ourselves than to be misrepresented by others," he said, "when the people of Utah, their faith and institutions are aspersed, maligned and unjustly attacked, we shall esteem it a solemn duty to present the truth in reply, when the source is worthy of a rejoinder." After 1890, following the official announcement by Mormon leaders that no new plural marriages would be performed, the *Herald* took an increasing interest in party politics and in 1891 announced that it was a Democratic newspaper. At the same time Mormons were more and more attracted to the Republican Party, and so the connection between paper and church decreased. In 1898 Alfred W. McCune acquired the *Herald* to aid his ultimately unsuccessful campaign for the U.S. Senate. After his defeat he sold it to Senator W. A. "Champ" Clark of Montana, also a Democrat, whose chief interest in Utah was the promotion of the Salt Lake, San Pedro, and Los Angeles Railroad. During Clark's ownership the *Herald* Building was constructed. In 1909 Clark sold the paper to a group of prominent Utah Republicans. Renamed the *Herald Republican* following a merger with the *Intermountain Republican*, the paper quickly declined as its longtime Democratic supporters withdrew their subscriptions and the editorial philosophy reflected only one segment of the Republican Party—Senator, and Mormon apostle, Reed Smoot's political machine, the "Federal Bunch." Still, it hung on until 1920, when it finally ceased publication.

Built in 1887, the Karrick Block, 236 South Main, was constructed for Lewis C. Karrick, Salt Lake City businessman and politician. Born in Iowa in 1848, he came to Utah in the 1870s and made what he later described as "considerable" money in the mines around Stockton in Tooele County. In the 1880s he moved to Salt Lake City and within a few years bought the Troy Laundry, established a men's clothing store, and founded the National Bank of the Republic. He also organized a local militia, the "Karrick Guards." Active in politics, he served on the Salt Lake City Council in the early 1890s as a member of the anti-Mormon Liberal Party. The original occupants of the building were a mixed group. Roberts and Nelden Drug Company occupied the first floor. A gambling hall was located on the second floor, as well as eight apartments that prostitutes maintained. Doctors and other professionals had offices on the upper floor.

Adjacent to the Karrick Block is the Lollin Block, 238 South Main, built

131

The Built
Environment

in 1894 for John Lollin. A native of Denmark, he arrived in Salt Lake City in 1857 and operated a succession of small hotels, restaurants, and saloons until his death in 1915. A variety of small businesses occupied the building following its construction, while the third floor served as the Lollin family residence. His son, Carl, lived there until 1960.

The David Keith Building, 242 South Main, was constructed in 1902 for David Keith as headquarters for the Keith-O'Brien Department Store. Keith was a native of Nova Scotia. Together with Thomas Kearns, he developed the Silver King Mine in Park City, which ultimately produced dividends of over $10 million and made both men rich. The two men also owned *The Salt Lake Tribune.* Keith was ultimately involved in a wide range of business ventures and was also a member of the convention that wrote Utah's state constitution in 1895.

The Clift Building, 272 South Main, was built in 1920 by Virtue Butcher Clift, who had converted to the Mormon church in 1849 and came to Utah with her family. One of Salt Lake's largest terra cotta-faced structures, its architect was James Chesbro, who had designed Salt Lake's East Side High School several years earlier. The first occupants of the building were a United

Salt Lake City built "public comfort stations" (or rest rooms) in the early 1900s for the convenience of people in the downtown area. Constructed underground, they were readily accessible on downtown street corners through men's and women's entrances. This one was located on the northwest corner of Main and South Temple, across from the Hotel Utah (now the Joseph Smith Memorial Building). According to city officials, they were kept in an "immediate state of cleanliness as an example of sanitary comfort in its most advanced form." (Courtesy Utah State Historical Society.)

Martha Hughes (Mattie) Cannon, shown here in 1899 with her infant daughter, Gwendolyn, was elected to the Utah State Senate from Salt Lake in 1896 as a Democrat and became the first female state senator in the United States. She went on to serve two terms and was particularly involved with public health issues. She was also a prominent physician, earning a medical degree from the University of Pennsylvania. She was the fourth of Mormon general authority Angus M. Cannon's six plural wives. He too had been a candidate in the 1896 election on the Republican ticket. (Private Collection.)

Cigar Store, Schubach Optical, Western Union Telegraph, and the Kinema Movie Theater.

Originally Salt Lake City's built environment was a clear projection of the values of the Mormon people, who sought to create a settlement pattern recognizable as distinctively Mormon. It was the product of a powerful sense of community and a set of values at odds with those of the larger society. As the above discussion makes clear, however, by the early twentieth century a rival interpretation had emerged as business interests, aligned with the language of progress and the forward look, became increasingly important. In a sense Salt Lake's Main Street became the Main Street of America. At the same time, however, the city retained certain distinguishing social and cultural features, most particularly the concentration of Mormon businesses at the north end of the business district and non-Mormon establishments at the south end, with 200 South a rough dividing line. In the first decade or so of the twentieth century, that division became even more firmly stamped on the face of the city than it had previously as non-Mormon businessmen, most of whom had made their fortunes in mining, deliberately built more than a dozen major buildings at the south end of the central business district near Fourth South as a coun-

133

This 1922 view of Main Street, looking south from North Temple, reflects the changes the automobile brought. In 1903 there were an estimated twenty cars in Salt Lake City. By 1929, 112,661 had been registered in the state. The Hotel Utah (now the Joseph Smith Memorial Building) is at the left in the photograph, and the Deseret News Building is at the right. (Courtesy Utah State Historical Society.)

The Gathering Place

terweight to Mormon concentration at the north end. Most of them still stand today.

In 1903 the Auerbach family, whose roots in Utah go back to the late 1850s, constructed the building on the southwest corner of 300 South and State Street that housed their department store until the early 1980s. Orange J. Salisbury built the New York Hotel on Post Office Place in 1906 and the Felt Building on Main Street near Fourth South across from the Post Office four years later. Mary Judge, who was soon to finance the building that ultimately became Judge Memorial High School, constructed the Judge Building at Third South and Main Street in 1907. First known as the "Railroad Exchange Building," it originally housed the Salt Lake offices of nearly two dozen railroad companies. With the completion in 1910 of the Denver and Rio Grande Railroad Depot four and one half blocks to the west, 300 South Street, as *The Salt Lake Tribune* pointed out, became "the railroad artery into the business section of the city." In 1910 mining man John J. Daly built the New Grand Hotel. Samuel Newhouse was responsible for constructing three buildings, the Newhouse and Boston buildings and the Newhouse Hotel, and he donated land for two others, the Salt Lake Stock and Mining Exchange Building and the Commercial Club Building, both located on Exchange Place. The Commercial Club, founded in 1902 by a group of Salt Lake City businessmen, was established to attract out-of-state companies to the city.

The intention of Newhouse and the others to create a non-Mormon financial district in Salt Lake City materialized at Exchange Place, which took its name from the Salt Lake Stock and Mining Exchange Building, the would-be Wall Street of the West, the Boston and Newhouse buildings anchoring its west end. By the beginning of World War I, then, the Hotel Utah on the north and the Hotel Newhouse on the south formed the terminals of Salt Lake's central business district. Prominent Mormon establishments, including ZCMI and the *Deseret News,* were clustered around one end, while non-Mormon ones were grouped around the other. Across the street from the Hotel Newhouse, and in a sense counterbalancing Temple Square, was the building housing the U.S. Post Office and other agencies of the federal government. It represented one of the earliest non-Mormon intrusions into Utah. To some extent the clusters exist even today—longstanding symbols of a significant aspect of Salt Lake City's life.

At the southeastern edge of the Exchange Place district is Federation of Labor Hall, a modest, three-story brick building, at the corner of 400 South and State streets. Albert Fisher, a German immigrant and owner of the Fisher Brewery, built it in 1903 and until 1913 leased it to the newly formed Utah Federation of Labor and its affiliated unions. In its February 1, 1904, issue, *The Salt Lake Tribune* offered the following description: "The west half of the second and third stories is occupied with an auditorium, or assembly hall, with a spacious gallery. This auditorium has a seating capacity of 500 and will be used for special meetings, balls, and other entertainments, the main floor being suitable for dancing. Its seating capacity is nearly 200 greater than that of any other available hall in the city, aside from the theaters, and it will fill a long-felt need in this direction. On the front half of the second floor are three lodge rooms and a reception room, while on the third floor are two more lodge rooms and an office and living rooms for the Federation's building manager, Carl Ostby, a veteran member of the organization representing the Tailors' union. ... The Electricians' Union will see to the installing of the most modern lighting plan with artistic fixtures."

135

The Built
Environment

By the early twentieth century, the labor movement was increasingly important in Utah. This photograph is of striking streetcar workers, September 1906, following Salt Lake City's Labor Day parade. (Courtesy Utah State Historical Society.)

Labor unions had been slow to emerge in Utah, but by the early twentieth century they were a growing presence, even though they continued to meet stiff opposition. As Thomas G. Alexander points out, in 1902 the National Association of Manufacturers announced that its goal was to break all union organizations. Following its lead, the Utah Copper Company refused to discuss wages or working conditions with its workers, while the Utah Fuel Company required coal miners to sign "yellow-dog contracts," under which, as a condition of employment, they pledged not to join a union. Perhaps of most importance, the Mormon church was unsympathetic to labor unions. As Alexander says, "When disputes erupted between management and labor, prominent Mormons tended to emphasize the rights of workers to organize and bargain, but they attacked labor organizers representing national unions ('walking delegates') and opposed union representation of workers in bargaining. More often than not, they sided with management in firing strikers and protecting property against picketers. Often, when workers bargained for a closed shop or union recognition, church periodicals and leaders condemned such efforts by

emphasizing the Mormon doctrine of free agency or likening the forced representation of those who opposed the union to emasculation. Apparently, neither the leaders nor the LDS church press condemned business people who forced their employees to sign yellow-dog contracts, to trade at company stores, or to live in company housing as conditions of employment."

Given the attitude of the Mormon church toward labor unions, the union hall's location at the south end of the business district where non-Mormon activities predominated is not surprising and was likely the result of a conscious decision to distance the union movement from the Mormon church. At the same time, as Exchange Place's "Wall Street" emerged, the proximity of Labor Hall served to remind capitalists of all stripes of the existence of a working class they not only could not ignore but would have to take account of and contend with.

Labor Hall was dedicated on February 22, 1904. The Reverend P. A. Simpkins of Salt Lake's Phillips Congregational Church was the main speaker.

These young shoeshine boys belonged to the boot blacks union, local no. 6. The photograph was taken on the steps of the City and County Building on September 2, 1907. (Courtesy Utah State Historical Society.)

137

The Built
Environment

He said, in part, "The working man of today is fighting a battle just as great as that fought by Gen. Washington in the Revolution. The industrial battle is not the same, but it is for the same purpose—the rights of mankind. Thank God, we are coming to the time when we know what brotherhood means, what manhood amounts to. America will not endure because it has ten hundred millionaires, but because it has ten million industrious men and ten million intelligent women."

Two other buildings are central to understanding the kind of place Salt Lake was becoming by the early twentieth century: the LDS temple and the City and County Building. Built on and off over a forty-year period, the temple was officially dedicated on April 6, 1893. As Jan Shipps points out, it was intended to carry Mormons away from the profane world of the everyday and allow them to enter sacred time and space. Though clearly not a public building, but a private and sacred one, and, while its style of architecture was intended to rival the grandeur of other great sites of worship, it was not a site of congregational worship analogous to cathedrals, but a place for the performance of certain sacred ordinances peculiar to Mormon faith, the channel through which Saints received special spiritual blessings. The theological importance of the ceremonies was so great that the religious life of those without at least occasional access to them was considered impoverished, and Mormons at the time saw the process of its construction as perhaps the most important symbol that the Kingdom of God had been established in the tops of the mountains. As Richard L. Bushman says, "The temple was early Mormonism's primal architectural space," focusing sacred power at a single spot where heaven touched earth. In addition, he points out, "Temples are similarly models for the body which is sometimes called a temple. People enter temples to divine the meaning of existence and to put themselves in touch with the holy." For Mormons the temple sacralized the landscape, but instead of all spaces having an equal amount of divine presence, God was present in greater intensity in one, sharply focused space. According to Brigham H. Roberts, speaking at the Mormon church's semi-annual general conference in October 1913, the temple was "a collective testimony in stones to God's presence and power and salvation, among the Latter-day Saints that is mightier, perhaps, than the verbal testimony of any man, because it might be seen by so many, unmoved through many generations, and has been established by the collective mites of a community." A labor of love, a monument to faith, and a striking ex-

ample of the skill of pioneer artisans, at the beginning it was the heart of the city. As Charles S. Peterson says, Salt Lake City was initially the place of Mormon church control and in many ways the very epitome of Mormonness, and, as Salt Lake grew, it grew in the shadow of the rising temple. It was intended to symbolize permanence and, indeed, to be a permanent feature of the city. Other buildings might come and go, but the temple would remain central to the city's identity—one way that the past would always stand squarely and securely in the present.

By the opening years of the twentieth century, the LDS temple was the most recognizable part of Salt Lake City's built environment. A distinctive landmark that could be seen for miles and a significant tourist attraction that church leaders from the first used to promote a positive public image of Mormonism, no other building was as easily or as widely associated with the city—and Temple Square remains today the most visited site in the city. Yet by the early twentieth century, the moment of the Mormon hierarchy's predominance was eroding. One building in particular to directly contest that dominance was the City and County Building, and it provides as much insight into

139

The Built
Environment

turn-of-the-century Salt Lake City as any single structure.

Ironically, planning for the City and County Building began in the late 1880s when the Mormon church's People's Party still governed the city. Construction was set to begin in the spring of 1890, but before it did a new mayor and city council took office and immediately questioned the project. Members of the anti-Mormon Liberal Party, including Mayor George M. Scott and nine of fifteen city council members, they were the first non-Mormons elected to public office in Salt Lake. During the campaign and afterward, Liberals attacked the People's Party for its decision to build the City and County Building, calling it extravagant and unnecessary and a demonstration of the incompetence of previous Mormon administrations. Eventually the new officials decided to go ahead with the project, and construction began in the spring of 1890. It halted in early November, however, when city and county officials fired the superintendent of construction, who was also the building's architect. Exactly why they did so is not clear, but a bitter debate followed divided along Mormon/non-Mormon lines. Mormon public officials and the Mormon church-owned *Deseret News* argued for proceeding with construction on the already completed foundation, following revised plans. To do otherwise, they said, would be a waste of money, evidence of Liberal Party incompetence and the folly of Salt Lake voters in abandoning forty years of Mormon rule. Liberal Party officeholders, on the other hand, wanted an entirely new building designed and a new site selected for its construction. Failure to do that, they said, would demonstrate the narrow vision and obstructionist tactics of Mormon office holders, and of the Mormon church in general. From the first, then, the City and County Building was entangled in one of the most striking features of the late-nineteenth century city: bitter division between Mormons and non-Mormons, both reflecting it and becoming an occasion for its expression.

After five months of debate, the mayor and city council decided to construct an entirely new building on a new site, Washington Square, one of the four squares set aside for "public purposes" when the city was first laid out in 1847. An architectural competition was held that attracted fifteen entrants from across the country. The design of the firm of Monheim, Bird, and Proudfoot was selected, and construction began in October 1891. Bird and Proudfoot were from the Midwest, while Monheim had been in practice in Utah for over twenty years. They joined forces for the City and County Building competition, rather than enter individually, in an effort to maximize their chances of being selected, since there had initially been some controversy over whether or not the competition should be restricted to local architectural firms only, or open to all. Ceremonies the next summer, on July 25, marked completion of the foundation and the laying of the cornerstone. All four speakers—governor, mayor, city council president, and county commission chair—were non-Mormons, and all made the same point. Construction of the City and County Building, they said, signalled the beginning of a new era in Salt Lake City's history. It meant the end of Mormon church dominance of political affairs and the triumph of civil government. Henceforth a firm division between church and state would exist, with no blurring of the lines. According to Mayor Robert N. Baskin, a founder of the Liberal Party twenty years earlier, the building would be "a temple of justice, and in some measure a representation of the majesty of the law. In its superstructure it will rise above its surroundings. And as it towers above its environment, so will the majesty and dignity of the law, as represented in the municipal, state, and national governments, rise above church influence and conditions."

Work proceeded steadily for a year following the dedication. During the summer of 1893, however, the effects of the nationwide depression, which would last four long years and remains the second worst economic downturn in U.S. history, began to be felt. The work force was cut in half, and construction slowed. Nonetheless, the City and County Building was completed in November 1894 and dedicated on December 28. Since then it has been firmly imbedded in the fabric of the community. The convention that drew up Utah's state constitution in 1895 met there. It housed the first Salt Lake City Public Library, and it served as Utah's first state capitol from statehood in 1896 until 1915 when the present capitol was completed. Visiting presidents of the United States, including Theodore Roosevelt and his successor, William Howard Taft, spoke from its steps. The 1914 trial of labor radical Joe Hill for the murder of a Salt Lake City grocer and his son took place in one of its first floor courtrooms. Hill's conviction on meager circumstantial evidence and his membership in the Industrial Workers of the World drew national and international attention to the case, while high unemployment and labor unrest in Utah and the nation helped foster a sense that the trial was a means for those in power to intimidate labor. On several occasions during the depths of the

141

The Built
Environment

Joe Hill, radical songwriter, labor activist, and member of the Industrial Workers of the World. On Labor Day, 1990, an event commemorating the 75th anniversary of his death was held in Salt Lake at Sugarhouse Park, site of his execution at the State Prison on November 19, 1915. Among the performers were Pete Seeger, Joe Glazer, Utah Phillips, and Earl Robinson, who wrote the words to the song, "I Dreamed I Saw Joe Hill Last Night," in the 1930s. Since then it has been performed by a range of singers, from Paul Robeson to Joan Baez, and remains a moving testament to Hill and the labor union movement. (Courtesy Will South.)

Great Depression of the 1930s, protest rallies of several thousand people were held on its grounds, some of which police broke up with tear gas. Its cafe remained closed to African Americans until the late 1940s, when protests by the Salt Lake branch of the National Association for the Advancement of Colored People (NAACP) finally succeeded in desegregating it. Since the early 1990s, the annual Living Traditions Festival has been held on its grounds each May to celebrate the traditional folk and ethnic arts of Utah. In recent years it has also hosted Salt Lake City's Gay Pride Day.

As Thomas R. Carter and Peter Goss point out, the City and County Building is Utah's best example of Richardsonian Romanesque architecture, which was the most popular style for public buildings in the United States in the late nineteenth century. Its most obvious characteristic is substantial weight and mass. It is heavy. It is also richly ornamented—alive with examples of the stonecarver's art: human faces and figures; gargoyles; animals; marine monsters; winged serpents; roses; scrolls; and carvings depicting various people, events, and themes in Utah's history. On the west façade is a beehive with a farmer standing on one side and a miner on the other. Behind them is a rising sun. The farmer carries a rake and a shock of grain and watches the flow of wa-

The Gathering Place

This photograph of the Salt Lake City and County Building was taken soon after its completion in 1894. The LDS temple had been dedicated a year earlier, and the City and County Building clearly contested the central place of the temple in the city at the turn of the century and, more generally, the dominant role of the Mormon church. (Courtesy Utah State Historical Society.)

West façade of the Salt Lake City and County Building. (Private Collection.)

ter from a dam. The miner holds a pick ax. A pile of ore lies behind him. On one level the farmer symbolizes agriculture, on which the territory of Utah was founded, but more generally the figure suggests the self-sufficient, egalitarian, and homogeneous commonwealth that the first Mormon settlers sought to establish, and for a time nearly achieved. The miner symbolizes not only the mining industry, which became increasingly important in Utah after 1869 following completion of the transcontinental railroad, but in a larger sense the new world that emerged in Utah in the late nineteenth century.

The LDS temple and the City and County Building were finished nearly simultaneously, the first in 1893 and the second a year later. As Lisa Bickmore points out in an insightful reading of the buildings, each yields a different story. One is clearly a sacred structure, soaring and aspiring, the other a public one, solidly rooted in this world. One invites entrance, the other conveys a sealing off. The City and County Building's clock tower orients the building and its business in human time and the world of the everyday, while the temple's guardian angel Moroni orients it and its doings to God's time. The two buildings comprise an opposition, each sharply diverging from the other. Each is a temple, but one is a temple of the sacred, the other a temple of the secular. Each governs, but one governs within a theology, the other within a politics, and life in Salt Lake City at the turn of the century could not fail to take account of that dialectic, which spun out its logic continually.

～

Recommended Readings

Carter, Thomas, and Goss, Peter. *Utah's Historic Architecture, 1847-1940: A Guide.* Salt Lake City: Center for Architectural Studies, Graduate School of Architecture, University of Utah, and Utah State Historical Society, 1988.

Davies, J. Kenneth. *Deseret's Sons of Toil: A History of the Worker Movements of Territorial Utah, 1852-1896.* Salt Lake City: Olympus Publishing Co., 1977.

McCormick, John S. *The Historic Buildings of Downtown Salt Lake City.*

_____. "A History of the Salt Lake City and County Building," 1989. An unpublished manuscript on deposit at the Utah State Historical Society.

Powell, Allan Kent. *The Next Time We Strike: Labor in Utah's Coal Fields, 1900-1933.* Logan: Utah State University Press, 1985.

Smith, Gibbs M. *Joe Hill.* Salt Lake City: University of Utah Press, 1969.

Chapter 8

HARD TIMES

During the decade of the 1930s the United States experienced the worst depression in its history, and Utah was one of the states hardest hit. Every generation before 1930 had seen periods of mass unemployment. Often it happened several times in one person's lifetime. Usually the slide into the pit was steep and the climb out slow, but the depression that began in 1929 was different. It came harder and faster; it engulfed a larger part of the population; it lasted longer; and it did far more and far worse damage than any before or since. Not until the U.S. entered World War II did the Depression end. As William Leuchtenberg says, people groped for superlatives to express the meaning and impact of the crisis. Writer Edmund Wilson compared it to an earthquake. Former governor of New York Alfred E. Smith said the Depression was equivalent to war, while Supreme Court Justice Louis D. Brandeis declared that it was worse than war. All agreed with Philip La Follette, governor of Wisconsin, that "we are in the midst of the greatest domestic crisis since the Civil War."

The chain reaction of unemployment spread rapidly. In 1929, 3 million people in the United States were without work; by 1933, between 12 and 16 million were unemployed, and, in 1939, 10 million people were still unable to find jobs. Underemployment was also widespread, and millions of people who had jobs found their hours of work and their hourly wages cut. By 1933 the average hourly wage and the average work week had both declined by 20 per-

The intersection of 300 South and State Street in 1925. The Knutsford Hotel, at the right, was built in 1880. Before its demolition in the mid-1930s for construction of the Centre Theatre, now also demolished, it commonly hosted visiting dignitaries, including several U.S. presidents. On the balcony above the entrance, speeches were given and bands performed. (Courtesy Utah State Historical Society.)

cent. In 1933 U.S. Steel Corporation had no full-time employees, whereas four years earlier there were 250,000.

Statistics can be mind-numbing, but they can also convey a sense of the magnitude of the crisis. In Utah at the beginning of 1930, about 8,700 people in a work force of 170,000 were unemployed. By 1931 the number of unemployed had quadrupled to over 36,000, and in 1932 it reached 61,500, or 35.8 percent of the work force, more than one of every three workers. It was the fourth highest unemployment rate in the nation. Unemployment was still 10 percent in 1940 and for the decade as a whole averaged 26 percent. Income per person fell sharply as a result of the decline in employment and the reduction in wages for those who had jobs. In 1929 Utah's annual per capita income was $537. By 1932 it had dropped to half of that, $276, and by 1940 had risen to only $480, just 82 percent of the pre-Depression level.

During the two years after the Utah Division of Employment Security began operating in 1938, one in every three Utahns was unemployed long enough to receive unemployment compensation. Nearly 60 percent exhausted their benefits before finding another job. Of those placed in jobs, only one-quarter were in permanent positions; the rest worked either in temporary government programs or at jobs in private industry lasting less than thirty days.

Sherman Avenue, between 1100 and 1200 East streets, was a typical, new residential development in Salt Lake City in the 1920s. (Courtesy Utah State Historical Society.)

When this photograph was taken in 1922 of Main Street from Fourth South looking north, Salt Lake City's growth rate was declining, and for the first time in Utah's history more people were leaving the state than were moving in. (Courtesy Utah State Historical Society.)

Unemployment office, early 1930s. Utah's official unemployment rate was 36 percent in 1933, and it remained difficult to get or keep a permanent job until the beginning of World War II. (Private Collection.)

Out-migration from Utah had begun in the 1920s and increased during the Great Depression as Utahns left the state hoping to find work elsewhere. Sometimes entire families moved away, sometimes only the unemployed breadwinner. By March 1933 more than 161,000 Utahns—32 percent of the population—were receiving all or part of their food, clothing, shelter, and other necessities from government relief funds.

To some the solution seemed to be a return to the farm, but the economic dry rot of the 1930s afflicted the countryside as well as the city. Between 1929 and 1932 gross farm income in the United States fell by more than half, to a point lower than it had been for forty years. Season after season farmers suffered from the miserably low prices they received for their products, and it made little difference whether they were Alabama cotton growers, Iowa hog farmers, Wisconsin dairy producers, California citrus ranchers, or Utah sheepmen. All considered themselves lucky if they could sell their products for enough to meet their costs of production.

Within a year after the stock market crash of October 1929, more than

6,000 people walked the streets of Salt Lake looking for work, double the number a few years earlier. At the same time major employers began to cut both wages and hours of work for those who still had jobs. Between 1929 and 1932 Utah Power & Light Company fired more than 25 percent of its workers. As one power company employee recalled, "People were always being laid off. No one really knew if they would have a job when they came to work the next day." For those who did not lose their jobs, the company reduced wages 10 percent in 1932 and another 10 percent in 1933. For Utah's workers as a whole, the wage level declined an estimated one-third by 1932 and the work week by 20 percent.

In its early years, public figures either expressed confidence that the Depression would be a short one or they ignored it entirely. At the beginning of 1930, E. O. Howard, president of the Salt Lake City Chamber of Commerce, described 1929 as a year of "healthy progress" closing a decade of accomplishment "unparalleled in the history of the state." A year later Gus P. Backman, secretary of the chamber, listed the city's accomplishments in 1930 and said he looked forward to continued progress in 1931. As Salt Lake City mayor John Bowman saw it, hard times would soon pass and "merge into a period of unprecedented prosperity." Instead the situation only worsened. In November 1932 a survey of the westside Southgate neighborhood found that more than 60 percent of heads of households were unemployed. In the westside LDS Pioneer Stake, more than half of all workers had no jobs. In January 1933, 12,000 families in Salt Lake County were receiving some form of government relief. Long lines of hungry men and women, their shoulders hunched against cold winds, edged along sidewalks to get a bowl of broth from private-charity soup kitchens or city-operated transient shelters, often named "Hoover Cafes" because people blamed President Herbert Hoover for the nation's hard times. Apple sellers abounded on city sidewalks. So did shoeshine "boys," ranging from pre-teenagers who should have been in school to men past retirement age. One kind of job remained plentiful—selling strictly on commission—and an army of new salesmen appeared on Salt Lake City streets peddling everything from large rubber balls to kitchenware to cheap neckties.

As in the nation as a whole, Utah's marriage rate dropped during the Depression. So did the birth rate, while the divorce rate rose. Women joined the work force in increasing numbers, even though the feeling was widespread that when jobs were scarce, women ought not to compete with men for them. Most school districts would not hire married women and stipulated that when single female teachers married they must resign. Women working in the home followed the old adage, "Use it up, wear it out, make it do, or do without." That meant practicing endless little economies: buying day-old bread; relining coats with old blankets; saving string, old rags, and wire in case they might come in handy some day; shopping creatively; and watching every penny. More than that, it meant constant anxiety for fear that some catastrophe, large or small, might completely swamp the family budget and send the family to the streets.

For Utah's ethnic minority men and women, the familiar pattern of discrimination, intimidation, and low-paying jobs persisted. Long near the bottom of the economic ladder, they suffered disproportionately through the hard times of the 1930s. The old saying among African Americans that they were "last hired, first fired" was never truer than during periods of high unemployment, and the black unemployment rate was much higher than that of whites. With jobs scarce and everyone desperate for the few available, even traditional "Negro" occupations—such as domestic service, cooking, janitorial work, and elevator operating—were coveted. In an interview with Leslie G. Kelen, Albert Fritz recalled his experience in Salt Lake City. "Even after the steel-workers organized in 1937, whites in the union were still promoted over minorities," he said. "Even when they had seniority. So I objected. The whites came at me with, 'What do you want? Aren't you satisfied that you have a job?'" In 1939 a petition containing several hundred signatures was submitted to the Salt Lake City Commission requesting passage of a city ordinance requiring blacks to live only in specified areas of the city. Though it did not pass, real estate covenants were adopted restricting sales of houses in many areas of the city to whites. (In 1966 the Governor's State Executive Committee on Civil Rights found that restrictive covenants, while then illegal, were still common. "Negroes experience discrimination when seeking to rent, purchase or finance housing other than in areas where Negroes now reside, ... and pay higher down payments or total cost than required from non-Negroes," the committee said.) "I've often thought of those years, because the Depression frightened me," said Ruby Nathaniel. "I was scared because Henry was gone so much and it was so hard to feed my kids. Oh, it was an awful time. I thank God my minister was there. He lived a couple of doors down from us, and people were always giving him food. So a lot of time, he'd give me part or all of what he got. And that helped. I never went on welfare, and I don't think my kids ever went hungry. But they sure didn't have much of what they wanted."

Utah's Hispanic population, many of whom had been actively recruited to Utah farms and businesses in the years after World War I, likewise found that they were not needed in the Depression decade. Signs inscribed "Only White Labor Employed" and "No Niggers, Mexicans or Dogs Allowed" expressed the hatred and fear that many encountered. In an effort to reduce unemployment, both federal and local authorities encouraged, and sometimes coerced, Mexican immigrants, including many who were U.S. citizens, into returning to Mexico. As Edward H. Mayer pointed out, "The Depression was a difficult period for all workers in America, but Hispanics were especially hard hit and were among the first to lose their jobs. Many Anglo-Americans displaced Mexicans in jobs they had earlier scorned." Dan Maldonado described what life was like for many Hispanic children at the time: "I remember a group of us, all about eight or nine years old, started going junking. We'd take our gunny sacks and pick up bottles, scraps of metal, copper wire, aluminum, anything we could sell. ... Those were rough times." Epiefanio Gonzales remembered travelling across the state as a teenager with his family looking for work. "Things were tough during the Depression," he said. "You swallowed a lot of pride, you suffered a lot and took whatever you could get."

In an article based largely on interviews conducted by Leslie G. Kelen and others with the Oral History Institute, Jorge Iber concluded that "during the depression, Utah's Hispanics, like other populations, wrestled with grim economic conditions. But they also faced problems unique to minority groups. Hispanics working in mining, transportation, agriculture, and the service industry were usually given the lowest-paying jobs, and the work they did was difficult, menial, and sometimes destructive to their health; at the same time, these workers were given few opportunities for advancement." In one interview, John Florez summarized his experiences: "People who talk about the 'good old days' do so because they didn't have to live it." He recalled that his father, Reyes Florez, came to Utah after World War I to work for the Denver and Rio Grande Railroad. During the Depression he managed to hold on to his job as a "traquero," and family members supplemented his salary by working the beet fields as "betabeleros" during the summer and early fall. The family lived on Salt Lake's westside in a boxcar divided into kitchen and living areas. The "house" was only twenty feet from the tracks, and Florez recalled his mother, Encarnacion, fighting to keep it clear of dust and dirt. She also stretched the family's budget, and beans and tortillas were the family's daily fare. Unemployed men frequented the Florez boxcar because they knew that the lady of the "house" provided food for anyone who asked. She also helped the community as a "curandera," or traditional healer. At the same time, she raised her children to have a deep sense of pride in their Mexican heritage. The Florez children faced a constant battle in school as teachers and peers humiliated them by claiming that their culture was "savage" and "barbaric," and their mother sought to counter those influences by teaching them Hispanic history, culture, and art.

As Iber points out, hard times led many Hispanics to turn to their church for help in meeting not only their spiritual, but also their physical, needs. The vast majority were Catholic, and Salt Lake's Guadalupe Mission provided much needed assistance, even though its own resources were limited. "The Sisters of Perpetual Adoration helped the children of the west side by teaching religion classes, Sunday school, and arts and crafts," Iber says. "The mission also sponsored a Boy Scout troop as well as Americanization classes. Father James Collins hosted sporting events, parties, film shows, and religious instruction. … The mission's major effort was a summer school held between mid-June and mid-August; attendance ran as high as 250 children per day, with all faiths and ethnic groups being represented." The LDS church also had a Spanish-speaking congregation in Salt Lake City, Rama Mexicana (Mexican Branch), formed in 1921, and it did what it could for those in need. Church officials helped branch members find work and arranged for the distribution of food, clothing, and other commodities, and as late as June 1942, with unemployment still running high among Hispanics, half of Rama Mexicana's members were exempt from paying the church's 10 percent tithing requirement.

During the hard times of the Great Depression, already existing Hispanic community groups were reinvigorated, and new ones founded, including El Centro Civico Mexicano. The fiestas, dances, and cultural events they sponsored served both as rallying points and as brief respites from hard times, reinforced traditional values, and helped preserve a sense of cultural identity. "As families and individuals worked together," Jorge Iber says, "struggling to maintain the last vestiges of normality, class and ethnicity proved to be strong bonding ties against the centrifugal power of economic adversity."

During the Depression the number of transients increased dramatically. According to the *Deseret News* of November 26, 1930, "More than 500 men who came to Salt Lake City looking for work from other sections of the country have been picked up during the last three days by members of the police department and sent on their way." Unable to pay rent or meet mortgage payments, many families were evicted from their homes. In the summer of 1933 the *Deseret News* wrote about hundreds of homeless families camped out on vacant lots throughout the city. Often evictions proceeded only over citizen protest, as on the afternoon of February 23, 1933, when Salt Lake County sheriff Grant Young and several of his deputies tried to conduct a tax sale from the west steps of the City and County Building. Six houses and a farm were to be sold for back taxes following mortgage foreclosures. By the time the sale was set to begin, a crowd of several hundred people had gathered to prevent the sale. Sheriff Young appealed to them to disperse. Instead they stormed the building. Deputies turned a fire hose on them, but they quickly wrestled the hose from the deputies, turned it into the building, and flooded the ground

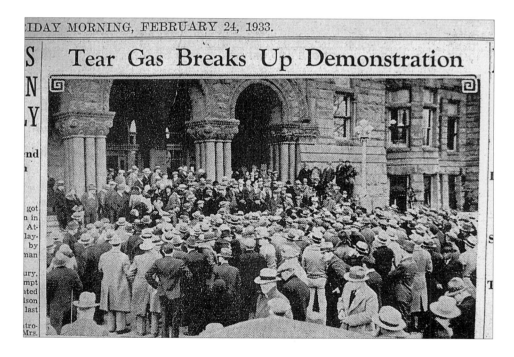

On the afternoon of February 23, 1933, a crowd of several hundred people who had gathered at the City and County Building to prevent homeowners from losing their houses at a tax sale clashed with police, who used firehoses and tear gas to disperse the crowd so that the sale could proceed. This photograph appeared the next day in The Salt Lake Tribune.

In February 1931 several thousand protestors gathered on the grounds of the State Capitol Building to make demands of the governor and state legislature, including a moratorium on mortgage foreclosures, a free school lunch program, and unemployment compensation. The speaker at the center of this photograph was Alfred Sorensen. A small businessman and an activist for most of his adult life, he had been active in the Socialist Party in the early twentieth century and in the 1930s was involved in a number of political organizations seeking to address the causes and effects of the Great Depression. According to a Salt Lake City weekly newspaper, *Progressive Opinion*, Sorenson "takes a prominent and capable part in progressive politics and human welfare, in which field he has been at the front for a long time." (Private Collection.)

The Gathering Place

floor. Police finally dispersed the crowd with tear gas and arrested more than a dozen people. Charged with "direct rioting," they were quickly found guilty and sentenced to jail. The next day's *Salt Lake Tribune* featured one photograph of the crowd gathered at the City and County Building and another of clouds of tear gas billowing from it. That afternoon a *Deseret News* editorial expressed sympathy for people who were losing their homes but characterized leaders of the crowd as "out and out communists."

In addition to tax protests, at least half a dozen demonstrations of the unemployed were held in Salt Lake City during the early years of the Depression. Typical were three in the spring of 1931 when groups of more than 1,000 unemployed men and women gathered on the grounds of the City and County Building to hear speakers and then marched up Main Street to the State Capitol carrying signs that read, "We Want Work, Not Charity," "Organize or Starve," and "We Want Milk for Our Children." Following more speeches on the Capitol grounds, lists of demands were presented to the state legislature then in session, including a moratorium on mortgage foreclosures, free school lunch programs, unemployment compensation, free state-operated employment bureaus, and thirty hours' work per week for forty hours' pay. The marches had been organized by a variety of groups, some of them Utah affiliates of national organizations and others local Utah groups, including the Unemployed Council, the Worker's and Farmer's Protective Union, the Working Women's League, the Worker's Ex-Servicemen's League, the People's Open Forum, and the Worker's Alliance. In addition to organizing such demonstrations, the Unemployed Council lobbied for an investigation of food wasting by wholesalers, an increase in relief work, and the establishment of a centralized

Platform of the Workers United Front in Salt Lake City's 1933 election. (Private Collection.)

system of relief. It also organized efforts to resist the eviction of families from houses and apartments, and in instances when people had been evicted and their furniture and other belongings placed on the sidewalk, they simply moved the furniture back inside.

People who had never had a radical thought in their lives began to reconsider. A radical weekly newspaper, *Progressive Opinion*, was founded in the early years of the Depression and continued publishing until the middle of World War II. A May 14, 1937, editorial reflected its point of view: "The present economic system is based upon excessive selfishness and private profit. The system has destroyed itself and lies in ruins all around us. The supreme need of the times is a new economic system, organized in accordance with the principle of cooperation." The 1930s never was a "Red Decade," but such a point of view found not only increasing expression throughout the country, and in Utah as well, but more and more support. In 1931, for example, M. P. Bales, a barber and long-time labor union activist, ran for Salt Lake City mayor on the Communist Party ticket. His platform stated, in part, "We realize that the economic depression is the logical outcome of capitalist economics and that the problem of unemployment cannot be cured in capitalist society. It is a social ill that we must reckon with as long as capitalism is in existence." Among his specific demands were the exemption of unemployed families from rent and utility payments; a ban on evictions; free milk and hot lunches for school children; thirty hours' work for forty hours' pay; a minimum wage of $30 a week for unskilled laborers; and unemployment compensation. In the primary election he ran fourth in a field of seven and received 15 percent of the vote. In a field of twenty-two candidates for the city commission, the two communists ran seventh and eighth. The day after Christmas in 1937, William Z. Foster, the head of the American Communist Party, spoke in Salt Lake City and drew a crowd of several hundred people.

In common with people throughout the country, Utahns, in the early years of the Depression, relied on wide-ranging voluntary charitable activities and local government to bring relief. The Salt Lake Chamber of Commerce canvassed the city block by block to identify people without work. Fraternal organizations held rabbit hunts and gave the thousands of animals killed to those in need. Public schools, private businesses, and hospitals held fund-raising events. High schools donated the proceeds from basketball games. Movie

theaters regularly contributed their day's receipts. Community fast days were held, and people contributed money they otherwise would have spent for meals. From the first, the Mormon church played an important role in providing help and support. The six LDS stakes (comparable to a Catholic diocese) in the Salt Lake Valley re-established the employment bureau that the church had first operated during the depression of the 1890s. The Mormon church also cooperated with Protestant, Catholic, and Jewish relief efforts, as well as those of private agencies. Its women's Relief Society was especially active in working with other organizations. In 1930 the Community Chest in Salt Lake City spent $150,000 on relief, while the LDS church spent an additional $250,000. Later, in 1936, it would establish its Church Welfare Plan to furnish employment and relief for its members.

In 1930 Salt Lake City set up a relief committee and in the next several years undertook a number of work projects that city money and private contributions financed, including construction of the Art Barn and several buildings at the Salt Lake City Zoo and in Memory Grove. A free school lunch program was started. Free vegetable seeds were distributed, and city land was made available for gardens. By March 1932 city officials had spent more than $450,000, but only $502 remained, and they saw little prospect of raising more money. Virtually every city and town in the state was in a similar situation.

Finally Utahns joined the rest of the nation in turning to the federal government for help as the problems of industrial capitalism proved too heavy for individuals, private charities, or local governments to handle. Washington responded with the New Deal, a barrage of government programs designed to provide relief and jobs and to reform the economic system in ways intended to prevent future catastrophes. The Great Depression, in other words, changed the American people's conception of the function and proper role of government. Tossed and torn by the Depression, Americans abandoned the doctrine of laissez-faire economics. The previous conviction had been that depressions were inevitable—much like dust storms and other natural disasters that occurred periodically, and about which nothing could be done. In 1931, for example, President Herbert Hoover criticized those who "have confidence that by some device we can legislate ourselves out of a world-wide depression." Such views, he said, "are as accurate as the belief that we can exorcise a Caribbean hurricane." Hoover's position, however, was soon rejected. From the experience of the Depression, Americans in general came to believe that something could and should be done when economic disaster struck, and the federal government was the one to do it.

Almost everything the federal government did during the Depression made inroads into the hitherto private preserves of business and the individual. It subsidized farmers, guaranteed bank deposits, provided unemployment compensation and social security, subsidized the arts and low-cost housing, and assisted labor unions in organizing. Most such measures survived the period of crisis to take their place as fundamental elements in the structure of American life, and much of what is taken for granted today as the legitimate role and function of government began with the legislation of the 1930s.

Because the Depression hit Salt Lake City and Utah so hard, federal programs were extensive in both city and state. Per capita federal spending in Utah during the 1930s was ninth among the forty-eight states, the percentage of Utah workers on federal work relief projects was far above the national average, and for every dollar Utahns sent to the nation's capital in taxes, the government returned at least seven, and by some estimates twenty, dollars through various federal programs.

The range of New Deal initiatives in Salt Lake was broad. A school lunch

program was established, and free classes in nutrition were offered. Adult education classes and children's summer recreation programs were set up. Thousands of miles of highways, roads, sidewalks, and sewer systems were constructed. Federal programs financed more than 250 public buildings throughout the state, including city halls, county courthouses, public schools, college and university buildings, fire stations, and national guard armories. More than half of them still stand, dramatic evidence of the New Deal's impact. In Salt Lake City they include the Administration Building of the Salt Lake School District and at the University of Utah the main library (now the Museum of Natural History) and the fieldhouse.

The Works Progress Administration (WPA) alone employed an average of 12,000 people annually in Utah between 1935 and 1942, with a peak of 17,000 in 1936. A 1939 survey revealed Utah's average WPA worker to be a white male, thirty-eight years old, married, with three children, and a member of the Mormon church. WPA workers undertook a variety of projects. The WPA Art Project was responsible for creating thousands of works of art, including the paintings of historic Utah figures and events in the dome of the State Capitol Building. The Utah Symphony Orchestra began as a WPA music project. The Federal Writer's Project sponsored the collection, cataloging, and

159

Hard Times

The Utah Symphony Orchestra began as part of the New Deal's Works Progress Administration (WPA) program for musicians, artists, and writers. Initially it performed across the city and state in parks, public halls, and schools. WPA artists, typically employed for $80 a month, created works of art and taught art classes. Writers collected pioneer diaries, made inventories of local archives, and wrote a first-rate state history. (Private Collection.)

publication of historical documents and the publication of an excellent state history. Some of Utah's most distinguished historians worked for it, including Dale Morgan and Juanita Brooks.

The Depression years saw a reinvigoration of Utah's labor movement. During the 1920s union membership in the state, as in the rest of the nation, declined dramatically as many companies adopted the "American Plan" under which they pledged to hire only non-union workers. Other employers simply refused to bargain with their unionized workers. In 1935, however, the U.S. Congress passed the National Labor Relations Act, also known as the Wagner Act. It outlawed blacklisting, yellow dog contracts, and a number of other practices, reasserted labor's right to organize and bargain collectively, and provided sanctions for companies that tried to prevent their employees from joining unions or penalize them if they did. Following its passage, union membership in Utah quickly increased, and by 1937 a higher percentage of Utah workers was unionized than at any time before or since.

The 1930s also brought political change. The Republican Party, which had dominated Utah politics since statehood in 1896, fell from favor, and from the early 1930s until the late 1940s Democrats were as preeminent in Utah politics as Republicans previously had been. During the 1937 legislative session, for example, Democrats outnumbered Republicans one hundred to five. Many of the new Democratic voters were first- and second-generation immigrants who had become politicized as a result of the hard times of the period and began voting for the first time. During the Depression also, those previously disenfranchised became involved politically in ways other than voting. As Helen Papanikolas points out, for example, "American-born children of Japanese immigrants actively began fighting for their civil rights. The Japanese American Citizens League succeeded in lobbying for a bill that amended the 1922 Cable Act, and American citizenship was restored to Japanese-American women who had married Issei (Japanese immigrants to the United States). American citizenship was also granted to seven hundred World War I Issei veterans."

The Depression years were a time of enormous difficulty for most Utahns. Almost no one escaped the trauma. Everyone was affected in one way or another, and as a result a new principle was established—that federal and state governments not only had a responsibility to provide relief from disaster, but also a duty to work to maintain the economic health of the nation. Even so, and though the scope of the New Deal was immense, it did not succeed in ending the Depression in Utah nor in the rest of the nation. World War II did that. More industrial plants were built during the war years than during the entire period from 1929 to 1941, and the country reached full employment for the first time in the twentieth century. Worker income increased by 50 percent, while corporate profits doubled. By the time the war ended, Utah, like the United States as a whole, had never been so prosperous.

~

Recommended Readings

Iber, Jorge. "'El diablo nos esta llevando': Utah Hispanics and the Great Depression," *Utah Historical Quarterly* 66 (Spring 1998): 159-77.

Kelen and Stone. *Missing Stories.*

Utah Historical Quarterly 54 (Summer 1986); a special issue on the Great Depression.

Chapter 9

THE WORLD WAR II YEARS

The experience of Americans during World War II was fundamentally different from that of most other people around the world. The war was not fought here. Planes did not bomb American cities. Foreign armies did not invade American soil. American cities and countryside did not become battlefields. No physical destruction occurred, no territorial lines were redrawn, no governments fell, and no civilians lost their lives in the fighting. Even so, World War II had an enormous impact on the United States, changing it and everyone in it. This was as true of Salt Lake City as it was of any place in the country. The massive mobilization of human and economic resources for war not only brought Salt Lake out of the Great Depression, it required an enormous change in the way its residents lived and influenced every aspect of their lives. Patterns of work, leisure, education, and family life were altered. Women working as welders, men building tanks, children stripping scarce tinfoil from empty cigarette packs, and the 30,000 residents of the Salt Lake Valley who served in the armed forces all felt the impact of the war in ways large and small. Women, African Americans, Hispanics, gays and lesbians, and others found new opportunities and also experienced continued prejudice and discrimination, as stereotypical images were both contested and reinforced. What Thomas G. Alexander and James B. Allen have called "the elixir of federal spending," to which Utah's economic well-being, and that of its capital city, had been tied since the beginning of the New Deal, continued, and by war's end almost 28 percent of civilian income in the state came from direct government employment, most of it military-related. The war not only extended government's central role in the economy, but also increased the cooperation between industry and government, creating what would later come to be called a military-industrial complex.

World War II restored prosperity to American workers. Unemployment vanished. Rather than too little work for too many workers, as in the Great Depression, the war years witnessed a booming economy and labor shortages. Factories running at capacity had a hard time finding people to fill jobs. One sure sign that a war was on was that people moved and took new jobs as never before. More than 15 million civilians in the United States relocated during the war, most of them in search of better jobs. Mainly they moved off of farms and away from small towns, flocking to cities, where defense jobs were readily available. Two hundred thousand people went to the Detroit area, nearly half a million to Los Angeles, and 100,000 to Mobile, Alabama. Salt Lake's experience was similar, though on a smaller scale, as military installations blossomed in the Salt Lake Valley and beyond and the city filled up with servicemen, new war-related industries were established, and existing companies hired more people.

Fourteen military installations operated in and around Salt Lake City during World War II. Fort Douglas became the headquarters of the Ninth Service Command and directed military operations in all states from the Rocky Mountains to the West Coast. Twenty miles to the southwest of downtown Salt Lake City, Kearns Army Air Base was established. By the fall of 1943 more than 90,000 airmen had received basic training there. It also provided specialty training to gunners and ground crews. Other military installations included Wendover Field, said to be the world's largest military base, where the team that dropped the atom bombs on Hiroshima and Nagasaki trained, the Ogden Arsenal, the Utah General Depot, Hill Field, the Clearfield Naval Supply Depot, the Tooele Army Depot, Dugway Proving Grounds, the Deseret Chemical Depot, and Bushnell Military Hospital near Brigham City, which became the Intermountain Indian School at war's end.

In 1941 the State of Utah established a Department of Publicity and Industrial Development whose job was to persuade war-related industries to locate in Utah. Its efforts met with considerable success, and military industries

163

The World War II
Years

A wide variety of goods, including tires and gasoline, as well as sugar, coffee, meat, butter, and canned goods, were in short supply during World War II and could not be purchased without stamps from monthly ration books, such as this one, dispensed by the U.S. Office of Price Administration. (Private Collection.)

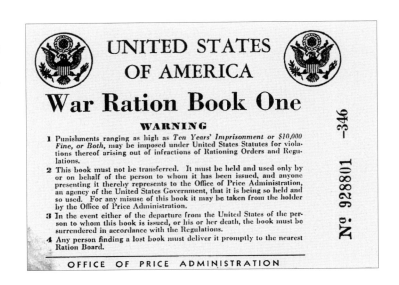

UNITED STATES
OF AMERICA

War Ration Book One

WARNING

1 Punishments ranging as high as *Ten Years' Imprisonment* or *$10,000 Fine, or Both,* may be imposed under United States Statutes for violations thereof arising out of infractions of Rationing Orders and Regulations.

2 This book must not be transferred. It must be held and used only by or on behalf of the person to whom it has been issued, and anyone presenting it thereby represents to the Office of Price Administration, an agency of the United States Government, that it is being so held and so used. For any misuse of this book it may be taken from the holder by the Office of Price Administration.

3 In the event either of the departure from the United States of the person to whom this book is issued, or his or her death, the book must be surrendered in accordance with the Regulations.

4 Any person finding a lost book must deliver it promptly to the nearest Ration Board.

OFFICE OF PRICE ADMINISTRATION

N° 928801 -346

blossomed around Salt Lake City, creating thousands of new jobs—12,000 in the first year alone after the United States entered the war, and 50,000 overall during the war years as total employment increased by 55 percent. One of the most important was the Remington Small Arms Plant on the city's westside, at Redwood Road and 1700 South. Constructed at a cost of $30 million, it manufactured 20- and 50-caliber small-arms ammunition and at its peak employed 10,000 people. One of them was Veda Swain. She and her husband had been unemployed during much of the 1930s. Just before Pearl Harbor she had found a job working as an elevator operator two hours a day at twenty-five cents an hour. When the Remington plant opened, she was hired there at sixty-nine cents an hour, forty-eight hours a week. Renee Christensen remembered the economic effect of her mother's job at Remington: the family bought its first record player, installed a telephone, and bought a natural gas stove, a water heater, and a typewriter. According to Gloria McNally, the war "set us up financially. We were never behind economically after that." They were not alone. In 1940 personal income in Utah was only 82 percent of the national average. By 1943 it had risen to slightly above it. Other important military industries in the Salt Lake area included the Eitel McCullough Radio Tube plant, a $5.5 million low-grade aluminum ore mill, and a tungsten retreatment plant. In addition, established companies expanded. For example, the American Smelting and Refining Company, the International Smelting and Refining Company, Kennecott Copper Corporation, and the Utah Copper Company

The Gathering Place

spent more than $15 million in facility expansion, copper mills at Magna and Arthur operated at 125 percent of their pre-war capacity, and the federal government financed a $20 million expansion of the Utah Oil Refinery, all of which provided thousands of jobs.

By mid-1943 Salt Lake City had nearly 40,000 new residents. As a result, a serious housing shortage developed, rents were high, and families often doubled up with parents or other relatives. One study estimated that one married couple in fourteen lived in a household other than their own. So scarce were apartments that for an extra fee taxi drivers became guides to up-to-the-minute vacancies. Able to set their own standards, landlords often discriminated against families with children and even more so against ethnic and racial minorities.

If establishing a household was difficult, supplying one, once established, was no less challenging. Although retailers extended their hours of operation into the evening and weekends, shopping had to be squeezed in between long hours at work. For the first time in years, many families had money to spend but less time in which to spend it—and there was less to spend it on. Production for war meant that many items, including cars, washing machines, and refrigerators, were no longer produced. The last new car rolled off the assembly line in February 1942. The experience of my own father, who camped out overnight on a doorstep so he would be the first person in line to buy a used refrigerator, was common. Everything worth having was rationed: coffee because of the shortage of ships available to carry it from Central and South America; canned goods because of insufficient tin; and shoes because of the needs of soldiers and sailors. In order to buy canned goods, as well as coffee, butter, cheese, meat, and many other food items, a consumer had to hand a grocer ration stamps as well as money. The color-coded stamps (red for meat and butter, blue for processed food, etc.) were issued regularly in books. In order to buy a pound of hamburger, for example, a shopper needed stamps worth seven "points" as well as the purchase price. A pound of butter cost sixteen points, a pound of cheese eight points. Gasoline was rationed, even though it was plentiful, in order to save rubber tires, which were not. Still, sugar, shoes, coffee, gasoline, meat, flour, and other items vanished from time to time, except on the thriving black market. Garment makers eliminated vests and shirt cuffs and narrowed the lapels on men's suits after the War Production Board estab-

The World War II
Years

lished fashion rules to conserve cotton and wool. Thermostats in houses and offices were turned down to 65 degrees. Conservation became a way of life. Women did without stockings because all suitable textiles were declared critical. Hairdressers used toothpicks instead of bobby pins. Shoes came in only six colors, three of them shades of brown. People saved fat in tin cans, and children brought it, as well as old newspapers, to school for collection and recycling.

In order to conserve both gasoline and rubber, a nationwide speed limit of thirty-five miles per hour was proclaimed, and pleasure driving was banned. The total miles a car could be driven was determined by the category of sticker issued to each owner. Ordinary motorists received "A" cards, limiting them to four gallons of gasoline a week. "B" cards were issued to workers in military plants for whom driving to work was necessary and allowed them a few more gallons, while physicians and others whose driving was essential got "C" cards entitling them to even more. Truckers got "T" cards and unlimited gas. Counterfeiting and selling of gas cards was common, as was theft from government warehouses. "Share the ride" clubs were organized. Ridership on Salt Lake City trolleys doubled in the face of fuel, rubber, and steel shortages, and in or-

During World War II, extensive efforts were undertaken to recycle scarce material. The Continental Oil Company paid one cent a pound for scrap rubber. This photograph was taken on June 19, 1942, six months after the U.S. entered the war. (Courtesy Utah State Historical Society.)

The Gathering Place

der to save gas the city eliminated some trolley stops and traffic signals. To discourage travel, the Mormon church curtailed large, church-sponsored gatherings. Beginning in April 1942, and for the duration of the war, its semi-annual general conferences were closed to the church's general membership, and attendance was confined to about 500 priesthood leaders. Due to shortages of gasoline, tires, repair parts, manpower, and even hot dogs and ice cream, the Saltair resort on the shores of the Great Salt Lake closed from the end of the 1942 season through 1945. With paper in short supply, the *Deseret News* and *The Salt Lake Tribune* reduced the length of their newspapers by half, to twelve pages, and eliminated special editions.

The war had other effects. Enrollment at the University of Utah dropped dramatically and by 1945 was down 70 percent from the prewar level. City high schools adopted a special wartime curriculum that divided the school day between academics and military-related vocational training. Periodic blackout trials were held in anticipation of enemy bombing raids. Labor unions pledged not to strike for the duration of the war. Except for murder, the rate of violent crimes increased. So did crimes against property. "Juvenile delinquency" climbed. The care of small children proved a major problem. Husbands and wives often lived apart for the duration, leaving children in the hands of only one parent, but even when parents were together, both adults often worked long hours, sometimes on different shifts, and little time was left for the family. In cooperation with federal government agencies, the Granite School District operated child care centers until war's end.

Downtown Salt Lake City was crowded during the war years. Sometimes it seemed that everyone was there, and one of the main reasons they went was for the movies. More than a dozen movie theaters operated in downtown, including the Utah, the Uptown, the Lyric, the Centre, the Gem, and the Rialto, and attendance soared. Gasoline might not be available for weekend trips or Sunday drives, but the whole family could ride the bus or trolley for an afternoon or evening at the movies. For children especially, movies were a major attraction during the war. As Thomas G. Alexander says, recalling his own childhood in Ogden, for a dime they could spend all Saturday afternoon at the movies, watching two features, five cartoons, and two serials. Musical comedies, westerns, and historical romances remained popular, but the war also intruded on Hollywood. Newsreels, offering a visual synopsis of the war news, always with an upbeat message and a touch of human interest, preceded most movies. Feature films often had a wartime theme. The basic message was that World War II was a good war fought against evil empires. The United States was right, the enemy wrong. It was an attitude that would influence the wartime generation for the rest of their lives.

Salt Lakers not only went to the movies during the war, they also listened to the radio—according to one survey, an average of 4.5 hours a day. "We'd listen to the radio every night," one man recalled. "My father would turn it on to find out what was happening." The war influenced most programming and even the advertising that took up more and more air time. Lucky Strike cigarettes changed the color of its package from green to white, because there was a shortage of green pigment, and its new slogan, "Lucky Strike Has Gone to War," became almost as famous as "Remember Pearl Harbor." The serials, the standard fare of daytime radio, adopted wartime themes. Dick Tracy tracked down spies, while Captain Midnight fought against the enemy on remote jungle islands. Superman outwitted Nazi agents, and Stella Dallas took a job in a defense plant. Music took up a large proportion of radio programming and also conveyed a war theme. There was "Goodbye, Mama, I'm Off to Yokohama" and "Praise the Lord and Pass the Ammunition," but more numerous were songs of romance and love, songs about separation, and songs of hope for better times after the war.

During World War II the number of Salt Lake households headed by women increased dramatically. Continuing to follow national trends, as it had since the early twentieth century, Salt Lake's marriage rate went up, despite the uncertainties of wartime, or perhaps because of them, and the birth rate soon followed as young couples started families as fast as they could. Some children were "good-bye" babies, conceived just before a husband left to join the military or go overseas. The increase in the number of births led area hospitals to reduce the stay for mother and child from fourteen days to five. The illegitimacy rate also went up, and from the outset of the war the divorce rate began to climb sharply as the circumstances of war placed unusual stresses on marriage. In Salt Lake County the divorce rate increased 25 percent during the war, from 25.3 per 100 marriages before the war to 31.7 by war's end.

During the war Salt Lake's population not only grew larger, but also more diverse. Utah's black population increased nearly fourfold, from about 700 in 1940 to 2,500 by 1945. As Ronald G. Coleman says, "World War II and the ensuing years had a dramatic impact on African-American life throughout the West. The development and growth of railroad centers, defense contract industries, and military installations in the region influenced a number of African Americans to relocate to the western part of the country in search of better opportunities." Nathan "Woody" Wright's experience was typical of many. Born in Cuba in 1916, he spent the first eight years of his life in New York City, joined the Civil Service in Missouri in 1942, and was sent as a machinist to Hill Field, where he spent the war years repairing machine guns, working on gun turrets, rebuilding batteries, and wiring the electrical systems of airplanes. By war's end he was an aircraft electrical inspector. After the war, like many African Americans who had come during the war years, he remained in Utah, working for many years at the Railroad Porter's and Waiter's Club on Ogden's Twenty-fifth Street and on an assembly line for Sperry Univac.

Even though World War II brought new opportunities for black men and women throughout the country, the United States remained a segregated society. African Americans could not live, eat, travel, work, or go to school with the same freedom whites enjoyed, and they needed no instruction about the chasm between assertions of freedom and equality and the realities of prejudice and discrimination. Nothing captured the reality more poignantly than the moment when a black soldier named Lloyd Brown, caught in the dusty heat of a Kansas summer day, looked past the restaurant owner who had refused him entry to see a row of German prisoners of war eating lunch at the counter. Salt Lake City was little different. There were no racial outbreaks, as there were in forty-seven U.S. cities in the summer of 1943, but as always a strong effort was exerted to keep black Americans in their place. On September 1, 1944, a petition was submitted to the Salt Lake City Commission requesting that African Americans be prevented from building houses in certain areas of the city. Throughout the war white and African-American soldiers were entertained in separate USOs, and as Emma Helwing, a Jewish immigrant from Eastern Europe, who volunteered as a cook with the black USO, said, "This was the only place they could get meals. They often told me their woe about not being admitted to any restaurant in town. I felt ashamed and bewildered that such things happened in a democracy." Myron Q. Hale worked as a clerk at the Hotel Utah during the war. It did not rent rooms to African Americans. When black men or women tried to register, his supervisors told him to say, even when rooms were empty, "I am sorry but we are filled to capacity, but I could attempt to obtain a room for you at another hotel," and he would direct them to the recently integrated Newhouse Hotel. He recalled one particularly agonizing experience: "I'll never forget the night sometime in 1942 that an army captain, who was black, with one arm missing, and on his uniform a chest full of ribbons, attempted to register at the Hotel Utah. I was ashamed, but I said, 'I am sorry, I cannot lie to you. Hotel policy prohibits my assigning you a room. ... I will, however, call another hotel and try to obtain a room for you.' The captain said nothing, and I made the call." Finding the Hotel Newhouse full that night, Hale allowed the captain to spend the night sitting in a chair in the hotel lobby.

After the war the situation did not change. Black entertainers coming to Salt Lake City to perform were routinely denied lodging. "I was at the Hotel Utah desk when Marian Anderson was forced to use the freight elevator after her performance in the Mormon Tabernacle," Myron Hale said. "During her stay at the Hotel, the rooms were 'blank'—no name—and no information was to be given to the newspapers or anyone else. ... She took meals in her room."

Marian Anderson was one of the premier classical singers in the United States. In 1939, after the Daughters of the American Revolution (DAR) refused to allow her to use their stage for a concert, Eleanor Roosevelt resigned from the organization and arranged for Anderson to sing from the steps of the Lincoln Memorial, where 75,000 people gathered to listen and to support civil rights for all black citizens. In the 1940s when Anderson came to Salt Lake City and performed in the Mormon Tabernacle, she was allowed to stay at the Hotel Utah (now the Joseph Smith Memorial Building) only after she agreed to use the back service elevator, and her name did not appear on the hotel register. (Courtesy Will South.)

One restaurant reluctantly consented to serve singer Nat King Cole only if he sat out of view of other customers behind a partition. The City and County Building's cafe did not serve black men and women until 1948, following a demonstration by the Salt Lake branch of the National Association for the Advancement of Colored People (NAACP), and the city-owned and operated Wasatch Plunge swimming pool did not allow blacks and whites to swim together until the 1960s. Blacks were not allowed at the Lagoon amusement park, founded in 1895, until the mid-1950s, except for one day after its "public" closing on Labor Day, and a 1956 poll revealed that 51 of 107 Utah restaurants surveyed refused to serve black men and women. Of his experience in the 1950s, John Oscar Williams recalled, "When we'd go to the Utah Theater, the Capitol Theater, all of the theaters, we had to sit in the balcony. That was the only place they would let us sit." According to Ruby Nathaniel, "Salt Lake City always had its segregation. We never had to ride in the rear of the bus or the streetcar (when we had streetcars), but you couldn't sit wherever you

171

wanted to. You couldn't go in dancehalls, you couldn't go to shows except in certain places. ... I learned to take it and do my best ... But I had my bad times, too. My bad times came, I guess, when white people would hurt my kids' feelings. Then I would just get really upset, and I would get in there and be ready to fight and argue with anyone." Albert Fritz recalled the way he felt: "I resented it when they told me to go upstairs in a theater. I resented walking into a cafe and being told, 'We don't serve colored here.' And I resented the way salesmen in the stores would take your money, with a smile on their faces, but wouldn't let you try on clothes before buying them."

Roy Hawkins was head waiter at the nationally franchised Coon Chicken Inn on Highland Drive from 1943 until 1949. A caricature of a black face was on the building's façade, with the main entrance to the restaurant in the middle of thick open lips. "Everything we used in the place had that face on it," said Hawkins. "The silverware, the plates, the menus, the napkins. And everything on the menu was named 'coon'—coon coffee, coon steak, coon, coon, coon." But Hawkins worked there and endured the insults of racist caricatures and sometimes of customers—he remembers adults coming in with their children, pointing to him and saying, "Look, there's a real live coon"—because the money was good and he had a family to support. "It was because of people like him, that someone like me could work here," said Wilfred D. Samuels, Professor of English at the University of Utah. "I can't imagine living and working there, facing my children when you drove by the restaurant. 'Coon' is synonymous with 'nigger,' but Roy went into the Coon Chicken Inn every day and held his head up high. I admire Roy and others—their fortitude, their sense of dignity and pride."

A 1953 article in the *Utah Law Review*, by University of Utah law professor Wallace R. Bennett, summarized the discrimination black men and women faced in Salt Lake City and throughout Utah at the time. Neither Lagoon nor Saltair, the state's two largest amusement parks, admitted blacks; neither did any college fraternity or sorority. With one exception, Salt Lake City movie theaters with balconies required blacks to sit in them when viewing a movie. State law upheld the practice of theaters throughout the state routinely refusing to sell tickets to blacks after a Utah court in 1933 held that theaters were not obligated to admit all applicants willing to buy tickets, but could exclude or segregate people of any race at their pleasure. A Utah miscegenation statute

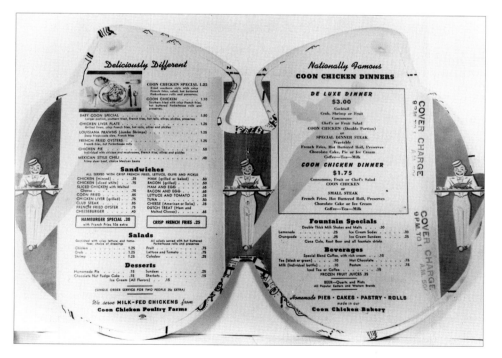

Salt Lake City's Coon Chicken Inn, 2950 Highland Drive, in 1930. A caricature of a black face was on the building's façade, with the main entrance in the middle of thick open lips. Other Coon Chicken Inns operated "coast to coast" throughout the United States. (Private Collection.)

prohibited marriage between blacks and whites. In 1935 the following restrictive covenant was incorporated into the standard Uniform Real Estate Contract, approved by the Salt Lake Real Estate Board: "The buyer, his heirs, executors, administrators, successors or assigns, agree that no estate in or possession of the said premises shall be sold, transferred, granted or conveyed to any person not of the Caucasian race," and the provision remained common in real estate contracts until the 1960s. In 1945 an "Equal Rights Law of the State of Utah" was introduced in the state senate. It expressly prohibited "discrimination on account of race, color or creed in the admission to, or the accommodation of, any person in any place of public accommodation," and provided criminal penalties for violations. It defined public accommodations to include "hotels, restaurants, hospitals, theaters, amusement parks." The bill died in committee. The same bill was introduced in the two following legislative sessions and died in committee each time. Hospitals admitted black patients but required them to take private rooms. The LDS Hospital and the Catholic-owned Holy Cross Hospital accepted donations of blood from both blacks and whites, but provided that blood from blacks could not be given to whites and vice versa. In 1947 a state legislative committee concluded that "there is a substantial body of unfair and discriminatory practice in the state's industry, which operates to deny minority groups among our citizens equal right to gainful employment. These policies affect somewhere between one-third and one-half of the state's employers, and a roughly equivalent proportion of available employment." On the basis of those findings, a bill was introduced in the senate proposing to make discrimination in employment on the basis of race, creed, or color a misdemeanor. It was soundly defeated, 16 to 6.

Utah's Hispanic population also grew during World War II as Mexican and Mexican-American workers were brought in to work—mainly in mining, railroads, agriculture, and military industries. As Edward H. Mayer says, "The sudden labor shortage impelled the United States to initiate the Emergency Labor Program of 1942 (the Bracero program) and to once again look to Mexico for agricultural workers. This influx of workers revitalized many Mexican communities throughout the United States." Mexican laborers were unable to meet all of Utah's wartime needs in agriculture and industry, however, and a large migration of Hispanos from northern New Mexico and Colorado began in the 1940s. "With the outbreak of World War II," Mayer says, "there was an immediate demand for a labor force. Recruiters from the defense industries went to the villages of New Mexico to entice Hispanic workers and their families to move to Utah. Not only did Hispanics contribute with their work to the war effort, but Hispanic soldiers actively participated in battle, becoming one of the most highly decorated groups in the United States Armed Forces."

After the war Hispanic soldiers returned home with new dreams and aspirations, eager to participate in the society they had fought to preserve. The GI Bill provided them with many opportunities in the areas of education, job training, and home loans, but they found that deep prejudices and discrimination still prevailed. When Epiefanio Gonzales attempted to purchase a house on Salt Lake City's eastside, a real estate agent told him he should stay with his "own kind" and look for a house in another neighborhood. A veteran of the U.S. Corps of Combat Engineers, he was devastated. "I mean, how would you feel," he asked, "if you came home decorated, you fought your heart out in the war, you said to yourself, 'Now, I'm American; I'm just as good as any one,' and then all of a sudden you're made to feel like a second-rate citizen with no privileges? That can have a terrible effect on a person. ... It can really take the starch out of you."

According to Mayer, "The negative attitudes of the majority population toward the Hispanics were especially destructive to the young, who were caught between two cultures, the Hispanic and the Anglo-American. The prejudice and discrimination they faced in the schools caused many first- and second-generation Mexican Americans to reject their culture. One of the most important, and most easily measured, cultural traits lost was language. The use of Spanish was discouraged on school playgrounds, and the demands placed on the students to speak English without an accent gave the bilingual Hispanics the wrong message—that Spanish was of no value."

More than previous conflicts in the history of the United States, World War II was a woman's, as well as a man's, war. One-quarter of a million women served in the nation's armed forces. Millions more entered the civilian labor force for the first time. During the Great Depression women working for a wage outside the home were accused of taking a husband's or father's job, but with the onset of war government and industry actively recruited women, and "Rosie the Riveter" became perhaps the best-known symbol of women's contributions on the home front during wartime. First drawn by Norman

Rockwell for a cover of the *Saturday Evening Post*, she was also the subject of a popular song of the same name. According to its lyrics, she was "making history by working for victory." In addition to doing traditional "women's work" as nurses, clerks, secretaries, and the like, women were bus drivers, welders, mechanics, lumberjacks, pilots, and train conductors. They worked in railyards, aircraft factories, automobile plants, shipyards, and ammunitions plants. A World War II movie ended with the heroine telling her Army Air Corps boyfriend as he was about to ship out, "While you're flying them, honey, I'll be building them."

During World War II women entered Utah's work force in unprecedented numbers. Many were married and had children. Near the war's end, almost 40 percent of Utah wage earners were women, many in areas of work previously closed to them. In November 1942 Utah Power & Light Company, which owned and operated Salt Lake City's bus system, announced that for the first time in its history it had hired women as bus drivers, or "driverettes," as the company preferred to call them. It would not normally have done this, it said apologetically, but "shortages of manpower caused by operators leaving to

In 1940 only one in six Utah women worked outside the home. World War II, however, brought a shortage of workers, and 24,000 Utah women became wage workers, many of them in military industries. Others repaired machinery, boxed ammunition, and drove trucks, buses, and taxis. After the war the number of women in Utah's work force steadily increased, and by 1960 had risen 57 percent since the end of he war. (Courtesy Utah State Historical Society.)

In 1943 World War II became the first war in which women were given regular military status when the U.S. Congress authorized full military participation for women, except for combat. They were persuaded to do so because of the military emergency and the argument that women could free men for combat duty. Nationwide about 350,000 women served in the armed forces, most in the Women's Army Corps (WACS) and the women's branch of the navy (WAVES), but some also in the coast guard and the marines. At war's end, more than 1,300 Utah women were in uniform. (Private Collection.)

join the armed forces and entering war industries have allowed the girls to invade this hitherto masculine occupation." By the end of 1943, it employed fifty women as drivers and in maintenance jobs that until then only men had held. All were doing a "man-sized job," it reassured its customers, and were performing well.

Even though women joined the work force in increasing numbers and made a crucial contribution to the war effort, they continued to be paid less than men. Nationwide, women's weekly wages averaged about $31, while men made $54, and it was no different in Utah. The Tooele Ordnance Depot Salvage Department, for example, paid women 67.5 cents an hour and men 85 cents. At the Rocky Mountain Packing Company women received five cents per hour less than men. The Cudahy Packing Company had different wage scales for men and women. At the Ogden Arsenal male ammunition loaders were paid $5.50 a day, while women doing the same job received $4.40.

The World War II
Years

In a recent study by Ann Chambers, Utah women pointed to their experience working during World War II as a turning point in their lives. "I developed more confidence in my ability to face new challenges," said one. According to Odessa Young Mower, "I knew I could do housework but not sure I could do work like this—but I did." Several others said war work brought them into contact for the first time in a meaningful way with people of various ethnic, cultural, and religious backgrounds. Others commented on the feelings of autonomy and independence that earning their own paychecks and not having to be dependent on their husbands for an income brought. For some, their paycheck paid for an education, not otherwise affordable.

At the same time, the war experience had a darker side. "War is terrible," said one woman. "For me it was awful as the first man I considered marrying was at Corregidor, and all the terrible things they were going through was in my mind constantly even though I was working ten hours, seven days a week at Ogden Arsenal and sometimes at a cafe in Ogden in between. ... I never heard from him again. Eventually he was listed as missing in action. ... I don't mention this much, because I just try to forget. ... It was hard work and a lot of tears." Some workers remembered that equipment salvaged from the battlefields often had blood stains on it. Ellen Jenkins recalled finding notes from American soldiers between gun parts. Pilots often left messages and drawings inside their planes. Workers on planes at Hill Field spoke of cleaning blood, skin, and hair out of cockpits. "This brought home the reality of what was happening," one woman said. Retha Nielson, who worked on B-24s, wrote, "I got a lump in my throat as I read the names of the men who had piloted them. Some of them had given the planes a name. ... I would walk up to the big plane and touch it and wonder if all the men had come out alive, what had happened and why they had named it what they had."

World War II provided many women with their first well-paying jobs. It pulled older and married women and mothers into wage-earning in large numbers, raised such issues as publicly supported day care and equal pay for equal work, and brought expectations that life could be better. In those ways it set the stage for changes to come in the following decades. Many women stayed in the work force after the war. In 1940 one in six Utah women worked for a wage outside the home—the second lowest percentage in the nation—while in 1950 the ratio was close to the national average of one in four.

Even so, women's work during World War II was not a breakthrough signaling the end of discrimination against women in the labor market. It did not revolutionize gender relations. The notion that a woman's place was in the home was barely dented, and in the end the rapid demobilization of both military and civilian economic sectors resulted in a basic restoration of former labor patterns. During the war women had been told that while their patriotic duty was to enter the work force, neither government nor industry expected them to stay in their jobs when the war ended. Recruitment campaigns addressed to "Mrs. Stay-at-Home" emphasized the patriotic, yet temporary, nature of women's wartime service, and also used conventional gender stereotypes to portray female war workers, depicting their new industrial labors as simply a variation of their domestic talents. Where once housewives sewed curtains for their kitchens, they now produced silk parachutes for the army, while their skills with a vacuum cleaner were viewed as easily translating into riveting on huge ships. "Instead of cutting a cake," one publication explained, "this woman factory worker cuts the pattern of aircraft parts. Instead of baking a cake, another is cooking gears to reduce the tension in the gears after use." Rosie the Riveter represented the model female citizen, working in industry, but only "for the duration" and in a way that made use of her uniquely female abilities. Thus it was only natural that following the war women were told that their patriotic duty was to leave the work force to make way for returning servicemen who would need jobs. Those who hoped to remain on the job were advised to seek traditionally female, or "pink collar," jobs. As the Mormon church's *Relief Society Magazine* said in an October 1944 editorial, "Home, After the War": "The great majority, it is hoped, of the men will be coming back; war industries will cease, and the returning members of the armed forces must be given the opportunity to once more earn livelihoods for themselves and their families. When this situation arises, the mother who has left her home should be prepared to face the situation and accept it."

Many women who learned what an extra paycheck meant for their family's standard of living would have preferred to keep working, but most women, and an even larger percentage of men, agreed at the end of the war that women did not deserve "an equal chance with men" for jobs. War work altered individual lives and attitudes, but it did not fundamentally change either gender's perception of women's proper role (just as it did not change the dominant perception of the proper place of blacks, Hispanics, Native Americans, and members of other ethnic minority groups).

During World War II propaganda campaigns sought not only to stimulate patriotism but also to demonize the enemy. Much of the hatred thus engendered carried over to certain U.S. residents of foreign descent. Though some negative feeling existed about German Americans and Italian Americans, the objects of greatest anxiety were Japanese Americans, not only resident aliens, but also American citizens of Japanese ancestry. Fear added to the racism Japanese immigrants had faced since the late nineteenth century when they had encountered hostility as economic competitors and intruders in a "white man's country," and during the war years Salt Lake City hotels and restaurants posted signs reading "No Japs Wanted Here"; Japanese employees were fired; Japanese school children were harassed; the Japanese section of the Salt Lake City cemetery was vandalized; the Salt Lake City Board of Realtors recommended that people of "Japanese ancestry" not be allowed to buy houses; and the Salt Lake City Chamber of Commerce asked city officials not to grant business licenses to "people of Japanese ancestry." Allowing Japanese Americans to operate businesses, it argued, would only attract more of them to the city and "create a problem not only now, but for the future, which would be a real challenge to law and order in this area." The Salt Lake City Federation of Labor endorsed the chamber's position. Earlier the Utah State Legislature had passed a bill prohibiting Japanese aliens from buying land, and Utahns overwhelmingly supported the federal government's decision in the spring of 1942, under President Franklin D. Roosevelt's Executive Order 9066, to forcibly move more than 110,000 Japanese Americans living on the West Coast and in Hawaii, two-thirds of them U.S. citizens, to so-called "relocation centers"— guarded camps isolated from other populations—for the duration of the war. The loyalty of all Japanese Americans, citizens or not, was suspect, the theory went, and internment was necessary to protect the United States from sabotage. More than fifty years later it is an episode that still haunts many Americans as a complete violation of civil rights under the pretense of military necessity.

One of the ten camps established in the United States was Topaz in Utah's Millard County, about ten miles northwest of Delta. At its peak it held more than 8,000 people and was Utah's fifth largest population center. Though

"military necessity" was the official reason for the move, the real motives, as Sandra C. Taylor says, were "economic greed, politics, and, above all, racism." As General John DeWitt, head of the Western Defense Command, headquartered in San Francisco, saw it: "In the war in which we are now engaged racial affinities are not severed by migration. The Japanese race is an enemy race, and while many second and third generation Japanese born on United States soil, possessed of United States citizenship, have become 'Americanized,' the racial strains are undiluted." As Nancy J. Taniguchi says, "The racist notion of 'Japanese' as an all-inclusive category promptly predominated. Physical appearance became the deciding factor, not citizenship, allegiance, or personal loyalty." The point Patricia Nelson Limerick makes is that without proof of actual treachery, government officials had to call on old patterns of thought, that is, "The fact that the Japanese seemed innocent proved that they were up to something." As Earl Warren, California's attorney general at the time, and later chief justice of the U.S. Supreme Court, said, some people "are of the opinion that because we have had no sabotage and no fifth column activities

The Japanese-American internment camp at Topaz, near Delta, in Millard County. During the war more than 100,000 people were evacuated from the West Coast to live in ten such camps. Most of them were in remote, often arid, sections of the West. (Private Collection.)

181

The World War II
Years

in this State ... that means that none have been planned for us. But I take the view that this is the most ominous sign in our whole situation." One curious feature of anti-Japanese sentiment was that although Japanese Americans were supposedly potential enemy agents, they were allowed to join the armed forces. They sustained enormous casualties in relation to their numbers and fought in some of the most decorated and decimated American units. Apparently they were fit to die for their country, but not to live in it.

During World War II homosexual Utahns faced challenges comparable to those of other marginalized groups. As James L. Roarke points out, the view that gays were a threat to good order and morale and were likely to crack under pressure had long dominated both military and corporate thinking, and, following Pearl Harbor, Secretary of War Henry Stimson reminded all commanding generals that they were expected to screen out homosexuals and prosecute soldiers who committed homosexual acts. At the same time the very crisis that renewed prejudice against gay men and women also worked against enforcing it thoroughly, and, like other disadvantaged minorities, gay Americans, though stigmatized, found the war to be a transforming experience in some ways. The need for as many people as possible in the armed forces made those in charge both less able and less willing to discriminate against potential recruits, and because screening procedures had been set up with only men in mind, lesbians volunteering for the newly formed women's branches of service had an even lower proportion of their numbers screened out. Likewise private employers, faced with a labor shortage, were less likely to purge gays and lesbians from their ranks. Gays in the military thus served in as many ways as did other inductees, and studies at the end of the war showed their records to be much the same. Like black, Hispanic, and Japanese-American servicemen and women, gays demonstrated their worth under fire. The brute experience of war also put issues of sexual inclination into a blunt new perspective. As one gay survivor of the Iwo Jima campaign put it, in the midst of life or death realities, "Who in the hell is going to worry about this shit?"

In a sense World War II was also a national "coming out" experience. As John D'Emilio and Estelle B. Freedman say, "For a generation of young Americans, the war created a setting in which to experience same-sex love, affection, and sexuality, and to participate in the group life of gay men and women. It offered a dramatic, unexpected alternative to the years of isolation and searching for others that had characterized gay life in the previous half century. For some, their wartime careers simply made more accessible a way of living and loving they had already chosen. For others, it gave meaning to little-understood desires, introduced them for the first time to men and women with similar feelings, and allowed them to embark upon a new sexual road."

~

Recommended Readings

Chambers, Antonette Noble. "Utah's Rosies: Women in the Utah War Industries During World War II." *Utah Historical Quarterly* 59 (Spring 1991): 123-45. Reprinted in McCormick and Sillito, *A World We Thought We Knew*, 321-36.

D'Emilio, John, and Freedman, Estelle B. *Intimate Matters: A History of Sexuality in America*. New York: Harper and Row, 1988.

Kelen and Stone. *Missing Stories*.

Powell, Allan Kent. *Utah Remembers World War II*. Logan: Utah State University Press, 1989.

Taylor, Sandra. *Jewel of the Desert: Japanese American Internment at Topaz*. Berkeley: University of California Press, 1993.

Chapter 10

CONTRASTING CULTURES
AND LIFESTYLES

W hile any number of things can be said about the history of Salt Lake City in the years after World War II, perhaps the main point is the one Robert Gottlieb and Peter Wiley make in their chapter, "Salt Lake City: Zion at the Crossroads," in their book, *Empires in the Sun: The Rise of the New American West*. After the war, they say, "a counterpoint of change and reaction set in. Salt Lake, unlike any other western city, resembled something of a battleground between contrasting cultures and lifestyles." The city was an example of what Mary Louise Pratt has called "contact zones," by which she means "social spaces where cultures meet, clash, and grapple with each other, often in contexts of highly asymmetrical relations of power." Various interests—some more powerful than others, including working class and racial and ethnic groups, Mormons, non-Mormons, local businessmen, outside corporate interests, and leaders of government—interacted, seeking to assert their legitimacy and authority. More than ever before marginalized groups acted on their own behalf, seeking a point of entry into the dominant culture, attempting to describe themselves in ways that engaged with the representations others made of them. In this, Salt Lake City both mirrored and was influenced by national and global trends. What occurred increasingly paralleled and reflected what was happening elsewhere and represented the localization of larger trends. Even so, Salt Lake retained what Dale L. Morgan had earlier called "a hard-gutted individuality."

Utah's economy boomed during World War II. The question was, what would sustain it afterwards? In the Cold War atmosphere of the postwar period, the answer, in effect, was "more of the same"—not necessarily more war, but more federal spending, especially for military purposes. Between 1945 and 1970 the federal government spent nearly half of its total budget on its armed forces, military industries rapidly expanded nationwide, and by 1970 the job of one in ten Americans was tied to the budget of the Department of Defense. In Utah, as elsewhere, the Cold War profoundly shaped economic priorities. The possibility of large government contracts encouraged businesses to focus their capital resources and technological know-how on producing armaments. By the early 1960s the military was the largest manufacturing sector in the state, generating 20 percent of all personal income, and more than 17,000 Utahns—20 percent of the state's work force—were employed in military industries. In 1962 Utah, by a variety of measures, was the second most military-oriented state in the nation and for a generation afterward continued to rank near the top. Among the companies locating in the Salt Lake area were the Sperry-Rand Corporation, which arrived in 1956 to produce sergeant missiles, anti-aircraft weapons systems, and radar systems, and the Hercules Powder Company, an important contractor of minuteman missiles. Hercules later worked with Thiokol on the trident and poseidon submarine missiles.

One of the most important features of the postwar period in the United States was the move to the suburbs. By 1970 more Americans lived there than anywhere else. As Herbert I. Schiller says, "The movement had been going on since the 1920s, but it accelerated dramatically after World War II. Cheap mortgages and subsidized highway construction that made the automobile the preferred mode of travel facilitated the growth of successive layers of bedroom communities outside and then well beyond the old city limits." While "street-car suburbs" had begun to emerge around Salt Lake City in the early twentieth century, suburbs really began to blossom soon after World War II and by the

After World War II a severe housing shortage existed in Salt Lake City, and many organizations cooperated in finding accommodations for returning soldiers and their families. (Courtesy Utah State Historical Society.)

186

1960s had overtaken the city in almost every respect. In 1960 Salt Lake City's population reached its historic high of 189,454. After that it began to decline—by 7 percent in the 1960s, when the county's population increased by 20 percent, and by 8 percent in the 1970s, when the county grew by 18 percent. Overall during the 1960s and 1970s, Salt Lake City lost an average of 1,200 people a year. In 1950 seven in ten Salt Lake Valley residents lived in the city. By 1970 only three in ten did, and by 1990 slightly more than two in ten.

School enrollment provides another measure of the magnitude of the flight from city to suburbs in the postwar years. Enrollment in Salt Lake City schools peaked in 1958 at nearly 45,000 students. By 1980 it had decreased by almost 50 percent to 23,000 students, and one by one more than two dozen elementary and junior high schools, as well as one of the city's four high schools, had closed because of declining enrollments. On the other hand, enrollment in the county's Granite and Jordan school districts increased nearly fivefold during the 1960s.

The town of Riverton provides a clear example of what the rush to the suburbs meant. So named because of its location near the Jordan River, it lies at the southwest end of the Salt Lake Valley, about twenty miles from Salt Lake City. One hundred years ago it was a Mormon community of several dozen families living on small farms, mostly along the river. In 1900 its population was about 600. A half a century later, in 1950, it had increased to only 1,666, and the town remained a small and relatively stable farming community. After that rapid change occurred. From 1950 to 1970 its population nearly doubled, to almost 3,000. It doubled again during each of the next two decades, reaching more than 16,000 by 1996, and its annual growth rate was 15 percent. Less than 1 percent of the population still farmed, and most of those who did were part-timers, either retirees or people with full-time jobs for whom farming was a supplementary source of income.

The move to the suburbs had a profound impact on the city. For one thing, it brought a change in the kinds of people who lived there. For the most part it was the middle class who moved to the suburbs. The rich could afford to live in the city, while the poor and disadvantaged could afford nowhere else. Thus by the mid-1970s the extremes in wealth and income in evidence in American cities in general—whether New York City or Lubbock, Texas—ex-

Contrasting
Cultures and
Lifestyles

isted in Salt Lake, and the population was increasingly polarized between rich and poor. In 1979, 13.6 percent of Salt Lake City's population was below the poverty level. Most of them lived in the central city and westside areas. In 1970 nearly 60 percent of central city families had incomes of less than $5,000 per year, and 16 percent were below $1,600, while at the same time 80 percent of families on the east bench had incomes over $5,000. Median family income in the upper avenues was more than $46,000 in 1979, the highest in the state, while in central city it was one quarter of that. By 1990 the situation had not changed. Median household income for the city as a whole was $22,697. In the upper avenues it was more than $78,000, while in central city it was about $11,000.

The move to the suburbs also led to deterioration in many of Salt Lake City's residential areas. As in cities across the country, decaying neighborhoods were more and more in evidence. A 1971 city-funded study concluded that 40 percent of Salt Lake's houses were "blighted"—either in need of major rehabilitation or beyond repair. In the central city and capitol hill areas, the figure was 60 percent. As Thomas G. Alexander and James B. Allen say, by the early 1970s Salt Lake City had become "a metropolis of blighted neighborhoods."

Suburbanization also affected downtown businesses. Fewer and fewer people shopped downtown, and more and more of them shopped in the suburbs, particularly at the half dozen large malls that dotted the valley by the 1990s. Since 1980 the city's share of retail sales in Salt Lake County slipped from 43 percent to 28 percent, according to a report by James A. Wood, senior researcher at the University of Utah's Bureau of Economic and Business Research. As *Salt Lake Tribune* reporter Phil Sahm observed, "Shopping used to mean going downtown. People came by bus or car to amble with packages along sidewalks, and to stop at restaurants and movie theatres. Furniture, hardware and clothing stores sold almost everything they needed. Salt Lake City's Main and State Street stores constituted the heart of the local service economy. But walk down Main Street some evenings, and it looks deserted. And it's not hard to figure where the shoppers are: They are at malls, neighborhood centers and national chains that dot the suburbs and dominate retailing." According to R. Thayne Robson, director of the Bureau of Economic and

Business Research, in terms of retail activity, "Downtown has reached and passed its zenith."

Historians often characterize the decade or so after the end of World War II, from 1945 to about 1960, conveniently referred to as the "1950s," as a time when Americans lost their taste for political change. They tend to see it as a period of consensus and conformity, a time of "the safe course, the safe thought, the safe life." Looking back on his experience growing up in the 1950s, Paul Goodman, author of an important collection of essays entitled *Growing Up Absurd*, remembered it as a time when his generation was taught: "WORK, don't play. STUDY, don't loaf; OBEY, don't ask questions; FIT IN, don't stand out; MAKE MONEY, don't make waves." At the same time, other things were going on. As Stephanie Coonz says in her book, *The Way We Never Were: American Families and the Nostalgia Trap*, in the 1950s we had just finished a world war, we were living with the threat of nuclear war, we were becoming involved in the Korean War, and we were living with the escalation of the Cold War. Women and children lived with the additional fear of personal violence. For many children, growing up in families of the 1950s was not so much a matter of being protected from the harsh realities of the outside world as preventing the outside world from learning the harsh realities of family life. Wife battering was not considered a "real" crime by most people. Psychiatrists in the 1950s regarded the battered woman as a masochist who provoked her husband into beating her. According to law, marital rape was impossible, no term existed for or acknowledged sexual harassment, and rape happened only to "bad" girls. What we think of as 1950s sexual morality was the sexual double standard. Women bore the burden of "drawing the line." Heavy petting was a normal part of dating, and the proportion of "white brides" who were pregnant at marriage more than doubled. Teen birth rates soared, reaching highs that have not been equaled since. A large wage gap existed between men and women, and women faced other problems as well. They were often denied the right to serve on juries, take out credit cards in their own name, or establish residence. They were excluded from a number of professions, and the policy of many national companies of not hiring women older than age forty violated no law. Some states gave husbands total control over family finances. A full 25 percent of Americans were poor in the mid-1950s, including a third of American children and 60 percent of Americans over sixty-five. Even when we con-

Contrasting
Cultures and
Lifestyles

sider only native-born, white families, one-third needed two incomes. Fifty percent of black families were poor, and poverty, discrimination, and suffering stalked most minority families. Because of the extreme segregation of the 1950s, the majority of Americans—anyone fitting into one of the following categories: disabled, racial or ethnic minority, migrant worker, female, young, poor, or practitioner of a non-Protestant religion—were discriminated against in employment, education, housing, travel, entertainment, and every other area of life.

All of this led to the intense unrest of the 1960s. In contrast to the 1950s, the 1960s, by which I mean the period from the mid-1950s to the early-1970s, was a volatile and passionate time when virtually every aspect of American life was challenged and questioned. It was a period of unprecedented optimism and activism. Significant movements for social change emerged, including an African-American civil rights movement, a women's movement, an anti-war movement, a gay rights movement, a consumer movement, a Native American rights movement, an Hispanic rights movement, and an environmental movement. Underlying much of that activity was the belief that "the personal is political," that was to say, the conviction that personal problems were not just personal problems. They were problems that millions of people shared,

Board meeting of the Crossroads Urban Center in the early 1980s. Founded in 1966, it has been important in addressing the needs of Salt Lake's poor and low-income residents ever since. Donna Land Maldonado is at the bottom, far left; Robert Velasquez is at the bottom, far right. (Courtesy Crossroads Urban Center.)

190

and because so many people faced them, their causes were not just personal inadequacy, and their solution not just individual. They were social problems with social causes and political solutions.

Salt Lake City was very much a part of the upheaval of the 1960s, both reflecting, and participating in, it. Thus, for example, a variety of citizen groups in virtually every part of the city was founded to combat the decaying neighborhoods that accompanied the move to the suburbs. They were part of a larger movement of grassroots groups emerging throughout the United States that one historian called "the backyard revolution." Some were short-lived. Others remain active today. The Central City Community Council, for example, fought to downzone the central city area, organized a Residents' Code Compliance Committee to work with city building inspectors, operated a job-referral service for the area's unemployed men and women, and founded People Against Redlining to fight against the common practice of banks and savings and loans of not providing loans to residents of "undesirable" inner city areas. The Senior Citizens' Coalition lobbied for issues of particular interest to older residents. An organization called "Cost-Off" sought the elimination of the sales tax on food. The Union of the Poor opposed the demolition of low-income housing, and a number of tenant unions were formed. In 1966 the

191

Contrasting
Cultures and
Lifestyles

Methodist church opened the Crossroads Urban Center, and it has remained to the present an important force within Salt Lake City's inner city neighborhoods, providing emergency food and clothing and a variety of social programs. Since its founding, it has also spawned a number of other advocacy groups, including Women Standing Alone, which later became Justice, Economic Dignity, and Independence for Women (J.E.D.I. Women); the Disabled Rights Action Committee; Utahns Against Hunger; the Children's Literacy Project; Wasatch Community Gardens; and the Coalition of Religious Communities; as well as groups that have not yet become fully independent, including the Utility Advocacy Program, the Salt Lake Area Alliance of Tenants, and Salt Lake Impact 2000 and Beyond. In the view of Glenn Bailey, the center's director since 1992, "You don't have to tell people what to do, just give them a direction and help them organize effectively so they can address their own issues and realize that change is possible." Bailey has always been willing to be confrontational. "I'm not one who believes in the rules of politeness," he says. "Sometimes you have to raise hell to get things done or bring attention to an issue. A lot of people in Utah are far too timid about that." Fundamentally, he says, "My beliefs are rooted in the gospels, and I've always been a Christian. One of the gospels' great themes is God's reconciliation with humanity. Reconciliation is also needed among people, but it's not possible when one person has power over another. Reconciliation happens when people are on an equal plane."

Another important organization founded to address problems of low-income residents of the state was Utah Issues. Organized in 1974, when an estimated 103,000 Utahns had incomes below the poverty level, Utah Issues provided information, research, and technical assistance to a variety of organizations concerned with specific problems of the poor. It continues today to monitor the actions of government agencies and the state legislature and publicize the activities of community action groups, and it sponsors an annual conference to address the variety of problems low-income Utahns face. Its twenty-fifth annual conference in May 1999 offered a number of workshops ranging from removing sales tax on food to improving laws to protect tenants from unscrupulous landlords. The workshop on landlord-tenant issues made a number of recommendations, including a "right to organize" law that would prohibit landlords from punishing tenants for organizing tenant-advocacy groups; outlaw the non-refundable deposit; end no-cause evictions; end landlord rules that banned older mobile homes from mobile home parks; and place a state-mandated freeze on rents prior to and during the 2002 Olympics.

During the 1960s Utah's African-American community and their supporters were active in ways and on a scale they had not been before to combat the prejudice they encountered and the discrimination they faced—in particular, the segregation that still made perfect sense to most Utahns and existed in every aspect of life. As Ronald Coleman says, "Black Utahns, like African Americans in other parts of the nation, began to focus their attention on issues of racial injustice on both the community and the national levels." According to John Oscar Williams, "We wanted our freedom. We wanted access into everything we were qualified to get into. We wanted to be able to go to schools. We wanted to be able to go to colleges. We wanted to be able to compete openly in the marketplace. And we wanted equal access to everything that the white power structure controlled without regard to race, creed, or color. On the other hand, the white establishment wanted us to wait. We called that gradualism. We had three hundred years of that. We weren't going to wait anymore."

In the early 1960s, African Americans revitalized the Salt Lake branch of the National Association for the Advancement of Colored People (NAACP). They gathered information about discrimination in housing, often using a technique called the "sandwich," where a black couple would try to rent an apartment or house and, if they were turned down, a white couple would be sent to see if they could rent the same place. They lobbied the state legislature to pass Utah's first civil rights laws, including a Public Accommodation Act in 1965, and to repeal anti-miscegenation legislation prohibiting marriages between whites and blacks or Asians. They held non-violent demonstrations in support of the national civil rights agenda and as a way of addressing local injustices. They picketed segregated facilities. Billy W. Mason, who has operated a barbershop in Salt Lake City since 1958, participated in some of them. "In the early '60s, people like me had a hard time, here, and just about everywhere else," he said. "In those days, black people didn't have any place to go bowling, you know. We didn't have a place to go roller skating. Oh, there was a Normandy Skating Rink on Sixth South and Main. The only time we could go roller skating there was from 12 o'clock at night until 1:00. One hour, yeah.

We couldn't eat at certain restaurants, or get into certain social clubs. Looking back, it would be interesting to see what their perspective was—to not let us in." Finally, Mason said, he had had enough and joined a group who picketed the Rancho Bowling Lanes. "With members of the NAACP, we went there to bowl. The guy says, 'You can't bowl here.' So, we picketed. We walked, and we walked, and we picketed. We had about 50 or 60 people with us. Blacks and whites. Boy, it's rough when you have to think about picketing a bowling alley to achieve equality." But, he said, it worked. "Finally, after some time, we got to bowl, just like everybody else. Then, as the movement continued, more changes came about. Segregation in housing changed and jobs got a little better."

From the first, Mason's barbershop was an important social center for African Americans in Salt Lake City. The NAACP gave newcomers the address and phone number. "When a brother comes into town, he needs a place to get his hair cut," said Utah Jazz professional basketball player Mike Brown. "He can't just go to Super Cuts for $9.99 and get a wash and blow dry." At the same time, said Thurl Bailey, also a Jazz player, "It's not just going and getting a haircut. It's like going over to a friend's house, in a way." According to Mason, "Back in the late '60s the social life at the U. was so bad that all the football team used to come to the barber shop even if they didn't need a haircut. They'd stay all day, come home with me, and eat what was there." Mason wanted children to meet his famous customers. When people like University of Utah vice president Ronald Coleman or Third Circuit Court judge Tyrone Medley came in, he always pointed them out. "I like the youngsters to know we do have black professionals here. When the judge comes in, I tell the kids, 'Don't you do anything wrong. This is the judge.'"

Charles Nabors, Professor of Anatomy at the University of Utah School of Medicine and a nationally recognized expert on cystic fibrosis, was one of the most active participants in Utah's civil rights movement. As Leslie G. Kelen and Eileen Hallet Stone say, "Intense, articulate, mercurial, Dr. Charles James Nabors brought verve and vitality into the fight for civil rights in Utah." He served on the executive board of the Salt Lake Branch of the NAACP, founded the Utah Non-Violent Action Committee, and was Utah's first black delegate to the Democratic National Convention. Nabors came to Utah in the mid-1950s to attend medical school. At first, he followed his father's advice to concentrate on his medical schooling and was not involved in community issues, but by the early 1960s that had changed. "I had seen enough crap in Salt Lake City by then," he said, "that I was not about to do that. There was gross housing discrimination here. Blacks were crowded into about half of Central City and near the West Side. Those were the only areas in town, with very few exceptions, where black people lived, and I was not about to put up with that. ... At that time, in Salt Lake City, they had given up segregation in most movie theaters and restaurants. But other types of public accommodations and facilities, like bowling alleys, had not, and housing discrimination, as I said, was rampant. Now, our activities were being absolutely, totally ignored by the local press. Nobody, and I mean nobody, would cover our stuff. 'That kind of segregation doesn't exist here,' they said. 'We don't have those problems in Utah.' ... I'd heard that blacks couldn't bowl at Rancho Bowling Lanes, over on North Temple. So we ran a sandwich on it with witnesses, and, no dice: Blacks couldn't bowl. I can't remember what day it was—it was summer. We put a picket line in front. ... And I led the picket."

The most dramatic public action, Nabors said, dealt with passage of Utah's first civil rights bill, the Public Accommodations Act of 1965. Support of the Mormon church was crucial if the bill was to be enacted. "Three or four of us went in to ask the leadership of the LDS church if they'd help us get the legislation passed. They told us, 'We only get into politics on moral issues.' It took me a minute to regain my voice. I said, 'Isn't the way one human being treats another a moral issue?' Well, we didn't get what we wanted, so on Friday morning I put a civil rights picket line in front of the office of the LDS church down on South Temple. I called United Press International and Associated Press, and they covered it. They put it on the 'A wire,' which means it went to all their subscribers nationwide. Three days later, on a Monday morning, the Civil Rights Act was passed by the Utah State Legislature's House of Representatives sixty-nine to nothing."

During the 1960s, Salt Lake City's Hispanic community was also increasingly active. As Edward H. Mayer points out, "A cultural awakening occurred within the Mexican community congruent with a movement to bring about political and social reform." It corresponded to a wave of Hispanic immigrants from Mexico and surrounding states to Utah in the years after World War II. By the end of the 1960s, more than 50,000 Mexicans and Mexican Americans

were living in Utah. Organizations like El Centro Civico Mexicano in Salt Lake City and its counterparts in other Utah cities and towns "planned social and cultural activities for the Mexican community to help maintain the Hispanic culture and language." The GI Forum, founded in Ogden in 1954 and the following year in Salt Lake City, was active in fighting discrimination and related problems. In December 1967 Father Jerald Merrill and a group of young Hispanos and Mexican Americans, who preferred to be called "Chicano," including Jorge Arce-Laretta, John Florez, Rey Florez, and Ricardo Barbero, said *Basta* ("Enough") and "set goals for demanding a rightful place for Chicanos in society." They established SOCIO (Spanish Speaking Organization for Community, Integrity, and Opportunity) to provide a voice for Hispanics and create a vehicle through which they might unify to meet their individual and community needs. Within six years its membership had grown from 400 to nearly 27,000 in nine local chapters. According to Robert "Archie" Archuleta, "SOCIO was the largest organization we've ever had in this state and the first real Chicano organization that purported to and did fight battles for our people here." Following its establishment, SOCIO formed the Utah Migrant Council, lobbied for a Chicano Studies Program at the University of Utah, argued for the creation of an Hispanic ombudsman position for the state, and worked to improve the public school system.

From the beginning, Archuleta was one of the most active and important participants in the Hispanic community's struggle for civil rights, and he continues today to be involved in a range of community issues. He is active, for example, in the Utah Coalition of La Raza, which was founded in 1991 to establish "a collective, unified voice to advocate for improved quality of life for La Raza communities of Utah"; in January 1998 he helped organize a march and rally at the State Capitol Building to protest a proposed bill designating English as Utah's official language and requiring that all state government business be conducted in English only; and in 1999 he ran for a seat on the Salt Lake City Council. In 1953 he was the first Hispanic the Salt Lake School District had ever hired as a teacher. Previously the district had hired Hispanics in maintenance positions only. He taught elementary school for fifteen years, was the first coordinator of the district's alternative high school, and then became a district curriculum specialist. In his view, "In the classroom we must do everything we can to help children learn as much as they can; we must give them all the skills we are capable of so they can confront their society—their environment—and cope with it. But outside the classroom, as a human being, ... I must also constantly struggle for better paying jobs, safer jobs, cleaner jobs, that can be done with a modicum of dignity for the good work people do and enough pay to feed, clothe, and house them. Without that, everything else is futile." So, he said, "I've been an activist." He was a member of the NAACP, helped establish a chapter of the GI Forum in Salt Lake, and was a founder of SOCIO and of the Joe Hill Club. He also became a member of the board of the Crossroads Urban Center, which, he said, "has a food pantry, feeds many of the down and out, and does a lot of advocacy work. I stayed with them because the social service bureaucracy plays games with people's dignity, enforces foolish rules, or overreacts to rules. For instance, when the food stamp emergency law was passed, it said there would be times when people could be given emergency stamps. It meant they were to be given the stamps now, not in ten days. Well, we found out our people were often being forced to come back over and over again, for as long as a week. In the meantime, what could they eat? What do they eat? Well, advocacy permits you to go in and shake those turkeys up. So we did that. We did that with Mountain Fuel as well. Before a moratorium was placed on Mountain Fuel to prevent them from turning fuel off in the winter, they had the nasty habit of cutting off people's utilities if they couldn't pay

197

Contrasting
Cultures and
Lifestyles

their bills. It didn't matter to them if a pregnant woman, or children, or an invalid was in there. What was important was profit and at the cost of human dignity. So we went to bat for them. We wrote letters, we negotiated, we telephoned. When all that failed, we took Channel 4 News down with their TV cameras. They broadcast it on the five o'clock news, and those buggers turned the gas on within two hours, which shows you the lesson that it was more important for them to save face, continue their profits, than to take care of people. People came last." Looking back from the perspective of the present, Archuleta says, "I never had any great aspirations in the 1960s and 1970s. I didn't believe we could instantly revamp the system. But I believed that the resolution of many of our problems was not entirely educational. Education was important. But it was not our main problem. Poverty and employment were our main problems. And we needed to spend as much effort in doing something about them as we did about education."

During the 1960s a majority of Utahns supported the Vietnam War, and Utah sent to Vietnam the fifth highest percentage in the nation of its young men eligible for the draft—a total of more than 47,000. Even so, the war was increasingly controversial in Utah, as it was throughout the United States, and a significant anti-war movement developed. The first anti-war protest march was held in downtown Salt Lake City on April 18, 1965, with about forty participants. Four and a half years later, on October 15, 1969, more than 4,000 demonstrators joined in a full day of protest, beginning with a "teach-in" at the University of Utah and continuing with a march from Reservoir Park on the west edge of the campus down South Temple to the Federal Building at 100 South and State streets where Reverend G. Edward Howlett of St. Mark's Episcopal Cathedral read the names of Utahns killed in Vietnam and other speakers called for an immediate withdrawal of U.S. forces from the war. The last major demonstration occurred on May 15, 1971, when an estimated 2,000 people gathered at the State Capitol building for a rally and then marched to Pioneer Park where 600 more people joined them at another rally featuring protest songs and speeches from local and national figures, including Robert Scheer, former editor of *Ramparts* magazine. Leading the march was a group of Vietnam war veterans wearing worn fatigues with their combat service medals attached and holding a banner that read, "G.I.s Against the War." Sponsored by the Wasatch Front Peace Action Coalition, the march was the culmination of eleven days of protesting by the group, "Common People," which had camped in front of the Selective Service Center in downtown Salt Lake.

Stephen Holbrook was one of the earliest and most active participants in the anti-war movement. Born and raised in Bountiful, Utah, he served an LDS church mission to Hong Kong and following his return worked in Washington, D.C., for Republican congressman Sherman P. Lloyd. While there he became increasingly interested in the civil rights movement and spent the summers of 1964 and 1965 in Mississippi as part of the Mississippi Freedom Project registering black men and women to vote. Upon his return to Utah, he became involved in protests against the war, participating in his first anti-war demonstration in the fall of 1965 when he and seven others were arrested for blocking the entrance to a local army induction center. "There were eight of us in '65," he said, "15 in '66, 3,000 in '68 and 5,000 in '69." Long-time political activist Wayne Holley has similar memories about the anti-war movement's slow beginnings and steady growth. "The opposition in Utah started with just a few of us going up and sitting on the Capitol steps with placards," he said. "It was a difficult thing to do. Not popular. But we kept working."

One role Holbrook played in the movement against the war, he said, was "the publicity side of it, both speaking on the radio and getting the marches known. I think I had some impact in increasing the size of the movement by utilizing mass media—producing ads on rock stations, getting people seen and heard on the war." One of his "precipitating experiences" was with KSL television. "They broadcast editorial opinion on the war. So we wrote a letter asking to give a counter opinion. They said that their policy was that only 'responsible parties' could respond, and that the very fact that we were against the war was proof we were not responsible. I'd have to say that the media were not terribly open at that point." Holbrook then helped stage "sit-ins" at local television stations, and eventually they each agreed to televise a debate about the war. He also led a sit-in at *The Salt Lake Tribune* offices to publicize what he and other protesters viewed as its biased reporting on the war and the anti-war movement. "Sometime in the early '70s was the last big anti-war march that I remember," he says. "That was the first march when all of the things that had been bubbling underneath on other issues began to surface in the anti-war movement. You had contingents for the environment, Women Unite, the Vietnam Veterans Against the War . . . which, after the war, then took on lives of their own."

199

Contrasting
Cultures and
Lifestyles

Ammon Hennacy demonstrating against the Vietnam War as part of his life-long campaign of "bearing witness" and calling those in power to account. (Courtesy Manuscripts Division, Marriott Library, University of Utah.)

Throughout the 1960s Christian anarchist Ammon Hennacy conducted his "one-man revolution" of fasting, picketing, letter writing, education, and acts of civil disobedience in Salt Lake City, culminating a life of social activism and protest that made him "An American Legend," as *The Salt Lake Tribune* said at the time of his death in 1970. A visible and important presence, he illustrates the complex place Salt Lake was becoming, the many layers found there, and was an example of the diverse voices increasingly seen and heard. Catholic activist Dorothy Day paid him what must have been the ultimate compliment when she noted he was "the most ascetic, the most hard working, the most devoted to the poor and the oppressed of any we had met. ... He was an inspiration and a reproach."

A pacifist as well as an anarchist—for him each entailed the other—Hennacy was born into a Baptist family in Negley, Ohio, in 1893. Early on he was exposed to the political side of life. On the first page of his autobiography, he proudly related that "a bewhiskered picture of John Brown hung in the family parlor, and I was ten years old before I knew the difference between God, Moses, and John Brown." At age sixteen he joined both the Socialist Party of America and the Industrial Workers of the World. He served time in the Atlanta Penitentiary, mostly in solitary confinement, because of his opposition to World War I, met anarchist Alexander Berkman there, emerged a Christian anarchist, and for the rest of his life dismissed all activism that was not anchored in a spiritual foundation, preferably that of the Christian gospel. Rejecting both the authority of the state and of a corporate capitalistic system in which, in his view, the dollar supplanted God, he thought it imperative for Christians to draw clear lines across which they would not step. When the state, the corporation, or society at large tried to compel them, collective public resistance was necessary. In that resistance, he thought, a community of belief was created, able to nurture its members in living out their faith, and a much-needed prophetic witness was offered to the larger society as well.

Throughout the 1920s and 1930s, Hennacy worked with Dorothy Day and her Catholic Worker movement in New York City. He spent most of the 1940s and 1950s in the southwestern United States as a day laborer, writing for *The Catholic Worker* and working for a variety of social justice movements. He came to Salt Lake City in 1960 and remained until his death in 1970. During his decade in Utah, he regularly fasted while picketing the State Capitol Building and the federal courthouse against capital punishment and in behalf of people on death row; he picketed and distributed literature at IRS offices and the Salt Lake City federal building at tax time; every year at the anniversary of the dropping of the atom bomb on Hiroshima, he fasted and picketed one day for each year since the bomb was dropped; he marched in front of the LDS Church Office Building to demand support for open housing and nailed lists of questions on the door of the chancery next to the Cathedral of the Madeleine asking why the Catholic church did not speak out against the Vietnam War. He continued to contribute prolifically to the national anarchist press, in particular *MAN*, and wrote two books, his autobiography, *The Book of Ammon*, and *The One-Man Revolution in America*, an examination of seventeen Americans, including Thomas Paine, William Lloyd Garrison, Malcolm X, Mother Jones and the Hopi Yukeoma, all of whom, in his view, had fought the good fight, displaying courage and integrity in living out their one-person revolu-

Contrasting
Cultures and
Lifestyles

tion in a world of compromise; he talked to anyone who would listen; he petitioned Salt Lake City church leaders of all denominations to prick their consciences and those of their "faithful" regarding the poor and disadvantaged in their midst; and he operated his Joe Hill House of Hospitality, first located in the downtown area on Post Office Place and later near the railroad tracks at about 3300 South, modeled on Dorothy Day's shelter for homeless men and women in New York City. Every Friday night Hennacy would speak. Afterwards, folksinger and fellow radical Bruce "Utah" Phillips and others sang songs "made up from what was going on around us"—songs like "Pig Hollow," the story of a group of citizens who burned down a hobo jungle near Ogden that had been there since 1900, and "Room for the Poor."

Phillips remembered Hennacy as a "wiry old man, tougher than nails, but with a heart of gold," who believed that as a white male in the United States, he was born "armed with the weapons of privilege—racial, sexual, and economic privilege—and he vowed to give up such privilege and go into the world disarmed." Brought before the legendary judge Willis Ritter on more than one occasion for unlawful picketing, he pleaded "anarchy," rather than "innocent" or "guilty," explaining that an anarchist was a person who did not need a cop to tell him what to do. He had broken the law, Hennacy admitted, but laws were unnecessary—good people did not need them, and bad people would not obey them, so of what use were they?

Hennacy often said that he wanted to die on the picket line. For him, the true test of a radical was whether he or she walked a picket line, and for him there existed no more honorable, or familiar, spot upon which to meet his maker. He was granted his wish. On January 5, 1970, at age seventy-six, he walked up the steep State Street hill to the Utah State Capitol to picket on behalf of convicted murderers Myron Lance and Walter Kelbach, who were scheduled for execution. On the fourth day he collapsed to the ground, struck by a heart attack, and died six days later.

Folksinger and storyteller, IWW organizer, labor activist, and candidate for the U.S. Senate in 1968 on the Peace and Freedom Party, as well as a friend and colleague of Hennacy, Utah Phillips was himself an important presence in Salt Lake City during the 1960s and in some ways is emblematic of the period. He came as a teenager in the late 1940s—his mother had been a Congress of Industrial Organizations (CIO) organizer and his father operated a series of

movie theaters in Salt Lake—and spent the next twenty years at a variety of jobs, including at the Utah State Archives, while working and performing in support of various social justice causes, including operating a draft resistance office. He strongly believed in people helping each other as a community. And he believed that much knowledge and insight came from hardship. In the liner notes to one of his albums, he wrote of a Wobbly friend who used to say, "When you're theorisin' on a full stomach, you hain't the least idea what you'd do if you was practicin' on an empty one."

Phillips's radicalization began in the late 1940s when Marian Anderson came to Salt Lake City to perform at the LDS church tabernacle and was not allowed to stay at the Hotel Utah and continued with his participation in the Korean War. "It was all wrong," he concluded about both racism and war. "It all had to change. And that change had to start with me. It all had to stop, and the stopping would begin with me saying, 'No.'" Much of what Phillips tried to do through his songs and stories was recover a certain sense of the past that had disappeared. He was interested in telling stories—the kind of stories that were usually left out—stories of strikes and labor leaders like Mother Jones and tramps and ordinary workers of all kinds. In his view, "The long memory is the most radical idea in the country," and he was impatient with those who tried

203

Contrasting
Cultures and
Lifestyles

to dismiss the past as irrelevant. "When someone says, 'Forget the past,'" he said, "they don't want you to remember something that if you did, they would be in trouble." The lyrics to the first and last verses of his composition, "All Used Up," illustrate much about his point of view:

> I spent my whole life making somebody rich;
> I busted my ass for that son-of-a-bitch:
> And he left me to die like a dog in a ditch
> And told me I'm all used up.
> He used up my labor, he used up my time,
> He plundered my body and squandered my mind
> And gave me a pension of handouts and wine
> And told me I'm all used up.
>
> And there's songs and there's laughter and things I can do.
> And all that I've learned I can give back to you;
> I'd give my last breath just to make it come true.
> No, I'm not all used up.
> They use up the oil and they use up the trees
> They use up the air and they use up the sea;
> Well, how about you, friend, and how about me?
> What's left when we're all used up?

In album liner notes introducing the song, Phillips wrote, "There is an old man who sits in the window ... and looks out on the parking lot day after day. I don't know if this song is his story. It's not going to be mine if I can help it, and I hope it's not going to be any of yours." Since the early 1970s, Phillips has lived in Nevada City, California. His two most recent CDs, *the past didn't go anywhere* and *Fellow Workers*, were collaborative efforts in 1996 and 1999, respectively, with punk rocker Ani DiFranco on her Righteous Babe Music label.

In addition to political movements for social change, a flourishing counterculture also emerged in Salt Lake City in the 1960s. It supported bookstores and "head shops" like the Cosmic Aeroplane, "underground" newspapers such as the *Electric News* and *The Street Paper* that were Salt Lake's counterparts to the *Berkeley Barb* and Atlanta's *Great Speckled Bird*, and clothing stores like

The Cosmic Aeroplane bookstore was at the center of Salt Lake's vibrant counterculture in the 1960s. (Private Collection.)

The Connection. An important part of it was the music scene. The Terrace Ballroom was Salt Lake City's equivalent of San Francisco's legendary Avalon and Fillmor ballrooms. It began in the 1930s as the Coconut Grove and later the Rainbow Rendezvous, where virtually every nationally known big band appeared. In the 1960s an array of groups played there and at other sites—the Fairground Coliseum (the "Dirt Palace"), Lagoon, the University of Utah Union Ballroom, and the Old Mill—including the Rolling Stones, The Doors, Jimi Hendrix, Led Zeppelin, Jefferson Airplane, Jim Morrison, James Brown, Big Brother and the Holding Company, Electric Prunes, Iron Butterfly, Santana, Ike and Tina Turner, Jethro Tull, Big Mama Thornton, the Mothers of Invention, and The Grateful Dead. Among the best known local groups were Holden Caulfield, Smoke, Tattered Souls, and Wood. Marv Hamilton recalled that "this music spoke to our guts, or hearts. ... Canned Heat at the Dirt Palace. Steven Stills at the Spectrum in Logan (set my date's hair on fire). Lynyard Skynyrd at the Terrace. The Dead; Neil Young; Emerson, Lake and Palmer at the Salt Palace. Eric Clapton and Carlos Santana tradin' licks! All this against a background of campus unrest, Students for a Democratic Society, Vietnam Vets Against the War, the Victimization of Vietnam (isn't that what it was?), Kent State, 'Four Dead in Ohio,' Nixon, Watergate, Angela Davis, George Harrison's 'The Concert for Bangladesh,' *2001 A Space Odyssey, Easy Rider, Hair*."

To publicize the concerts, Mikel Covey, Kenvin Lyman, Rob Brown, Richard Taylor, Neil Passey, and other local artists forged a dazzling body of poster art that rivaled anything produced in the country and helped define the Salt Lake 1960s. According to Ken Sanders, one of the organizers in the fall of 1995 of an exhibit of more than 200 concert posters and other memorabilia, including tickets, contracts, photographs, and handbills, "Even though they were inspired by the Bay area scene, they created their own unique style." They were "swirls of surrealist, idyllic scenes," Marv Hamilton said, "dream-like, ethereal visions of the natural world juxtaposed with earthly circumstances." Other local artists produced psychedelic light shows that were both a part of the concerts and could, and did, stand on their own, including the legendary "The Dance of the Desert Prophet," by Mikel Covey and Nik Thayne, and Richard Taylor's "Rainbow Jam."

In the generation after World War II, Salt Lake City's population continued to diversify. The largest new group was Polynesians. They had begun coming to Utah a hundred years earlier as converts to the Mormon church, and by the late 1880s nearly 800 Polynesians, mostly Hawaiians, lived in Utah, many near Beck's Hot Springs in northwest Salt Lake City. In the 1960s Polynesians from some of the islands in the South Pacific began to arrive. Since then perhaps 20,000 have come, settling throughout Utah, but mainly in the Salt Lake Valley. The largest group were Tongans who came mostly, though not entirely, as Mormon converts. People also arrived, though in smaller numbers, from Samoa, New Zealand, Hawaii, and Tahiti. In addition to religion, economic factors played a role in their immigration—in the 1960s unemployment in Tonga, excluding subsistence farming and fishing, was as high as 75 percent, land was difficult to acquire, and inflation was high.

As Carol Edison points out, Polynesians in Utah fall into two groups. The first group is composed of Hawaiians, Maoris, and Tahitians—who historically experienced early and intensive contact with European cultures—and the second of less "westernized" Tongans and Samoans—who underwent less intervention from the outside. In twentieth-century Utah those historical differences resulted in different experiences in terms of assimilation, acculturation, and the maintenance of cultural tradition. Today, Hawaiians, Maoris, and Ta-

Immigrants to Utah from the islands of the South Pacific brought with them a tradition of quilting that embraced bright colors and bold patterns, as in this Tahitian flower quilt made by Henriette Munanui. Many quilters from the Pacific have adapted their designs to the availability of American colors and materials. (Courtesy Utah Arts Council; photograph by Hal Cannon.)

hitians are small in numbers, still more westernized, and are more removed from their own traditional cultures than are other Pacific Islanders. This has led them to seek ways to recover their traditions through organizations such as the Hawaiian Civic Club and the New Zealand-American Club. On the other hand, the more numerous Tongans and Samoans, in general, struggle to some degree to fit into the society that surrounds them. Their traditions remain an integral part of their daily life, and they live in Utah in enough numbers to maintain a vibrant, thriving subculture that develops and reinforces a strong sense of cultural identity.

Hawaiians, Maoris, and Tahitians today reside mainly in Utah's urban centers, primarily in the Salt Lake Valley. Most are members of the Mormon church and attend non-ethnic, English-speaking congregations. As a group they have acculturated relatively easily. Culturally their main difficulties are related to the challenge of perpetuating Pacific traditions in their children. On

Contrasting
Cultures and
Lifestyles

the other hand, the Tongan and Samoan populations are geographically concentrated on the west side of the valley. Most hold jobs in the service sector. The majority also belong to the Mormon church, but many attend foreign-language services in a handful of Tongan and Samoan wards. There is also a large Methodist population, as well as smaller Catholic and Seventh-Day Adventist groups. Since the mid-1980s several pan-Polynesian organizations have been founded to serve the needs of all of Utah's Islander population, including the Governor's Polynesian Advisory Council, the Iosepa Historical Society, and the Utah Polynesian Choir, which specializes in Mormon hymns sung in English, Hawaiian, Samoan, and Tongan. Soon after its founding in 1979, radio station KRCL began broadcasting a regular program of Polynesian music.

While Salt Lake City changed in important ways in the generation after World War II, one thing did not change: the influence of the Mormon church remained strong and its place predominant. Wielding power was not as easy as it had once been and required more compromise and negotiation with various individuals and groups. Still it was difficult for public projects of any kind to succeed without at least the church's passive support and, conversely, difficult for them to be successful in the face of its opposition. Any number of examples could be cited. In 1946 a professional football team, the Salt Lake Seagulls, was organized in Salt Lake City as part of the nine-team Pacific Coast Football League, a western counterpart to the eastern National Football League. The team's coach and manager, Fred Tedesco, was also a Salt Lake City commissioner, and before the season began he used city employees and resources to install sod and a sprinkler system and improve the bleachers at the Utah State Fairgrounds field where games would be played. Some city workers, feeling that city resources were being used inappropriately to benefit a private company, arranged a meeting with David O. McKay, second counselor in the LDS church's First Presidency. McKay in turn met with the mayor, city commission, and city attorney. Tedesco quickly made a public statement, presented a detailed report, and gave the city a check to cover the expenses involved. Even so, talk spread of calling a grand jury to investigate the situation. Tedesco's wife, Klea, who was also president of the ladies' auxiliary of the Utah Municipal League, met with McKay, and then she and her husband met with him again. After that, writes Linda Sillitoe in her recent history of Salt Lake

Presidential candidate John F. Kennedy with Mormon church president David O. McKay, center, and Mormon church general authority Hugh B. Brown, at the Mormon Tabernacle, October 1960. Though Kennedy received an enthusiastic welcome, Richard Nixon carried the state by a wide margin in that year's presidential election. Since 1948, when Salt Lakers voted for Harry Truman, Lyndon B. Johnson in 1964 has been the only Democrat to carry Salt Lake City in a presidential election. (Courtesy Will South.)

County, "The controversy ended as abruptly as it had begun. ... Clearly the city officials, the media, and the legal system responded to McKay's concern with vigor, and the resulting tumult was quelled just as quickly." What is particularly telling in this incident, as she points out, is that city employees sought the intervention of a top Mormon leader rather than follow a grievance procedure within city government, and a Mormon general authority felt comfortable convening city officials to discuss the situation.

The place of the Mormon church was also evident when the 1960s ushered in a new era of construction in the downtown area. More money was poured into concrete, steel, and mortar than during any previous period, and the Mormon church was deeply involved in changing the city's face. Through both its own real estate activities and its links with individual real estate developers, it moved from being a passive supporter of downtown redevelopment to playing a leading role in the dramatic facelift the central business district underwent. It leased land to Salt Lake County for the $19.2 million Salt Palace

209

Contrasting
Cultures and
Lifestyles

convention center; built the ZCMI Center mall that occupied a full city block; leased land on the block to the west of the ZCMI mall to Mormon developers to build the Crossroads Mall, in the process demolishing, or allowing to be demolished, a number of historic buildings, including the Amussen Jewelry Building (1869), the oldest remaining commercial building in the city and one that a Salt Lake City-commissioned study had identified as the most architecturally significant structure in the downtown area; and it built new high-rises, notably its own twenty-eight story office building, completed in 1973, adjacent to Temple Square. As Sillitoe says, "It dwarfed other structures, symbolizing not only the religion's worldwide status as depicted by the hemispheres carved on the front, but also the bureaucratic complexity and power of the corporate church."

Many of those projects were discussed at weekly breakfast meetings in Lamb's Cafe on Main Street that for nearly two decades, until his death in 1970, church president David O. McKay held with Gus Backman, executive director of the Salt Lake City Chamber of Commerce, and John F. Fitzpatrick, publisher of *The Salt Lake Tribune*. Following Fitzpatrick's death in 1960, his son-in-law and successor, John W. "Jack" Gallivan, replaced him at the meetings. The intent of the three was to keep abreast of city affairs and direct them in appropriate ways. As Sillitoe points out, "Between them, these men linked the interests and resources of religion, the capital city, and the media in a locus of power fused entirely outside democratic channels." In her view, "The importance of this triad in affecting development and policy in the valley cannot be overstated though their decisions were informal and largely undocumented." After McKay's death ended the meetings, "an LDS general authority, a Salt Lake City commissioner, and a state senator individually bemoaned the end of the breakfasts as the loss of a single group that could 'consistently get anything done.'" Even so, Thomas G. Alexander and James B. Allen report, "After his appointment as executive vice-president of the chamber of commerce, Fred S. Ball met regularly with Nathan Eldon Tanner, a counselor in the church's First Presidency who died in 1982, or Gordon B. Hinck- ley, who became a member of the First Presidency in 1981, to discuss city affairs." Clearly Salt Lake City was a place where close personal ties were still important. It was what Mayor Ted Wilson would later call a "city of brothers-in-law."

So the church continued to exercise enormous political influence in the post-World War II years. According to Robert Gottlieb and Peter Wiley, "'Clear it with the church' became an unwritten rule for politicians in the 1960s in areas where Mormon church policy was directly involved." Historically, the church had opposed labor unions, first as a gentile (or non-Mormon) phenomenon unnecessary in the Saints' cooperative commonwealth, then as competitors for the loyalty of their members and as avenues to radical politics. In the mid-1960s, the church played a prominent role in defeating the effort to repeal section 15b of the federal Taft-Hartley Act, which sanctioned state "right-to-work" laws, and in the passage of right-to-work legislation in Utah, as well as in Nevada, Idaho, and Arizona. Likewise, a statewide referendum in 1968 to reform Utah's liquor laws, initiated by the tourist, restaurant, and public accommodations industries to provide "liquor-by-the-drink," and supported by Jack Gallivan and *The Salt Lake Tribune,* was soundly defeated after church authorities mounted a strong campaign against it. Jennings Phillips, a non-Mormon member of the city commission, reported that he often conferred with Mormon general authority Gordon B. Hinckley on pornography; Mayor Ted Wilson, a practicing Mormon, consulted regularly with the church's Special Affairs Committee and met with them at least once a year to show them the city's budget; and, as Sillitoe points out, the common understanding among politicians was that the church, although it would not necessarily endorse particular candidates, might lend them support and might actively oppose those who attacked or threatened church interests. Thus it seems fair to say that Wilson, a Democrat with a youthful liberal image, could be elected mayor of Salt Lake City twice in the 1970s precisely because of the absence of active church opposition. And it was not without significance that the manager of his reelection campaign was the Mormon church's comptroller.

In the 1970s the church created a new institutional mechanism— the Special Affairs Committee—to take the lead in looking after its interests in the political arena, and it proved very effective. As Gottlieb and Wiley say, the committee "served as the intelligence arm of the church, with a staff that gathered information on social trends that affected the church. It also acted as a contact point for politicians." In 1974, for example, it opposed passage of the Equal Rights Amendment (ERA) and helped defeat it in at least five

Contrasting
Cultures and
Lifestyles

states, including Virginia, Florida, Missouri, Nevada, and Utah. Three months before the 1975 legislature's vote on the ERA, a *Deseret News* poll showed that a majority of Utahns supported it, including 63 percent of Mormons, as well as a majority of legislators. Ten days before the vote, however, the *News* editorialized against it, and objections by the LDS hierarchy were read from Sunday pulpits. The next poll revealed that a majority of Utahns now opposed the amendment, and it failed in the legislature. Many of those who had worked for ratification said that they had expected that if the LDS church opposed the ERA it would cost votes, but they had not expected a poll reversal of twenty points in only three months. As James H. Joy, head of Utah's American Civil Liberties Union (ACLU) affiliate said, "I knew I was witnessing power."

That power was also evident in June 1977 when on short notice the Special Affairs Committee mobilized nearly 14,000 women to attend an International Women's Year (IWY) convention in the new Salt Palace. According to Gottlieb and Wiley, "Beginning with a letter sent out on church stationery over the signature of Quorum of the Twelve President Ezra Taft Benson, an organized Mormon network was put into motion. Word was put out through both the ward structure and the local Relief Society organizations. The Relief Society itself sent out a letter that called for at least ten women to attend from every Utah ward. Barbara Smith, the Relief Society President, worked through both the Priesthood Executive Committee and the Public Communications Department of the church to orchestrate the entire affair." Voting as a block, they defeated all forty-seven resolutions offered, including those opposing pornography, attacking racism, supporting child care, and providing support for incest victims, and as delegates to the national convention, they elected prominent LDS women. In response, the IWY national steering committee, citing a need for diversity, appointed at-large delegates to accompany the elected delegation to the national convention in Houston, Texas. As Linda Sillitoe says, "Thus it was that Utah—at the end of the twentieth century as well as at the end of the nineteenth—sent to a national forum two delegations generically (if inaccurately) known as Mormon and non-Mormon. As had happened a century earlier, the dividing issue in the public mind involved the role and the rights of women."

Finally, the influence of the LDS church was seen when the Jimmy

Carter administration announced plans in 1979 for the MX missile system, a huge, $100-billion national defense project to be built in the desert west of the Salt Lake Valley. Though there was some opposition to it from the first, its construction seemed inevitable until in May 1981 the church officially opposed placement of it in Utah and issued a strong statement, attacking not only it, but the proliferation of nuclear weapons as well. As Sillitoe says, "The church's posture bucked decades of valley partnership with military and defense industry and effectively halted the enormous project."

~

Recommended Readings

Friel, Laura. "All Fall Down: Money Wins and History Loses at Canyon Road." *Utah Holiday*, December 1980, 42-58. Reprinted in McCormick and Sillito, *A World We Thought We Knew*, 377-92.

Gottlieb, Robert, and Wiley, Peter. *America's Saints: The Rise of Mormon Power.* New York: G. P. Putnam's Sons, 1984.

_____. "Salt Lake City: Zion at the Crossroads." In Gottlieb and Wiley, *Empires in the Sun: The Rise of the New American West.* New York: G. P. Putnam's Sons, 1982, 140-64. Reprinted in McCormick and Sillito, *A World We Thought We Knew*, 452-80.

Hennacy, Ammon. *The Book of Ammon.* Salt Lake City: n.p., 1965.

_____. *The One-Man Revolution in America.* Salt Lake City: Ammon Hennacy Publications, 1970.

Kelen and Stone. *Missing Stories.*

Sillitoe, Linda. *Friendly Fire: The ACLU in Utah.* Salt Lake City: Signature Books, 1996.

_____. *A History of Salt Lake County.* Salt Lake City: Utah State Historical Society, 1996.

Contrasting
Cultures and
Lifestyles

Chapter 11

AS COMPLEX A PLACE AS CAN BE IMAGINED

What can be said of Salt Lake City as it now faces the challenges of of a new millennium? One answer is that it has been "a generally well-ordered, hard-working, family-centered, and friendly community at a time in the history of the United States and the world in which those qualities are increasingly rare." There is much to this view, but for me a more fruitful way of looking at Salt Lake City during the last generation is as what might be called a "contested site." It has been, and in the future will continue to be, complex, fragmented, and deeply unsettled—where luxury hotels are juxtaposed with junked cars, and the towers of multi-national corporations coexist with homeless shelters and shanty towns—and, at the same time, a place of vitality and possibility. Perhaps the central questions facing Salt Lake City during the last generation, and into the future, are: "Whose city is it? Who will be acknowledged and heard, and who will not be? Whom does the city serve, and who pays the price?"

Salt Lake City has long been a place of "othering." By that I mean a place where, on the basis of a variety of factors, including race, class, gender, ethnic background, and sexual orientation, an effort has been made to define various people and groups as "other"—as unworthy, inferior, subordinate, and thus assign them to certain places and confine them to certain roles. It has also been a place with many examples of the ability of people to construct their own mean-

214

ings of self and social relations, a city where various people have sought to make a position for themselves and resist the ways others have seen them and the stations to which others have tried to confine them. This has been true throughout the city's history, and has continued in recent years to be its central feature. Cooperation has existed in many ways, of course, and on many levels—in moments of disaster, for example, as in the floods of 1983 or the tornado that swept through the city on August 11, 1999, killing one person, injuring eighty others, damaging nearly 400 buildings—from the Delta Center to houses in the Avenues neighborhoods—and causing an estimated $170 million in damages; among economic and political elites; among churches working to provide supplies for homeless shelters; among individuals in their everyday lives—but more striking has been the constant interplay of power and resistance, discipline and undiscipline, order and disorder.

The percentage of members of the Mormon church in Salt Lake City declined during the 1980s and 1990s until, for the first time in its history, it was slightly under 50 percent, but it remained a place where religion continued to make a huge difference, pervading and shaping people's lives in every imagin-

IN UTAH,
THEY KNOW HOW
TO PUNISH A
WOMAN WHO HAS
AN ABORTION.

SHOOT HER.

In the early 1990s, debate about abortion heated up throughout the United States, and in Utah as well. This advertisement appeared in The New York Times, *March 24, 1991. The first paragraph reads, "On April 28, a new law goes into effect in Utah. Under it, a woman who has an abortion could be sentenced to the death penalty. In Utah, that means the firing squad. (Or she may choose lethal injection as an alternative)."*

able way. As David Rich Lewis observed, Mormonism, even though many would deny it, influenced virtually every facet of life. It affected everything, from who one's friends were to how people spent their leisure time, how they voted, whether or not they belonged to a labor union, who was elected to public office, and who served on the Olympic Committee. Mormonism, in other words, remained the city's most conspicuous feature and more than anything else was what set it apart from other U.S. cities. Robin Blumner came to Salt Lake City in 1986 to head the Utah affiliate of the American Civil Liberties Union. "I have never before lived in a place where one's religion so affected one's social choices," she said. "One's religion here seems to dictate the choice of friends, associates, activities, and even business contacts. ... Of all the places I've lived where there's a majority religion, none comes anywhere close to what happens in Utah." In her view the influence of Mormonism in Salt Lake City was greater than the Jewish influence in parts of New York

City, the Catholic influence in Boston, or the Baptist influence in areas of the South.

And the lines of demarcation between Mormons and others remained clearly established, relatively rigid and inflexible, easy to see and hard to breach. This has been a complex and controversial subject, uncomfortable for many to consider. And not everyone's experience is the same. Still, in a very real sense, Salt Lake City's population continued to be divided into two groups: those who are Mormons and those who are not. It remains a place comfortable for believers yet difficult for others. As Phyllis Barber said in a 1981 essay entitled "Culture Shock": "All non-Mormons in Utah share one thing in common, that supersedes race, creed, or religion, the fact that they are not Mormons." She asked the question, "How well does Utah assimilate newness and differences, accept and provide for newcomers?" The answer she suggested, based on interviews with three dozen people, was that newcomers experienced what could, without exaggeration, be called "culture shock."

For Hugh Gillilan, a practicing psychologist and a former Unitarian minister in Salt Lake City, "That I am a guest on Mormon turf is a pervasive feeling." Judy Hagerman said, "It hit me after six to eight months. Suddenly you

State Street and Fourth South, looking west, during the spring 1983 floods that transformed downtown Salt Lake City streets into sandbagged rivers that sped through the city for weeks. As Governor Scott M. Matheson said in a much-quoted statement, "This is a hell of a way to run a desert." (Courtesy Utah State Historical Society.)

217

As Complex a Place as Can Be Imagined

realize that you're happy in your work, but you don't have a social core unless you are LDS. People are friendly and say, 'We've got to have you over,' but they never do." According to Noel de Nevers, Professor of Chemical Engineering at the University of Utah, in his "Suggestions for Outsiders Moving to Utah—A Purely Personal View," "You will probably not be able to have close personal friends among Mormons. They are not unfriendly, simply busy." The message many non-Mormons, especially children, perceived, Barber said, was, "This is the way to be; you're not this way; what's wrong with you?" While living in Utah, a Northwest Energy Company executive and his wife felt as if they were "strangers in a strange land," while a non-Mormon Utah Power & Light Company official compared his feelings about working in a state of pervasive Mormon cultural, political, and economic influence to the feelings of a young man he read about in *National Geographic* magazine for whom, after walking across the United States, crossing into Utah felt like entering a foreign country. According to Thomas L. Allen, in Shannon R. Hoskins's important collection of essays, *Faces of Utah: A Portrait*, "We have been recognized as being different, our differences have been respected, and we have been integrated into this community. ... We will never be natives, but we are welcome here." Still, he said, Utah was a place where non-Mormons "come to feel their Otherness—sometimes overtly, but usually completely unconsciously." Stephan M. Borton put it more strongly: "All too often being a non-Mormon in Utah is similar to being black in Mississippi in the 1950s." The tension between Mormons and others was periodically played out in the letters to the editor section of local newspapers. One letter to *The Salt Lake Tribune*, May 14, 1999, expressed a common response to such comments: "If all the non-Mormons out there are so opposed to the Mormons in this area, why do they live or stay here? The Mormons were the first settlers here. They were driven from their homes in the East, and no one wanted this 'God-forsaken' desert which had only one scaggly tree, and miles and miles of nothing else, until the Mormons came and built it up into a beautiful city. Then when the non-members came in, they were welcomed as long as they were law-abiding citizens. Now many of the non-Mormons are still law-abiding citizens, but to those who spend their time in sneering and ridiculing the Mormons, I would like to ask again, why do you stay here?"

Since 1980 Salt Lake City has remained Utah's most ethnically diverse

New Pilgrim Baptist Church choir at a 1993 Voices W.E.S.T. concert sponsored by the Utah Arts Council. (Courtesy Utah Arts Council; photograph by Hal Cannon.)

community. In 1980, 70 percent of the state's Vietnamese, 44 percent of both African Americans and Japanese, 42 percent of Filipinos, 54 percent of Koreans, 68 percent of Samoans, 52 percent of Hispanics, and 23 percent of Native Americans lived in Salt Lake. Only Ogden had a higher population of African Americans, and no other urbanized area had a higher population of any other ethnic group. Evidence of this diversity was visible at every turn. Helen Zeese Papanikolas made the point in her commencement address at the University of Utah in 1984: "As I look at you graduates, I recognize in your faces, full-blown in some, slight in others, the ethnic people of your past. Among you sit men and women whose sorrowing ancestors were summarily sent to federal reservations when settlers arrived. Those settlers ploughed the land on which for centuries your people had picked berries, gathered nuts, and hunted small animals. ... A great many of you, though, are progeny of those celebrated American Mormons and the later-arriving English converts. ... Many of you may be descendants of persevering converts from other parts of Europe who were drawn to this new Zion. Some of you may descend from those few blacks, freeborn servants or slaves, brought west by unbelievers and by southern converts in the first migrations. Others may come from those blacks recruited years later by the railroads to work as porters and waiters. Surely several of you

Cannon LDS Second Ward Tongan Singers at the 1993 Voices W.E.S.T. concert sponsored by the Utah Arts Council. (Courtesy Western Folklife Center; photograph by Carol Edison.)

Salt Lake City's Japanese Church of Christ Taiko Drum Group at a Utah Arts Council's "Monday in the Park" concert, August 3, 1998. (Courtesy Utah Arts Council; photograph by Carol Edison.)

Dancers at the Basque Club's annual dinner-dance in 1989. (Courtesy Utah Arts Council; photograph by Craig Miller.)

can trace your roots to those early Jews who drove precariously loaded wagons to army posts and mining camps. ... Perhaps among you are great-great-grand-children of those Chinese railroad workers who rushed to Promontory. ... Many more of your forefathers were young men from the Balkans, Mediterra-nean, Middle East, and Japan who began coming to Utah at the turn of the century. ... Then the Mexicans came to follow this pattern of immigrant experience. Several of you come from those first Hispanics, who drove covered wagons from southern Colorado and northern New Mexico to teach the Monticello Mormons the nurture of sheep and in time homesteaded there themselves."

One group that continued to be drawn to Salt Lake City in the last two decades was Native Americans from throughout Utah and surrounding states. They came seeking both education and employment. Katchee Mitchell, a Na-vajo, was born and raised on a reservation near Winslow, Arizona. After work-ing for twenty years in the construction industry, including several years in Ja-

221

As Complex a Place
as Can Be Imagined

Gerlyn Tsosie watches Francis Smith demonstrate Navajo weaving. (Courtesy Utah Arts Council; photograph by Anne F. Hatch.)

pan, he moved to Salt Lake City to study business and communication at Salt Lake Community College before moving on to the University of New Mexico. Born to parents who spoke no English, Bertie Kee-Lopez lived in her family's hogan on Arizona's Navajo reservation until going away to a government boarding school and then moving to Salt Lake City in search of work. She eventually enrolled in business college and then became a paralegal for Utah Legal Services, particularly helping Native Americans with legal concerns. She also operated a Navajo translation business.

Southern Paiute Gail Russell was also reared on an Arizona reservation. After graduation from high school, she worked as a secretary in Phoenix, in northern California, and in the history department at the University of Utah where she was also a student. In 1972 she and her husband marched to Washington, D.C., with thousands of activists on the Broken Treaties Caravan, sponsored by the American Indian Movement (AIM), for a week of demonstrations, including occupation of the Bureau of Indian Affairs. The experience helped her gain a renewed pride in Native American heritage. "For the first time I saw all these masses of Indian people," she said. "And for the first time, we all identified with more than just our tribes. We had so much in common. All of us were Americans and Indians."

A year later, in the summer of 1973, Russell quit her job at the university, packed her kids into a station wagon, and joined the AIM-initiated occupation of Wounded Knee, South Dakota, where, in 1890, the U.S. 7th Cavalry had massacred the Sioux. The reservation surrounding the town was mired in poverty. Half of the families were on welfare, alcoholism was widespread, and four out of every five students dropped out of school. The occupation was meant to dramatize those conditions and draw attention to the 371 treaties with Native Americans AIM leaders said the government had broken since the United States was founded. Federal officials responded by encircling the area and, when AIM tried to bring in supplies, killed one protester and wounded another. The confrontation ended with a government agreement to reexamine the treaty rights of Indians, although little of substance was ever done. Russell's experience was "a real eye-opener," she said. "The point was to change federal Indian policy, but we also stayed indoors swapping stories and customs. It was a spiritual renewal for many city people who had lost touch with their cultures on the reservation. That's where I witnessed the Sioux healing ceremony, and the medicine man blessed my children. We had never seen anything like that."

Today Russell runs Salt Lake City's Indian Walk-In Center. Founded in 1983, it joined the University of Utah's ethnic-studies program (established in 1973) the Indian Health Care Clinic, which opened in 1976, and KRCL-FM radio's program *Living the Circle of Life* to help meet the needs of the city's Native American population. The KRCL broadcast features American Indian news, music, and cultural commentary, hosted by Donna Land Maldonado, who is an Affiliated Ute. The show went on the air in 1979. "Most people think we're a church," Russell said, "and in a way we are sort of a sanctuary." Each year the center has fed, clothed, and counselled nearly 25,000 people. It has also sponsored powwows, support groups, and classes on Native American ceremonies and traditions. Russell compared her clients to "seekers." For her, "the essence of Indian culture is this seeking. It always has been. But it's more difficult for Indians in the city. Many of us tend to isolate ourselves. We lose the spirit that enabled our people to endure for centuries. But the culture never disappears. You just have to go out and find it."

While existing groups have grown in numbers in the last twenty years, new groups have also continued to join Salt Lake City's population. Those who have come in the largest numbers have been Southeast Asians and peo-

223

Members of the Sae See family, Lahu tribespeople from Southeast Asia, typify recent immigration to the Salt Lake Valley, 1981. (Courtesy Utah Arts Council; photograph by Carol Edison.)

ples from throughout Central and South America. By the mid-1990s Southeast Asians in Utah numbered between 8,000 and 9,000. Most of them lived in the Salt Lake Valley. As Carol Edison says, "The community originated in the 1920s and 1930s when a handful of migrant laborers from the Philippines settled in the state. For the next fifty years this small community experienced only sporadic and modest growth. But war in Southeast Asia in the 1970s changed many things, including Utah's demographics." In the fifteen years after the Vietnam War ended in 1975, an estimated 600,000 Vietnamese, Cambodians, Laotians, Thais, and Hmong have immigrated to the United States. Approximately 12,000 of them settled in Utah, mainly in the Salt Lake Valley, and Utah ranked behind only Washington, D.C., California, and Washington state in the number of Southeast Asian refugees resettled in proportion to its population. Those who arrived first were mainly educated city dwellers who were part of Vietnam's technical, managerial, and military elite. Following them were farmers, fishermen, and mountain tribespeople, roughly half from Vietnam and half from Laos and Cambodia. According to Edison, "By the early 1990s, most arriving refugees were either Amer-Asian children (fathered by U.S. troops) accompanied by family members or individuals who had been detained in Communist reeducation camps." Most were sponsored by American families and lived with them for a time before finding work and homes. Many were young people under the age of sixteen who came alone or with some family members and waited for the others to join them.

The Guadalupe and Rose Park neighborhoods northwest of the city center, the Chesterfield area on South Redwood Road, Midvale, ten miles south of Salt Lake City, and West Valley City were where they commonly first moved, and where they have continued to live, most often in extended family groups, as was the custom in their homelands. Most were Buddhists, and by the late 1980s three temples in the Salt Lake area provided fellowship and served the spiritual needs of the several language groups.

Life was difficult for them at first as it was for earlier generations of immigrants. They worked at entry level jobs and faced culture shock as they tried to adjust to ways of life different from ones they had known. Like earlier immigrants, they turned inward to their own community while they struggled to adapt to new ways and build a life for themselves here. According to 1990 census figures, less than half of the 12,000 Southeast Asians who immigrated to Utah decided to stay. "A combination of climatic, economic, and cultural factors seems to have prompted many to leave the state," Edison said. "Utah's cold winters and dry climate were difficult for people accustomed to tropical surroundings to adapt to, and the short duration of the state's public assistance program failed to provide adequate time for many to develop needed language and occupational skills."

During the 1980s and 1990s, Salt Lake City's Hispanic population also grew dramatically, and it became much more diverse than previously. During the decade and a half after 1980, Utah's Hispanic population grew by 40 percent and in 1995 was estimated to be a minimum of 120,000, while in 1990 in Salt Lake City the Hispanic population was officially 15,508, nearly 10 percent of the city's total, and growing. Until the 1970s *Manitos* from New Mexico and Colorado comprised two-thirds of the state's Spanish-speaking residents. By

Johnny Whelan (left), Tony Rodrigues (right), and some of their children entertain audiences at the June 1979 Utah Arts Festival. (Courtesy Utah Arts Council; photograph by Carol Edison.)

Members of Club Peru, Salt Lake City—left to right, Bertha Hurtado, director, Ballet Folklorico; Yolanda Robles, Maruja Luis, and Augusto Robles—at the 1991 Living Traditions Festival. (Courtesy Utah Arts Council; photograph by Craig Miller.)

the mid-1990s their absolute numbers had risen considerably, but in terms of percentage they were less than half, as immigration from Mexico and virtually every country in Central and South America increased. The largest groups were Argentines, Peruvians, Chileans, Guatemalans, and Salvadorans. According to Sonia Alarcon Parker, a native of Equador who came to Utah to attend Brigham Young University, received a B.A. degree in broadcast journalism, edited *America Unida*, and in 1997 began work as an academic advisor at Salt Lake Community College, "With such diversity, it becomes a little easier for the immigrants to adapt to this new culture without feeling forced to lose his or her own heritage. Certainly there are some who wish to forget their country, happy to leave behind the problems of education, employment or difficult family life. But for many of us, we want to remember our origins." For Alarcon Parker, "Of the many things we miss from home, traditional foods are among the most difficult to forget. We yearn for the foods we grew up eating and often resort to asking visiting friends and family to bring ingredients to replenish our kitchens. Without *ajf amarillo* Bolivians cannot prepare their *sajta de pollo* (chicken with rice); without *morada* flour Equadorans cannot prepare the *colada morada*, a popular drink on November's Day of the Dead celebration. And without *hierba mate* Argentines cannot drink their traditional hot *mate* tea. The list is endless." In addition, she points out, Latinos have sought to preserve their ethnic identity by forming groups like *Circulo Argentino de Utah* (Argentine Circle of Utah), *Club Deportivo Socio-Cultural Peru* (Social-Cultural Peruvian Sport Club), and *Mujeres Latinas* (Latin Women's Club). "Like many Latinos," she concludes, "though I choose to live in Utah, it is important for me to remember the ways of my homeland and to share these traditions with my family. By doing this, not only do we enrich ourselves and our ethnic communities, but we are contributing to the larger Utah community by sharing our unique cultures and talents."

A reflection of Salt Lake City's growing ethnic diversity is the "Living Traditions Festival: A Celebration of Salt Lake's Folk and Ethnic Arts." Held over a three-day period each May since 1986, the intention has been to present the traditional music, dance, art, crafts, and foods of the city's ethnic communities, from African-American gospel music and Jewish klezmer music, to Navajo weaving, Chilean embroidery, and Chinese brush painting, to food from France, India, and Switzerland. As the 1993 program said, "As you move

Members of Salt Lake City's Tibetan community perform at the 1993 Living Traditions Festival. (Courtesy Utah Arts Council; photograph by Carol Edison.)

about the festival, from stage to food booth to craft tent, you'll realize that the people you meet are your neighbors. The traditions ... represent cultural resources—deep reservoirs of community identity and artistic expression. ... They are not just for festivals or for festive occasions, but are a part of everyday life, linking both generations and members of each ethnic group within their communities. They are symbols of the community's past, its origins and its heritage. Through these traditions, individuals gain a sense of their own identity, and communities perpetuate themselves."

During the 1990s Salt Lake City's population, after two decades of decline, began to grow—to an estimated 172,000 in 1996, up from an official 159,936 in 1990. Still the county's population grew at a much faster rate, and the city's population continued to be a smaller and smaller percentage of the county's. Even so, Salt Lake City remained the vital heart of the larger metropolitan area. Every hour traffic moved in both directions as commuters drove to and from jobs in office buildings, factories, warehouses, and shopping malls. After 5:00 p.m. the city's population may be 172,000, but during the day it exceeded 400,000. It is still the metropolis's hub of transportation, the magnet of sellers and buyers, the world headquarters of the LDS church, and the destina-

The Gathering Place

tion of tourists. It has welcomed the young in search of careers and excitement, sheltered the aging whom the suburbs no longer suited well, and accommodated the poor whom the suburbs rejected. And it remained the haven of interest, contrast, and stimulation, a lively meeting place, the heart of the valley. It is the focus of cultural activities: nightclubs and dance halls; professional basketball and baseball; the opera and the symphony; premiere classical and modern dance companies; a vibrant jazz scene that has included both local clubs and a monthly concert series that since 1995 has included such performers as Wayne Shorter, Milt Jackson, Roy Hargrove, Clark Terry, George Shearing, Ray Brown, Monty Alexander, Diana Krall, Sue Raney, Joey De-Francesco, Pancho Sanchez, Chick Corea, Dave Brubeck, and Joshua Redman; the Salt Lake Arts Council's "Brown Bag" series that has presented music, poetry, and dance performances every weekday at noon during the summer at various locations in the downtown area; the week-long Utah Arts Festival each summer, featuring music, food and drinks, an art exhibit, booths selling a variety of arts and crafts, costumed street actors, and poetry readings; live the-

V. Douglas Snow at work on his "extraordinarily expressive" painting for the new Salt Lake City Public Library, August 1964. (Courtesy Utah State Historical Society.)

229

As Complex a Place
as Can Be Imagined

ater; restaurants, cafes, and delicatessens; museums and art galleries; the First Night New Year's Eve Celebration that features music, dance, poetry, and food at a dozen locations in the downtown area and each year since its beginnings in the early 1990s has attracted more than 70,000 people; two colleges and a major university; libraries; coffeehouses and taverns; bookstores—new and used, large national chains and small, locally-owned independents offering everything from a $2 paperback edition of *Tom Sawyer* to a $2,000 first edition. The Gilgal sculpture gardens, which *Catalyst* magazine called "one of the local wonders—and one of the top 3 gardens of its kind in the United States," is there. Begun in 1945 by stone mason Thomas Child, the most famous of the twelve finished pieces is a sphinx carved with the face of Mormon church founder Joseph Smith. The city is where lively alternative magazines and newspapers are published, including *The Salt Lake City Observer, The Event, Salt Lake City Weekly,* "an independent publication dedicated to alternative news and news sources," the wide-ranging *Catalyst,* with its coverage of the arts, health and environmental issues, and politics, and *Slug,* described by one observer as "an in-your-face local music magazine soaked in attitude," and short-lived ones, like *The Salt Lake People's Press.* It is a place of old neighborhoods—the Avenues, 9th and 9th, 15th and 15th, Marmalade Hill, and Sugarhouse—with their older houses, big trees, and commercial pockets based around small, owner-operated businesses—whose community fabric and architectural integrity have, at least to a considerable extent, been maintained, and whose neighborhoods are alive and organic, with history and personality— neighborhoods of many pleasures where one could wander. The Marmalade district, for example, is the most architecturally varied area in the entire state. Architectural styles there include Greek Revival, Victorian Eclectic, Carpenter Gothic, and Gothic, as well as a former LDS meetinghouse that features Byzantine onion domes, while house types include single-cell, hall-parlor, double-cell, central passage, cross wing, and side passage/entry hall. The 9th and 9th neighborhood includes the Tower Theatre, the only movie theater in the valley to offer independent, avant-garde, and "art" films, and successor to the Blue Mouse and Cinema In Your Face, as Sean P. Means said, it "blends the residential with the commercial, the quirky with the conventional, the higher mind and the bottom line" (though how long that will be true is unclear, as small, locally-owned businesses have periodically closed and been replaced by national franchises). It is the location of Westminster College's Anne Newman Sutton Weeks Poetry Series, which has brought to campus for several days of readings, lectures, workshops, and discussions such poets as Adrienne Rich, Robert Pinsky, Carolyn Forche, Lisa Bickmore, Mark Doty, Jackie Osherow, Louise Gluck, W. S. Merwin, Mark Strand, Robert Haas, and Czeslaw Milosz; as well as monthly poetry slams at a westside coffeehouse "packed with different facets of society—social, economic, racial, and age diversity all gathered around the spoken word"; and weekly poetry readings sponsored by the group, City Arts, that have helped create a vibrant literary community.

According to Barry Scholl and Greta Belanger deJong, City Arts began in 1990 when friends of musician and poet Sandy Anderson suggested she oversee a series of poetry readings focusing on local writers, and under her direction it became a significant cultural force. She had organized Salt Lake Younger Poets in the 1960s, with readings at the Phillips Art Gallery and the University of Utah, and then Word Affair in the 1970s and 1980s, which began at the Campus Christian Center ("because Father Ed was a poet," she said) and then moved first to St. Mark's Cathedral and later to the Art Barn.

City Arts's beginnings were inauspicious. One of its early homes was the basement of the Perseus Opera House at 222 South Main Street. Previously the Peter Pan pool hall, where my own father spent many profitable lunch hours and afternoons hustling other newspapermen and anyone else bold enough to challenge him, its walls were covered with fading photographs of professional baseball and football players. When City Arts took it over, it was being rented by an operatic rock composer who had used curtains of plastic sheeting to mark off his work and living spaces. When City Arts's board of directors considered ways to raise money for operating expenses and, since it was winter, to provide heat for the then unheated room, one member remained unconvinced of the need for fundraising because, after all, "We can't see our breath yet." In February 1992 the weekly readings moved to the basement of Mount Tabor Lutheran Church. Since then the group has maintained an ambitious schedule of weekly readings featuring every kind of poet—unknown and established, street and academic, musicians and performance artists—and attracts a diverse audience. "Once I sat between a guy with a half a haircut, looked like roadkill on his head, and an older woman in a dress and high heels," G. Barnes, Literary Coordinator for the Utah Arts Council, remembered. "There are Mormons, radicals, street poets, academics, all enjoying the same show." One night three ministers read. Another evening was Spanish night, with all the poetry in Spanish. The Chilean and Equadoran consul generals and their families were there. "The place was packed," recalled one person. "Two-thirds of us didn't understand any Spanish, but we had a great time anyway." According to Craig Crowther, "It's a very good vehicle for poets, especially those who are sometimes considered underground. Even if you're a well-known poet, it's hard to find a place to read. In the last couple of years, it's become pretty well-known. Some of the best poets in the Intermountain West have read there." Ken Brewer, Professor of Creative Writing at Utah State University, regularly drove the ninety miles from Logan to Salt Lake to attend the Thursday night programs. "I like the combination of reading and music," he said. "I've read there a couple of times with (jazz guitarist) Keven Johansen. I'll read a set of two or three poems and then Keven will respond with a jazz number, and then I'll respond to his music. We go back and forth like that for an hour." As Scholl and deJong say, "Former University of Utah writing professor Ed Lueders, himself a musician, has read to Dan Waldis's jazz piano. Jerry Johnston of the *Deseret News* and G. Barnes played folk tunes from the '40s, '50s, and '60s to accompany Bruce Jorgensen of BYU; performance artist Mark C. Jackman has done interesting things with chest hair and electronics; bass player/poet Harold Carr mixes the two and sometimes includes a dancer in his performance."

Once a year City Arts sponsors a "Poetry Meltdown." Ballots are handed out at the weekly readings and attendees nominate their favorite poets. The top twenty have five minutes each to perform, "making for a fast and delicious night of poetry smorgasbord." The September 15, 1999, Meltdown kicked off the tenth season of readings. The readers included Margaret Aho, Sandy Anderson, Jeffrey Berke, Lisa Bickmore, Karen Brennan, Ken Brewer, Alex Caldiero, Bill Coles, Joan Coles, Katherine Coles, Greta Belanger deJong, Rich Hallstrom, Andy Hoffman, Joel Long, Jacqueline Osherow, Donald Revell, Nancy Takacs, Jennifer Tonge, Rob Van Wagoner, and Ralph Wilson. In addition to the Meltdown and its weekly series of readings, City Arts also publishes a literary journal and sponsors writers' workshops and a poetry contest for elementary, junior high, and high school students.

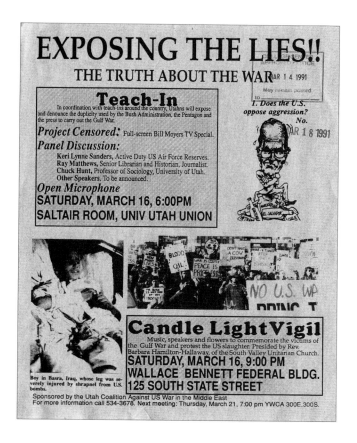

This handbill advertised a teach-in at the University of Utah, followed by a candlelight vigil in downtown Salt Lake City, March 16, 1991, to protest the Gulf War.

The predominant position of the Mormon church, the continued division between Mormons and others, growing ethnic diversity, and the city's cultural vitality all illustrate what I mean in suggesting that during the last generation Salt Lake has been a city of many worlds and that the central question driving much of what has happened has been, "Whose city is it?" Any number of other examples abound. Consider the following:

■   In the spring of 1977 a feminist publication, *Network* magazine, was founded. Born in the aftermath of the 1977 International Women's Year Conference (IWY) in Salt Lake City, it was aimed at a particular group: upwardly mobile career women—those who had been vilified at the conference as undermining the family. According to its former editor and publisher, Karen Shepherd, "*Network* was conceived at the IWY and created nine months later under the leadership of Jinnah Kelson, Lynne Van Dam, and Mary Gaber as a resource for women who wanted to be full, not partial, participants in life. *Network*'s first issue carried the faces of women who had already chosen career paths that set them apart, women whose lives were proving opportunities ex-

233

As Complex a Place
as Can Be Imagined

isted and that they were up to the jobs they had taken." Linda Sillitoe recalled that "when I became aware of *Network* in the late 1970s it seemed like a brave new world—a small publication willing to cover women's issues in the polemical environment surrounding the ERA. At that time it took courage to write about women's issues openly and honestly. One women whose story I had been asked to complete because she was fearful of the consequences showed up on my doorstep literally shaking. 'What have I gotten myself into,' I thought." In the spring of 1997 *Network*'s new owner, Murray Printing Company, ceased publication on the eve of the twentieth anniversary issue. According to Andy Bernhard, "We don't feel proud about shutting it down, but in Utah feminism is somewhat of a crusade. It was bleeding us. We gave it a good try, but we just couldn't support it anymore. I'm sure there's a lot of pissed people out there, but none of them have stepped up to the plate to say they'd take it on." For Elouise Bell, author of "In Our Prime," *Network*'s longest running column, "The demise of *Network* is a great personal loss to those of us involved with the publication over the last twenty years. For some of us, writers and editors, it was the only forum for our most authentic voices. For regular readers, it was connection on subjects that mattered to us, and connection to people who shared the fullest range of our values. But the disappearance of *Network* will be a great general loss to the community and the state as well, a loss to people who may never have read a single issue. The influence of a publication like *Network* cannot be measured on a balance sheet, cannot be understood without a broad view of what civilization truly means. These may seem like big words about a little magazine. But I stand by them. ... Sadly, *Network* has been taken from us; but, happily, the network remains."

■ Radio station KRCL was founded in 1979 as a not-for-profit, "listener-supported community radio station." According to Diane Orr, the idea for it came out of the experience of the anti-Vietnam War movement in Salt Lake in the 1960s, whose members found it hard to get media coverage of their views and difficult for alternative views in general to get disseminated. Stephen Holbrook began to formulate the idea for it as a way of opening the local media to groups outside the predominant culture. "I was marching down the street in Berkeley one day," he said, "and I heard coverage of the anti-war march. It was a local community radio station, KDFA, in Berkeley. I thought, 'Wouldn't it be great if we did more than hand out leaflets on the street corners in Salt Lake, if we had a wider audience.'" According to its mission statement, the station's goal is to provide a voice to individuals and groups whose access to the media has traditionally been limited, including racial and ethnic minorities, women, gays and lesbians, the disabled, and working class and low-income people; to present a diverse range of cultural and musical programming in an effort to expose people to alternative lifestyles and points of view; and cover local current events and affairs while encouraging dialogue from a variety of points of view. "People have called us an oasis," said Donna Land Maldonado, KRCL's program director. As a Native American woman, she called the station's programming a "touchstone": "I turn on the Native American program on Sunday and it validates my existence. It takes me home and says it's OK to be what you are."

■ Filmmaker James Meredino was part of Salt Lake City's "fringe, weirdo, punk movement" in the mid-1980s and described it in his 1998 film, *SLC Punk*. Punks were rebels, he said, full of anger and angst, but they did not march on anything because "it was too overwhelming. What was there to march on? It was understood at that time that Ronald Reagan was going to blow up the world. With the hypocrisy of the Baby-Boomers, selling out was so clear to us. All we could do was to be ironic and self-destructive. Slam into each other to show our aggression, because we felt invisible. We were such a fringe group, maybe the only way anyone would notice our existence at all would be if we dyed our hair blue."

■ On September 3, 1984, during U.S. president Ronald Reagan's visit to Salt Lake City to speak at the national convention of the American Legion as part of his campaign for re-election, a group of several hundred people marched along West Temple Street to protest his interventionist policies in Central America, while passers-by shouted at them to "Go home." That evening an estimated 500 people gathered at a Rock Against Reagan punk and hard rock concert in front of Symphony Hall. Early in the concert, a line of people held up cards spelling "RONALD WILSON REAGAN" and on cue switched positions to spell out "INSANE ANGLO WARLORD." According to one participant, "It's a beginning. That's how it started in the '60s. People just got together and voiced their doubts. This is the first open, public meeting of this type opposing Reagan that I've seen in Utah."

■ Threatened with a law suit in 1987, the Alta Club admitted women to membership for the first time in its history. For the previous 103 years, since its founding in 1884, only men could join. Though women were allowed as guests of members, they were required to enter through a specially designated "Women's Entrance." According to Nancy Mitchell, who served on the editorial board of *Network* magazine, "I can see the sign so clearly in my mind: 'Women's Entrance.' It was on the west side of the Alta Club. We had just walked right across the grand steps leading to the front doors, and I was bewil-

235

dered and then shocked to learn that I, as a woman, could not enter through the front door." Though it was 1980, she felt as if she had moved back in time to an experience in Ontario eighteen years earlier. "I learned that to go for a drink, a woman could only go to the Ladies and Escorts side of the hotel. Even in 1962 at my young age and with my inexperience that felt like an affront and 'Stone-age.' But here I was in Salt Lake City, Utah, and my freedoms were limited. Not only mine but every other woman's."

■ During the late 1980s the Disabled Rights Action Committee staged a sleep-in at Governor Norman Bangerter's Office to protest his lack of support for their concerns, and they organized a number of civil disobedience actions, including "crawl-ins" to protest the absence of lifts on Utah Transit Authority buses.

■ In 1988 a not-for-profit, urban forestry organization called TreeUtah was founded. Its goal was to "improve Utah's quality of life for present and future generations by enhancing the environment through planting, stewardship and education." Since then it has been involved in a number of projects, including a 1998 effort to restore a natural migratory song bird habitat by planting 12,000 native scrubs and tree seedlings along the banks of the Jordan River. Among those involved in the project were students from Parkview Elementary School on Salt Lake's westside. In a small nursery on school grounds that TreeUtah helped build, they grew golden currant plants and cottonwood tree seedlings and helped plant them along the river. "Kids love getting their hands dirty," said Toni Sage of the school staff. "They don't even notice how much they are learning about science and the environment. Parkview is right by the Jordan River, and they have seen the pollution. The project created a sense of 'This is our area. We're taking care of it.'" TreeUtah also worked with several Salt Lake City schools in a program called Naturescapes that gave children an opportunity to plant and care for their own trees and native plants in hopes of instilling in them a feeling of connection with nature and with their urban environment.

■ In the early 1990s the Crossroads Mall in downtown Salt Lake City began playing recorded classical music at its entrances. The intent was not to give pleasure to visitors, but to drive away teenagers and young adults, specifically those deemed to be undesirable "mall rats" who hung out at the mall but had no intention of buying. Because they were without purchasing power, they were considered uninvited guests who invaded the space of those who did have the ability to buy. It was part of the mall's effort, while claiming to offer public space, to provide a carefully controlled area designed to enhance mer-

chandising. The effort did not succeed in driving away what one observer called "proletarian shoppers," however, and was eventually abandoned. The larger point, though, is that, like shopping malls in general, the Crossroads Mall became an arena of cultural significance—a place where a cultural struggle was played out that paralleled and reflected similar struggles going on in other contexts, and in the contest a variety of people and groups have proven remarkably adept at using mall space for their own purposes, even, or especially, when those uses have contradicted the carefully planned commercial purposes of owners and developers. As cultural theorist John Fiske points out, malls are places where the strategies of the powerful have proven vulnerable to the tactical raids of those presumed to be weak. The young people whom the Crossroads Mall was concerned about were not just there, invading space intended for, and seen as rightfully belonging to, others. They were there with a purpose—to assert their identity and place and challenge the way others defined them. Their own clear pleasure in parading up and down, offending "real" consumers and the agents of law and order, asserting their difference within, and their different use of, commercial space, became what might be

237

As Complex a Place
as Can Be Imagined

called an "oppositional cultural practice." The mall was where "tricksters," in M. De Certeau's term, exploited their knowledge of the official "rules of the game" in order to identify where the rules could be mocked and inverted and thus used to free the very people they were designed to discipline.

■ In 1991 Salt Lake City voters elected businesswoman Deedee Corradini as the first female mayor in the city's history. *Newsweek* magazine named her one of "America's 25 Mayors to Watch." She was narrowly re-elected in 1995. Controversy surrounded her from the first. Soon after she took office, Bonneville Pacific Corporation, the company she worked for before her election, and had helped to found, declared bankruptcy. Criminal investigations by the FBI, the U.S. Justice Department, the Securities and Exchange Commission, and the Internal Revenue Service followed. Eventually several company executives were indicted, and one pleaded guilty and went to prison. Corradini was not indicted, though she was plagued by rumors that she would be, but after two years, to avoid being targeted in a civil lawsuit on behalf of Bonneville's investors, she and her husband agreed to pay a civil settlement of $800,000. Early in her second term, she came under fire for soliciting $231,000 in gifts and loans over a two-and-a-half-year period, from November 1993 to March 1996, from more than two dozen wealthy business executives and friends, many of whom had business dealings with the city, to help her pay the trustee. The episode raised a storm of criticism and for many reinforced the idea that Salt Lake City government was a place of privilege and self-seeking that differed from the city that "ordinary people" inhabited and led to calls for her resignation.

■ During the 1994 session of the state legislature, members of Justice, Economic Dignity, and Independence for Women (J.E.D.I. Women), a grassroots activist organization made up mainly of low-income women whose goal was to improve the lives of women and include them in public policy debate on issues that impacted their lives, staged a sit-in at Governor Michael Leavitt's office until he agreed to meet with them. During the fifteen-minute meeting that followed, he lectured them on what constituted appropriate behavior. According to a member of the group, "The perception here is that you shouldn't rock the boat. It's not ladylike." The next year the group held a three-day "camp out" on the State Capitol Building lawn, where thirty families pitched tents to call attention to the lack of affordable housing in the city and statewide.

■ In 1994 a Salt Lake City branch of the national organization Food Not Bombs (FNB) was formed and began serving free, hot vegetarian meals to homeless men, women, and children at various locations in the downtown

area. City officials threatened to shut them down and arrest FNB volunteers because they did not have proper city licenses. The group advocated a "nonviolent and egalitarian society that knows neither rich nor poor, homeless nor landlord." In 1999 its website bore the motto, "Dice the onions, crush the garlic, and smash the state."

■   Salt Lake City first established a homeless shelter in 1982 when the homeless population was estimated to be about 500. Ten years later the shelter served nearly 8,600 people. By the mid-1990s, families with children were one-third of the city's homeless, 60 percent of homeless men with families worked but were not paid enough to afford an apartment, and city services to the homeless had expanded to include not only shelters and meals, but outreach by Intermountain Health Care and the Salt Lake Community Services Council; the School With No Name, which educated a shifting student body of homeless children; legal help from Utah Legal Services; and participation in the Homeless Veterans Stand Down, a two-day event at Salt Lake's National Guard armory that provided veterans a warm place to sleep for two nights, eat, shower, get new clothes and a haircut, medical and dental exams, legal advice,

239

As Complex a Place
as Can Be Imagined

job counselling, and information about social services available to them. In the fall of 1999, shelter workers said they expected to serve an additional 1,000 families beginning in January 2000 when benefits would run out for the first wave of welfare recipients under state and federally mandated reforms.

■   Each winter after the opening of the first homeless shelter in 1982, more people sought room in the permanent shelters than was available, and temporary "overflow" shelters were established for the winter months. Every year finding a building to use as a temporary shelter and funding to operate it was difficult. By late November 1997, with nighttime temperatures plunging toward freezing, homeless shelters began pulling cots out of storage to serve what was expected to be a marked increase in the number of people needing to come in from the cold. The cots—set up in crowded hallways, kitchens, and offices of several facilities—violated Salt Lake City ordinances, but Mayor Corradini agreed to suspend enforcement since the committee charged with finding sites for an overflow shelter for single men had come up empty after looking at fifty-seven possible buildings. In each case, either landlords or neighbors objected. The People's Freeway Community Council vowed to fight any plans to open another shelter in their neighborhood. "Our community and Salt Lake City are inundated with all the services for the homeless," it said. "It's time for another community, another city, to step up and let a shelter in." According to Palmer DePaulis, who, with Pamela Atkinson, of Catholic Community Services, led the Salt Lake County Council of Government's long-range planning committee, "We need a place for a winter shelter that we can count on for a few years to provide us the stability to plan. This constant crisis each winter just exhausts us." Atkinson suggested that in order to move beyond a short-term perspective, Utahns not regard the homeless condescendingly or dismissively, as vulnerable and ultimately insufficient objects of charity, thus keeping them at an emotional distance. "They share the same dreams, goals, and hopes we all have," she said.

■   The Homeless Youth Resource Center was founded in 1994 as Visions of Attitude. Since then it has offered a daytime shelter, shower facilities, food, warm clothing, counselling, and free long-distance telephone calls to more than 350 homeless youths annually. Brad Simkins, director of the center, says many of them are what he calls "porcupine kids. They're tough, and they have all these spikes and quills, but underneath they have a very soft side. They're very loving, compassionate, caring people with each other and with anyone they trust. The thing that makes them different than other kids is that rather than fretting about what they're going to wear to the prom or whether Dad's going to loan them the car keys for their Saturday night date, these kids are worried about survival, staying warm, and avoiding getting beat up."

■ In 1991 Nancy Boyasko, a refinery worker at Kennecott Copper Corporation and a member of the United Steelworkers union, ran for the Salt Lake City Council as a member of the Socialist Workers Party. Her platform included proposals to shorten the work week with no cut in pay as a way of spreading available jobs among the unemployed; a massive public works program to build child care centers, hospitals, and schools in order to provide both jobs and needed services; affirmative action programs; "building solidarity with working people around the world"; full rights for immigrant workers; union rights for farmworkers; and a moratorium on farm foreclosures. She received more than 40 percent of the vote, and for a time it looked as if she would be elected.

■ In May 1996 *The Salt Lake Tribune* announced that it would cease publication of its column, "Utah's People of Color," which had appeared every Sunday for the previous two years and dealt with a variety of groups and issues. On July 30, 1995, for example, Taniela K. Fiefia, a graduate of Brigham Young University law school, a former prosecutor in Hawaii, and editor of Salt Lake City's *Tongan News*, issued a call for Polynesians in Utah to work to preserve their language, history, culture, and customs in the face of serious obstacles. "Ours is a wonderful opportunity to reverse the trend and make sure that uniqueness of our identity and richness of culture is taught to our children," he said. "They have a right to enjoy it just as our ancestors did and just as we do. As the present possessor of that culture, it behooves us to preserve as much of what we know and have, and continue our Polynesian culture to the next generation." On February 4, 1996, Karen Kwan-Smith discussed the position that people of color, in particular Asian Americans, occupied in Utah. "Our presence is only confirmed as an afterthought," she said. "For the most part, we are thought of and treated as visiting foreigners, or migrant workers, not as people who live here. Sometimes we feel as if we are not welcome and at these times Utah can be a hostile place. It isn't about mean spirited people calling us names, it's about respect—respect for our way of life, our culture, our diversity, and individuality." On July 16, 1995, LeNora Begay, a freelance writer in Salt Lake City and former managing editor of *Navajo Nation Today*, who grew up in the small Navajo community of Sawmill, Arizona, discussed the way she was taught to introduce herself: "Ya'at'eeh. My name is LeNora Begay. I am Tachii'ni (my mother's clan is the Red Running Into Water People) and born for the To'dich'ii'niis (or my father's clan, the Bitter Water People). The Ta'neeszah niis (The Tangle People) are my grandparents and Kinyaa'aanniis

241

(The Towering House People) are my paternal grandparents." The lesson she was taught, she said, was that "a person who knows oneself is never alone. 'Wherever you go, you will find relatives,' my maternal grandparents often repeated to me and my siblings. 'If you are not willing to know yourself, you will not only be lost but alone in this world.'" When she told her grandparents that because she would eventually move away from the reservation she had no need to remember her clans, her grandfather responded, "You still have to remember who you are and where you came from. If you find yourself lost and lonely out there, you will always have a home to come back to. You have a place in this world. Your family and relatives will always be here."

In the view of the column's editor, Andrea Otanez, "The value of the canceled *Tribune* column was that we were included in the mainstream, even though what we said might have run against its current. In fact, it was valuable because what we said often ran against its current. The column enriched the dialogue by putting a face on at least some of the non-white communities within our borders. More importantly, we accomplished this on the pages of the state's largest daily, right along with everyone else. To lose that avenue is to be cut out of the conversation. We didn't leave the table; the table was taken away. ... We have a lot more to share. Too bad we won't be doing it in *The Tribune* anymore in the near future." According to Otanez, only three people called or wrote to protest the column's cancellation.

■   In 1996 three predominantly African-American churches—Calvary Baptist, New Pilgrim Baptist, and Trinity A.M.E.—were plastered with white supremacy literature, swastikas, and pictures of hooded Ku Klux Klan figures. "We also received a hate letter from the KKK," said Calvary Baptist's Rev. France Davis. "And we've had people, while we were having services, coming up to the windows of the church heckling us about our singing and worship." Rev. Corey Hodges, of New Pilgrim, said his church had been vandalized numerous times. In 1998 crosses were burned on the front lawns of at least two black families in the Salt Lake Valley. In February 1999 the Senate Judiciary Committee of the Utah State Legislature voted against a hate crimes bill. Modelled on similar legislation in most of the other forty-one states in the U.S. with hate crimes laws, it would have expanded and enhanced penalties for felony hate crimes, as well as changing the definition of a "hate crime" to specifically include those crimes motivated by sexual orientation.

■   On June 16, 1995, the International Olympic Committee announced that Salt Lake City had been chosen to host the 2002 Winter Games. City officials, business leaders, and a variety of organizations, ranging from the Utah AFL-CIO to the LDS church, supported the decision. So did most city and state residents, though a significant minority, nearly half, according to some polls, had serious reservations or were opposed. Concern increased in the fall of 1998 when it was learned that members of the Salt Lake Organizing Committee (SLOC) had handed out nearly $1 million to members of the International Olympic Committee (IOC) to secure the bid. The gifts included cash, university tuition payments, free medical care, expensive firearms, and all-expense-paid trips for IOC members and their families. Half a dozen investigations were launched, including those by the U.S. Justice Department and the Internal Revenue Service. In the view of G. Robert Blakey, a Notre Dame University law professor and one of the chief architects of the United States' racketeering law, the RICO Act, SLOC's efforts to land the 2002 Winter Games fit the federal definition of organized criminal activity. "This is an enormous embarrassment to Salt Lake City and to Utah," he said, "and if the prosecutors want to bring racketeering charges, it would fit." While there initially seemed to be a possibility that the scandal might lead to the games being transferred to another city, it soon became clear that changing the site of the games was unlikely and that they would go on as scheduled in Salt Lake. It also become evident, however, that SLOC might face a shortfall, at taxpayer expense, on its multi-million dollar budget as scandal-shy companies rethought their sponsorship, and at the very least sponsors were expected to use the scandal to negotiate better deals for themselves. It was also increasingly obvious that preparations for the games would have an enormous impact on Salt Lake City, affecting almost every aspect of the city's life. It was a driving force behind the construction of a $300 million light rail system that began operation December 1999 and changed the face of the city and reconfigured the way people moved through downtown Salt Lake City and throughout the Salt Lake Valley. It led to the complete reconstruction of Interstate 15—scheduled to be finished on the eve of the Olympics. Liquor laws were redrawn. A portion of the Salt Lake County sales tax was designated to help fund the games. Rice Stadium at the University of Utah was expanded so that the games' opening and closing ceremonies might be held there. As Glenn Bailey, director of the Crossroads Urban Center said, "Every decision is tied to the Olympics. From homeless issues to publicly financed projects, it all seems to revolve around those magic two weeks in 2002." For that reason in 1996 a group called Salt Lake City Impact 2002 & Beyond was organized to monitor the activities of the SLOC as it prepared for the games. It was particularly concerned that the games benefit all groups equally. Thus, for example, in December 1997 it charged that SLOC's thirty-one-person board lacked diversity and was dominated by rich, white, male, Mormon businessmen, and it asked that people representing other groups be added. "The point of our request is not to create a

243

'rainbow coalition' on the SLOC board," it said, "but rather to ensure that qualified, committed individuals from a variety of perspectives have the opportunity to contribute to the development of the Olympics." In May 1999 the group issued a "report card" for the committee: though Olympic organizers had made "slow progress" on proposals to convert media housing into affordable units, they had sought $23 million in federal funds for housing options; the SLOC board was slightly more diverse than it had originally been, but "rich, white insiders still dominate"; SLOC had yet to adopt a clear policy on the displacement of low-income residents, but had hired an Americans with Disabilities Act (ADA) coordinator in an effort to insure that the 2002 Olympics were accessible to all; and there had been no concerted effort to hire Utah's women- and minority-owned companies, or vendors who offered livable wages and full benefits.

■   On February 18, 1997, a group of Native American elders and their supporters marched from downtown Salt Lake City to the State Capitol Building to protest what they regarded as unfair policies at the Utah State Prison regarding Native American religious services and sweat lodge ceremonies.

■   In the spring of 1997, a group calling itself Artists Against Visual Pollution was founded. Its goal was to eliminate billboards entirely from Salt Lake City streets and throughout the entire state, and to accomplish that it called for a consumer boycott of companies that advertised on billboards. "Are you sick of the ugly billboards along streets and highways?" the group asked. "Would you rather see the Utah landscape resemble Oregon or New England with trees, instead of signs along the highways? Help boycott all products, services, and establishments which advertise on billboards. Send the message to all elected officials and companies who use billboards that they are polluting the visual landscape and annoying the public, rather than accomplishing their desired goal. If the public sends this message, money for billboard advertising will begin to dry up. This has worked effectively in other states, and it can work here. Notify city, county, and state officials that billboards are an unpopular and unnecessary blight."

■   When Lee Martinez was chosen to fill a vacancy on the Salt Lake City Council in the spring of 1997, he became the first Latino on the council. "I hope I can provide an insight, a different perspective from the standard fare," he said. "It's a big charge for me." For Mexican consul Anacelia Perez de Meyer, the selection of Martinez was important. "It reflects the role that the Hispanic community has in Salt Lake City. It reflects our presence." Six months later Martinez was defeated for election. At a time when the city's population was at least 25 percent people of color and one-half non-Mormons, the new city council was composed of five Anglo men and three Anglo women, five of them members of the Mormon church.

■ The Rose Park neighborhood on Salt Lake's westside was originally home to mostly white, blue-collar workers. In the 1970s and 1980s, it became more ethnically diverse. By 1990 its population was 15 percent Latino, and growing. In the fall of 1997 Latino residents of the area complained that its Neighborhood Watch Program unfairly targeted them. It seemed to them to be designed to, in effect, "Keep an eye on the Mexicans." Equipped with cellular phones and free gasoline that the city supplied, volunteers were sent off to reconnoiter their neighborhoods in private vehicles and report "suspicious activities" to police dispatchers. "The people actually volunteering for this were all white. The people being targeted were people of color, our people," said Robert "Archie" Archuletta, and, according to Lee Martinez, many Latinos felt under siege. "If we're drinking beer in the park, if there are several single men sitting in front of a house, they get reported as something suspicious," he said. At the root of the problem, he believed, were radically different ideas of what constituted "appropriate" behavior. In his view, "The fear for many people in the community is that 'they' are coming. It scares some people when they walk around their own neighborhoods and they see Latinos and they hear Spanish spoken. There is so much anger. I'm afraid that it's becoming 'us' vs. 'them.'"

■ In fall 1997 Salt Lake City officials announced a long-range project, using a projected $100 million in taxes and public subsidies, to completely redevelop the "Gateway District," a sixty-block, largely industrial area of the city's westside that had begun to emerge in the late nineteenth century with the coming of the railroad and had pretty much assumed its present shape by the turn of the century. It also included scattered, low-income residential areas. City officials saw it as the next big upscale growth area in Salt Lake, and envisioned about 1 million square feet of office space and 700,000 square feet of retail space. One question a number of individuals and groups raised was what impact it would have on downtown Salt Lake City. Would it compete with downtown merchants and lead to a decline of the central business district? Another question was what impact it would have on the current residents of the area. The plan focused on the real estate opportunities in the district and mentioned only in passing that real estate developers' plans for the area might not coincide with those of the area's residents. Glenn Bailey, for example, director of the Crossroads Urban Center, pointed out that under the plan, many residents, including the homeless, would be displaced. In 1996

245

Pioneer Park was shut down for two weeks for "maintenance reasons" and everyone in the park was evacuated. Bailey was suspicious of the maintenance excuse and thought that it was actually an experiment to see where the park's large contingent of homeless people would go, pointing out that a similar experiment happened in Atlanta, Georgia, before the 1996 Summer Olympics. A third question was whether or not funding the Gateway project would divert money from other projects and other areas of the city. According to John deJong, in *Catalyst* magazine, "The $100 million of improvements slated for the Gateway district are a reward to the speculators and developers who have been sitting on their assets for the last twenty years. The rest of Salt Lake City will have to fight over budget scraps to keep their neighborhoods in decent repair."

■   In the fall of 1997, after the galvanizing effect of a women's studies class at Salt Lake Community College, a group of perhaps a dozen young women formed a feminist group they called Twisted Sisters. They took the name because it was "funny, but at the same time memorable." Their goal, they said, was equality for everyone, not just women. They believed that stay-at-home mothers, professional women, lesbians, Latina wage-earners, and men could all stand together for common feminist goals, and consequently they sought to connect with similar groups in other parts of the country. As part of their effort to redefine and reclaim feminism, they published their own self-titled "zine," *Twisted Sisterrrs.* According to Ben Fulton, "Thoroughly irreverent, politically aware, jarringly, humorously honest and stuffed with haphazard graphics and art, it's a joyous tour through a newspaper, collective diary, call to action, plus an anatomy lesson all rolled into one." It included personal essays on virginity and feminine beauty, suggestions for activism, polls about masturbation, Angela Davis's latest lecture in Seattle, poems, pointed jabs at the right wing, an Ani DiFranco concert review, and a 1950s era advertisement for a vibrator. Utah's coordinator of the National Organization for Women (NOW), Anne Marie Straight, said she respected the tone of young feminism even as she was amazed by it: "It's kind of an in-your-face feminism, whereas when I was in my late 20s we felt as strongly, but we found quieter ways of expressing it. Now we've got this great group of women who say, 'Wait a minute, we don't feel quiet. We don't need to fit inside society's norms.' They embrace what's going on inside of them even though it may not fit nicely into our social constructs. In how many magazines do you get to read a tampon review? How often are women completely honest about how they feel, and about what kind of obstacles they're coming into contact with? These young women don't try to couch their feelings in appropriateness."

■ In early December 1997 the Salt Lake City Parks Department announced plans to remove stairs around a tree that had become a popular religious shrine in a small, city-owned, inner-city neighborhood park, saying they posed a liability. Many people believed that the stump of one of the tree's branches contained an image of the Virgin Mary. Candles, handwritten prayers, photographs, rosary beads, flowers, and crosses surrounded the tree. Scores of people offered prayers each day at the shrine and lined up to climb the stairway and touch the image in the wood or dip their fingers or handkerchiefs in the weeping water that oozed from the image and rub it on their bodies as balm. A wave of criticism followed the city's announcement, and a petition with more than 2,000 signatures protested the dismantling of the stairs and the removal of offerings. One letter to the editor called it "yet another sad reminder of the unconscious racism that seems to pervade local seats of power" and an example of "a double standard here, one that, I fear, must make minorities feel less than fully appreciated in our community. And it can only be harmful for all of us." Three days before Christmas, Mayor Corradini announced that the stairs would not be torn down and that city workers would

Religious shrine in Salt Lake City's Tauffer Park where many people believe that the stump of one of a tree's branches contains an image of the Virgin Mary. (Courtesy Utah Arts Council; photograph by Carol Edison.)

247

As Complex a Place
as Can Be Imagined

keep them swept and salted during the winter months. "Christmas is a time of hope," she said, standing before the shrine. "And hope is something we need a lot more of. This tree has given a tremendous amount of hope to more people than we ever realized." On May 15, 1999, the second anniversary of the shrine, several hundred people from throughout Utah and surrounding states visited it. "I believe Mary is here. I feel better after being here," one of them said. "My soul is calm. I feel safe around here," said another who came often.

■   On January 30, 1998, Abdal Fattah Amor, a professor of law at the University of Tunis, was in Salt Lake City on assignment from the United Nations to hear testimony about religious tolerance and discrimination in Utah. Representatives of various religious and ethnic groups were invited to the State Capitol Building to speak about their experiences. Many reported the difficulties they faced and the discomfort they felt. According to one Jewish resident, "This is not Bosnia. But neither it is an ideal place to live. There are many reminders that we are other."

■   In 1998 the Pagan Community of Utah adopted a portion of Foothill Boulevard as part of the state's Adopt-A-Highway Litter Control Program. By then Utah Pagans was a growing presence in Utah. They included the University of Utah Student Spirit Alliance, the Unitarian Universalist Pagans, and the Pagan Action Network, and they maintained an information hotline and a website and published a monthly newsletter, *Moonrise News*. After participating in a Gay Pride March in Salt Lake City, Goddess Circle facilitator Gretchen Faulk said, "By coming out and marching, we're helping create a space for people to live their lives the way they choose to."

■   In May 1998 the Faculty Association at Salt Lake Community College voted by a margin of more than two-to-one to affiliate with the American Federation of Teachers (AFT), a union with more than 900,000 members nationwide. Two weeks later the Utah State Board of Regents, following a closed meeting, voted unanimously not to recognize any union at SLCC or any other public college or university in Utah. The decision was made without discussion with faculty. As Lisa Bickmore, professor of English at the college, said, "I think it's fair to say that they did not request a shred of faculty input before they made that policy." According to Paul Henderson, executive director of the Utah chapter of the AFT, "The Regents have drawn a line in the sand. They have set up a confrontational situation which could create all kinds of labor unrest." On June 8, 1998, the community college's Faculty Senate published an open letter to the regents in *The Salt Lake Tribune* and the *Deseret News*. It discussed reasons the faculty had voted to affiliate with the AFT and the concerns they had about working conditions at the college—most importantly, the lack of a faculty voice in decision-making—expressed "regret that the Board of Regents and our own administration have chosen not to recognize the voice of the professional faculty at SLCC though they clearly have the option to do so," and asked regents to reconsider their decision. At a meeting several weeks later, on June 25, that included faculty leaders and SLCC president Frank Budd, Charlie Johnson, chair of the Board of Regents, said regents would not change their mind. When asked by *The Salt Lake Tribune* why he thought the faculty had voted for affiliation, Budd said, "I can't give you a good, direct answer to that. Maybe it's growth. When you get larger, there may be some feelings [by faculty] of not being in the communication loop." The problem was deeper, said Dean Huber, president of the SLCC Faculty Association. "The only way for [morale] to get better is for faculty to be given a voice back and have some say in the institution." On June 26, the Faculty Association filed a lawsuit against the Utah State Board of Regents and representatives of the SLCC administration alleging that the actions taken by the defendants after the vote to affiliate violated Utah's "Right-to-Work" statute.

■ On May 10, 1998, *The Salt Lake Tribune* reported the results of an analysis it had undertaken of traffic tickets the Salt Lake City Police Department had issued in 1997 and concluded that police had engaged in racial "profiling"—targeting people based on their race. According to the paper, "A random sample of 1997 tickets shows that blacks are twice as likely as white drivers to get a ticket and that Latinos are nearly three times as likely as whites to receive a traffic citation." According to Jeanetta Williams, president of the Salt Lake City branch of the NAACP, "It has been a problem for a long time. Most of the complaints we receive are from African Americans—mainly men—who are being stereotyped and stopped for minor reasons." Latinos reported similar experiences. "This is something that we have been talking about for years," said Jesse Soriano, president of the Utah Coalition of La Raza (UCLR). "There is a perception in the ethnic-minority communities that police target them. And the perception is correct. There's no question about that." Police officials disagreed, saying that officers did not "profile" or discriminate when stopping drivers, and complaints about "DWB"—driving while black—violations were unfounded; the tickets issued simply indicated the nature of violations committed and did not reflect bias against particular groups. Studies in others areas of the country found similar situations. According to a 1995 study, 73 percent of cars stopped and searched by Maryland state police were driven by blacks, while only 14 percent of people on the road were black. Seventy percent of searches of black-driven cars turned up nothing. Another

249

study of traffic stops in one Florida county showed that nearly 80 percent of drivers who were stopped were black, that their stops lasted longer than those of white motorists, and that they were twice as likely to be searched.

■ On July 6, 1998, the first issue of a newsletter, *Bridges: Building a Neighborhood Through Story*, appeared. It was a collaboration among Artspace, Inc., and faculty, primarily professor of English Tiffany Rousculp, and students at Salt Lake Community College. Artspace was a not-for-profit organization that sculptor Stephen Goldsmith founded in 1979 to create affordable housing and workspaces. Its first project transformed an abandoned warehouse into living and workspaces for artists and their families. It then developed another warehouse into fifty-three affordable housing units, with commercial space on the ground floor. Its current Bridges Project will house families, a child care facility, businesses, an art gallery, not-for-profit organizations, including the National Conference for Community and Justice, the Center for Community Dialogue, TreeUtah, and KRCL 91 FM Community Radio, and a new Buddhist temple. "I really like Stephen's idea of creating a new neighborhood, a new community," said the Rev. Jerry Hirano, head of the Buddhist temple. "It's a rare opportunity for us to become part of something like that." The newsletter's goal, and the larger goal of Artspace, was to help strengthen the process of neighborhood building in Salt Lake City's Gateway District west of the downtown area. "What is a neighborhood?" it asked. "Many years ago, this was an easy question to answer. A neighborhood was where we lived, shopped, played, socialized, and spent our time living our lives. Now, with increasing suburban sprawl, commuter lives, and electronic access to just about everything, it becomes hard to define what a neighborhood is, and nearly impossible to consciously develop one. If we add to this the common neglect of urban spaces, a neighborhood can become fragmented, isolated, and invisible. Artspace, Inc. has been working for several years to revitalize this sense of neighborhood in the western corridor of downtown Salt Lake City. ... This newsletter is a piece of the process of neighborhood-building. It is through story that we find out who we are, what our history is, what differences we have, and what similarities we share. ... When we know who we are we can begin to build relationships that are at the very core of neighborhoods. We become our neighborhood, and make of it what we wish to make of ourselves." The first issue of *Bridges* highlighted the history of the area and of community organizations there, including El Centro Civico Mexicano and Our House, a not-for-profit child care center for children of homeless families.

■ On Thursday, August 20, 1998, more than 200 people gathered at a downtown Salt Lake City hotel as part of President Bill Clinton's "One America" initiative on race to hear forty panelists from Utah and surrounding states. Similar groups met in cities and towns across the country. After each gathering, a report was sent to the White house. "This is a great meeting, but it is a group of minorities complaining about discrimination by the people who are not here," said Utah State Supreme Court justice Michael Zimmerman. "Where are the concerned whites? Why aren't they here? Nothing is going to change until whites sit down and listen to minorities and minorities hear the perspective of whites." Michael Martinez, a Salt Lake City attorney and a former member of Salt Lake Community College's Board of Trustees, lamented the state of affairs in Utah. "We have a very low tolerance level," he said. "We don't tolerate diversity—diversity of language, diversity of ethnicity, diversity of culture." Many panelists asserted that whites in Utah had a problem acknowledging racial discrimination. "If there is anything that you need to take back to the Clinton administration," said Forrest Crawford, professor of education at Weber State University in Ogden, "it is that the issue needs work and that there is a pattern of discrimination based on race." Uinise Langi, a Tongan doctoral candidate at the University of Utah, spoke about the many Pacific Islanders with college degrees who were unemployed or worked in low-paying, fast-food restaurants. "The message sent to our children is that education doesn't matter," she said. "Mom and Dad can go to school all they want, and they will still struggle." Moon Ji, a native of Korea and director of the Utah State Office of Asian Affairs, said he did not want his name to be identified as "foreign." "All names are American names," he said. "Moon Ji is not a foreign name. Sometimes people look at Asian Americans not as American but as Americanized Asians." Attorney Martinez feared the discussion would make no difference. "We've all been at meetings like this," he said. "And it's always the same people. Talking, talking, and talking." It was not to President Clinton that a message needed to be sent, he concluded. "We need to send a message to our state and local leaders."

■   Concerned that in a variety of ways Salt Lake City and County governments favored national and multi-national corporations and large companies at the expense of small locally-owned ones, the owners of several dozen small, neighborhood businesses formed the Salt Lake Vest Pocket Business Coalition in the spring of 1999 to try to reverse the trend. "Vest pocket means close to the heart," said Lorraine Miller, a founder of the organization and owner of a greenhouse and nursery, "because these businesses are close to our hearts." And, she said, "Across the country, there's a movement growing to protect neighborhood businesses, to 'think small.' I think people are getting tired of superstores." The impetus to the coalition's founding was the closing of three local bookstores in the last six months of 1998. In all three cases, owners saw the problem as the "corporatization" of Salt Lake City and reported not being able to compete with supergiants like Borders, Barnes and Noble, and Amazon.com. About Amazon, Patrick de Freitas, owner of Waking Owl Bookstore, one of the three stores that closed, said, "They're losing money hand over fist, but they're buying market share. I'm losing money hand over fist and losing market share. Capitalism is weird."

■ At noon on a cold day in February 1999 a small group of demonstrators gathered on Main Street in front of the ZCMI department store to protest its sale of fur coats. Members of the Utah affiliate of People for the Ethical Treatment of Animals (PETA), they carried black cardboard coffins to the store's front doors, stripped to their black underwear, lay down in the coffins, covered themselves with flowers, and displayed a banner that read, "Don't be caught dead in fur." Said one of the group, "We're freezing and cold, but it's not anything compared to what animals go through who are killed for their fur." The group was fresh from a victory at a local junior high school where, after weeks of demonstrations, school officials agreed to take down a McDonald's flag that had flown over the school because the company was one of the school's corporate sponsors.

■ A March 10, 1999, *University of Utah Human Resources Bulletin* was sent to all university supervisors, including the president, vice presidents, deans, directors, and department chairs. Its stated purpose was "to remind supervisors of the University's position in regard to unions and to provide some guidelines on how to respond if union activity should occur." According to the bulletin, the university "does not formally or legally recognize unions as agents for individual employees or employee groups," and supervisors were "expected to be able to recognize the signs of union organizing activity in the work place. Activities that may indicate early union organizing include: employees who have not had previous relationships suddenly becoming very involved with each other; increased use of phones, photocopies, or fax machines for personal business; increased number of complaints or grievances (may be used as a union rallying point)." The bulletin went on to say that "if union activity is suspected, it is the supervisor's responsibility to immediately report the activity to Human Resources." If suspicions were confirmed and union activity was found to be taking place, supervisors had a number of responsibilities, including informing employees "that you are opposed to unionization and that the University has taken a position that it does not recognize unions for the purposes of collective bargaining"; telling employees that "they have a right to refrain from joining a union, and that they do not have to sign an authorization card," and that "it is their own personal choice to opt not to speak to union organizers—even at home"; and informing the Department of Human Resources "of any union activities or rumors of such activities." Exactly what prompted the bulletin is unclear, though a former part-time instructor in the English Language Institute who had earlier filed a lawsuit against the university arguing that she was fired for publicly questioning working conditions in her department and for discussing with other employees the possibility of organizing a union said she thought it was her actions that had led to the university's explicit statement of its anti-union policy.

■   On April 13, 1999, the Salt Lake City Council voted to close one block of Main Street and sell it to the LDS church for $8.1 million. The vote was split along religious lines—the five council members who voted in favor of the sale belonged to the Mormon church; the two who voted against it did not. The section of the street sold ran between two city blocks that the church owned. Temple Square was located to the west, and on the block to the east were church headquarters and several other church buildings. The church announced it planned to build a parking garage beneath the street and on the surface construct a plaza with a large reflecting pool and garden that would link the two church blocks. According to Mormon church architect Kerry Nielsen, "It will be a high-quality, world-class open space." The city council also approved more than a dozen conditions of the sale, including allowing the church to ban demonstrations, skateboards, smoking, sunbathing, and "illegal, offensive, indecent, obscene, vulgar, lewd or disorderly speech, dress, or conduct" on the plaza. The sale and the conditions governing behavior on the proposed plaza were controversial from the beginning and drew national attention. One supporter wrote that "When I first read about the LDS church considering the purchase of Main Street for a pedestrian mall and gardens, I applauded it. I am always in favor of more green space, especially in an area filled with concrete. I also envisioned what a golden opportunity it would be for Utah's majority faith to show the world their love for and acceptance of diverse cultures and religions. This area could be used to honor all the other faiths that exist here. It would enhance our tarnished image and, forevermore acknowledge the existence of all the 'others' who live and work here." Another person found it "very hard to believe all the resentment against the idea of this plaza. Heaven knows, there is precious little open space in any urban area. LDS church officials, it seems to me, are offering it as a gift to the citizens of and visitors to this city, and people are spitting (or blowing cigarette smoke) in their faces. ... It may not be the Boston Common, but it is in that spirit, the spirit of beautiful municipal gardens which all can enjoy. They may be owned

253

by the LDS church, but they are open to all, and the city could certainly not afford to build or maintain such spaces." A third supporter said, "Consider a new park in downtown Salt Lake City where one need not stumble over a drunk in a sleeping bag, plastic cups, fast food containers and paper napkins. ... Cigarette stubs claiming the lives of planted tubs of flowers and shrubs? None. No semi-nudity to shock. No swearing or putrid language befouling the air. No barefoot flower people, no marijuana groups. Here will be a park to connect two of the most beautiful areas of the state. A person is restricted to just enjoy and relax, without fear of unpleasant or dangerous contacts. If you enter you will be surrounded by flowers, shrubs, lawn, statuary and benches by trees. ... All in all, how wonderful for the seekers of peace and quiet. Me? I vote for the park." Critics argued that adequate studies had not been conducted on the impact of the street's closing, that public spaces should not become private ones, that the decision demonstrated the ability of the Mormon church to work its political will in the city, and that public debate prior to the city council's decision to sell was a mere formality. According to one critic, "Religious power triumphed over civic sensibilities. Religion broke loose from the realm of private beliefs and exploded upon the public arena like a clumsy giant crushing small people in its wake. ... Now with Main Street a Mormon thoroughfare, [it] flows into one enormous display of power." The new plaza would not be a public space, he said, but, in reality, a Mormon space, "a connecting moat in the sea of Mormon dominance." As Rev. Tom Goldsmith of the First Unitarian Church saw it, the sale and conversion of a public thoroughfare into a private space meant the Mormon church would overwhelm the downtown with its presence. He also objected to the process by which the decision was made. "Everyone is dumbfounded by how quickly it went and how poorly the process was followed," he said. "It's unthinkable that church-state separation can be violated in such a fashion. It's comparable to New York City selling Fifth Avenue to St. Patrick's Cathedral. ... We live in a very delicate balance living here in Salt Lake City. And church authorities have exceeded their boundaries. The church needs to be respectful of a growing diversity and multicultural focus in this community. They need to be sensitive to a greater public than they have in the past." The *Salt Lake City Weekly* agreed, asserting that both the Mormon church and the city council seemed blind to the "ill will" and divisiveness the sale would bring. One writer described the sale as "the most blatant of church power-plays in recent memory" and said it testified "to a lack of perspective and even arrogance in the highest of LDS councils." In a letter to the editor of *The Salt Lake Tribune*, Karen Wildfoerster wrote, "The Salt Lake City Council votes 5 to 2 along religious lines to sell a city block to the Mormon church. OK, can we finally stop pretending that religion isn't the most prominent feature of our local government?" According to Deeda Seed, one of the two council members to vote against the sale, "Who else would we sell a public street to? We are making a special exception, selling Main Street, because it is the LDS church asking." One person asked, "Since the Salt Lake City Council decided, 5-2, to sell the Mormon church a street in Salt Lake City, I was wondering if I could possibly purchase the street in front of my home. The traffic is horrible and all of the cars zipping up and down are a real nuisance. I don't have $8.1 million but I could cough up $100 or so." Still another person said that "taking a main, public street from the taxpayers who paid for it, and then restricting its usage to those willing to live LDS standards is no gift." In early May, the ACLU of Utah threatened to sue the city because of the restrictions placed on public expression on the new plaza. "Main Street, like all public streets, is and always has been a traditional public forum, a uniquely American institution central to the 'marketplace of ideas,' open to the unorthodox as well as the conventional," ACLU legal director Stephen C. Clark wrote to the mayor and city council. "It never has been, is not now, and must not be allowed to become an extension of Temple Square." He was particularly concerned about a clause in the easement accompanying the sale specifically protecting church-related activities, "including, without limitation, the distribution of literature, the erection of signs and displays by [the LDS church], and the projection of music and spoken messages"—under which music and speeches from the church's semi-annual general conferences could be broadcast on the plaza, and allowing the church to permanently bar anyone who threatened harm or damage to church leaders and members or their property or who violated the rules governing the plaza more than once. As *The Salt Lake Tribune* wrote, "You can't carry a boombox blaring rap onto the LDS Church's new Main Street pedestrian plaza. But the church can send conference speeches and Mormon Tabernacle Choir performances wafting over the block. You won't be able to pass out fliers with pictures of your lost dog, notice of yard sale or even vegetarian propaganda. But The Church of Jesus Christ of Latter-day Saints can distribute copies of *The Book of Mormon* and brochures on the Word of Wisdom. And before you get any ideas of protesting those rules with a public rally—don't. Church security guards will take your signs and send you packing. If you come back, you can be banned for life from the plaza. But church signs and groups are just fine. That's the deal Salt Lake City attorneys worked out with LDS Church officials. And they are sticking by it." In the view of the ACLU, those conditions were unconstitutional—in violation of the First Amendment's free speech provisions and its establishment clause that prohibited government from favoring one religion over another. City council chair Keith Christensen disagreed and stood behind the vote. "The deed has been transferred, the money has been received, and the deed has been recorded," he said. "We have done what we've done. We're not going to undo it. And we'll defend it if we need to." According to city attorney Roger Cutler, "That property is no longer public. Like any other owner of private property, the [LDS church] has the right to determine what activities it will or will not allow on its property, subject to the terms of the easement reserved by the city. As the owner, the [LDS church] may also engage in activities on its own property that it will not allow by others." Further, he said, "The City Council knew, understood and acquiesced in the terms of the limited public access easement, including the fact that it was not to constitute or be used as a public forum."

■   Habitat for Humanity is an international ecumenical Christian organization that builds "simple, decent houses" for low-income families. Volunteers build the houses with donated materials, and people purchase them through no-profit, no-interest mortgages while contributing hundreds of hours of "sweat equity" labor working on their house and the houses of others. Mortgage payments are placed in a revolving "Fund for Humanity" to finance the construction of more houses. During the 1990s the group's Salt Lake Valley affiliate built thirty-two houses, including, in the spring of 1999, a "blitz build" of a 1,300-square-foot house in fifty hours by Salt Lake Community College building trades students. In the future the organization says it will find it difficult to build as many houses. According to an annual report published in December 1998 by the U.S. Conference of Mayors, lack of affordable housing was on the rise among thirty major U.S. cities surveyed, including Salt Lake City, and the strong U.S. economy of the 1990s had had little or no positive effect on the number of hungry, homeless, and marginally-housed. For the lowest 20 percent of wage earners, inflation had outpaced wages by 100 percent, and Utah's own strong economy had pushed rents to record highs. As a result, more and more people worked but remained poor. At the same time, prices for land had skyrocketed. "It's hard to find an affordable lot that a developer doesn't want," says executive director Yasamina Roque. "We used to buy lots for $15,000. Now we're lucky to get some at $39,000." According to Ken Adlam, "We have to compete just like everyone else, except in the rare case where a lot is donated. That doesn't happen very often." Part of the difficulty, too, is local zoning regulations. As a general rule, Adlam says, municipalities and neighborhood community councils favor lower density, while Habitat for Humanity favors higher density so as to be able to serve as many people as possible. "Sometimes we want to put in five houses and they say two," Roque says.

"It took us two years to get a subdivision built in one area because of the intricacies of planning and density."

■	Beginning in the mid-1990s, a drum circle, sometimes with as many as several hundred people, met each Sunday afternoon in Salt Lake City's Liberty Park. In the spring of 1999 *The Salt Lake Tribune* described the gathering as "a haven for counterculture neo-hippies, aging hippies, the homeless, young families and curious onlookers. The event is disorganized. Music starts whenever more than one drum is present and winds up when the drums leave. Food is communal. Recycling is encouraged. Pierced body parts, hemp, backless tops and drug pipes are everywhere. The smoke from cigarettes—traditional and marijuana—wafts through the crowd." On April 18, 1999, about fifty Salt Lake City policemen armed with nightsticks, riot gear, and tear gas cleared the drum circle and everyone else out of the park, about 500 people in all, and closed it for several hours. Police said that some members of the drum circle were selling drugs and had weapons, and when they tried to arrest them, the crowd taunted and threatened them, and they were forced to call for help from other officers. The action aroused bitter controversy. According to city police chief Ruben Ortega, "We cannot afford to let that park deteriorate to open lawlessness, to where drugs and weapons are being brought into that park. It was just a matter of time for these folks to take over the park. Every year [the drum circle] is a major problem. Others in the park feel intimidated, and we need to take control of the park." Acting mayor Kay Christensen backed police, saying that administrators and police decided to send a zero-tolerance message to the drum circlers. "The idea was to get a handle on it in the spring," she said. Though several members of the Salt Lake City Council said they were uncomfortable with what the police did, most of them supported its actions. "As a citizen, I appreciate your efforts to uphold the law, no matter how ugly it might appear," said Councilman Bryce Jolley. "Everyone overreacted," said Deeda Seed. "Clearly the people in the drum circle shouldn't have forced police officers out of the park. But then I wonder why we called in SWAT teams." In Joanne Milner's view, "There had to have been some other means. We didn't need to go in there with billy clubs. It reminded me of the war protests of the '60s and '70s. I just didn't want to see that." Mayoral candidate Ross Anderson blamed Chief Ortega and promised to remove him if elected in November 1999. "The police essentially victimized everybody in that park with their show of force and terror," he said. Several weeks later a second mayoral candidate, Jim Bradley, also promised, if elected, to remove Ortega. In the view of one member of the drum circle, the police were driven by their prejudices against certain kinds of people. "It appears that the police in this instance

257

ended up losing their cool and lashed out at innocent people based upon some prejudice which unfortunately seems to be shared and even encouraged by their leadership." For another critic, "The actions of the Salt Lake City Police in Liberty Park were an offense to every citizen of the city and the state. The police force used a small illegal drug incident as an excuse to attack a segment of society that the conservative establishment does not like. The segment includes youthful anti-establishment activists, libertarians, environmentalists and peace activists, the very people who protest the fascist police mentality that pervades Utah law enforcement agencies and which was in evidence that Sunday. ... The police need to be reminded that the Constitution and Bill of Rights also protect the disenfranchised, youth, liberals, the poor, students, musicians, crafts-people, protesters, sun-bathers, children, face-painters, dancers, and pet-owners. These were the people that my wife and I saw in Liberty Park while taking our usual afternoon walk there." Chief Ortega was particularly criticized. "I have some suggestions for Police Chief Ruben Ortega in response to the incident at Liberty Park on April 18," one person wrote. "He could have a wall created around all public places to ensure only the 'right kind of people' will be able to enjoy them. Maybe he could take a page from *Mein Kampf* and force all undesirables like the drum circle hippies to wear a peace sign at all times to distinguish them from proper citizens. After all, if you are going to have storm troopers in riot gear with billy clubs, you may as well go all the way." The *Salt Lake City Weekly's* interpretation of the event was that Ortega sent police "into Liberty Park like storm troopers to frighten and club whomever they might come across on a Sunday afternoon, just because, earlier in the day several park patrons misbehaved. It was a brazen move by Ortega that displayed the chief's open disregard for civil liberties." In their view, the Liberty Park incident was part of a pattern visible since Ortega had been appointed chief several years earlier, and they called for his removal from office.

■ In April 1999 Chief Ortega proposed to the Salt Lake City Council an "anti-cruising ordinance," which the council approved on June 8. Under the ordinance, anyone who drove past police checkpoints more than twice on streets in a 200-block, four-square mile area from 11:00 p.m. to 4:00 a.m. would be ticketed. Cities nationwide, including Portland, Oregon; Phoenix; and Los Angeles had similar laws. The ordinance was controversial. According to Ortega, "We're having to take drastic measures. Unfortunately, we have to curtail movements we enjoyed before." Police official Roy Wasden agreed: "It is unfortunate the problems are so great that we need to do something like this, but the time has come. The city has an obligation to keep the streets safe."

258

The Gathering Place

Many residents in the area supported the ordinance, as did mayoral candidate Stuart Reid. "The problem is so intense now," he said, "that we need to keep the streets safe. It's not just cruising that takes place. It's cruising and confrontation happening out there." Other candidates for mayor in the November 1999 election disagreed. According to Jim Bradley, "I can fully appreciate the nuisance factor, but steps can be taken short of prohibiting people from using public streets. If the problem is the nuisance people are creating, then address that issue by itself." The strongest statement came from Ross Anderson, who said, "Once again, as in the Liberty Park incident, a whole group of people are being painted with a broad brush because of the actions of a few. [Cruising is] one of those choices that shouldn't be restricted because of a police chief who wants to impose more and more of a police state on our city." City council member Joanne Milner called the ordinance and the thinking behind it "brute mentality. There is a pattern, and it's indicative of the administrative style of the mayor and the chief. It's dictatorial," she said. For Glenn Bailey, Crossroads Urban Center director, the residents of the city should be apprehensive about the proposal. "They would rather have nobody out, doing, moving anywhere," he said. "All of this is unnecessary. It's restricting everybody's freedom, and we should all be concerned about that." The Utah chapter of the ACLU agreed, seeing the ordinance as an improper restriction on the fundamental constitutional rights of freedom of movement, assembly, and expression. "We're not insensitive to the problems surrounding cruising," said ACLU executive director Carol Gnade. "We just feel this response will not be effective, or appropriate." On Saturday night, July 10, about 200 people marched along State Street from City Hall at 400 South to 2100 South and back, chanting, carrying posters, and calling for repeal of the ordinance. The march was organized by Sherry King, founder of Citizens to Repeal 12.12.090. "State Street is a state highway, paid for by tax dollars," she said. "If [police] would enforce the other ordinances—like speeding, noise, and racing—they would not have to worry about this one. We believe as taxpayers we should be allowed to drive those roads any time of day or night." At the Salt Lake City Council meeting three days later, on July 14, mayoral candidate Ken Larsen presented a petition signed by more than 800 people opposed to the cruising ban. If the petition did not work, Larsen said, he expected the law to be thrown out in court. "There are so many ways the cruising ordinance is unconstitutional," he said to the council. "And I will fight this in the courts. And I will win. You'll lose this one. You'll lose this one in court. You'll lose this one in the public eye."

■ In the summer of 1999, the Friends of Gilgal, as part of its effort to raise

$600,000 to purchase Gilgal Gardens and turn it into a city park, rather than see it razed for a condominium development, asked the Salt Lake County Commission for funds to help purchase it. The garden featured a collection of sculptures by Thomas B. Child, an LDS stonemason who brought his religious convictions to life in quartz and granite. From a sphinx with the face of Mormon church founder Joseph Smith to a headless heavenly messenger to a sculpture of the artist himself, the garden abounded with works that Robert Olpin called "provocative and delightful, and very telling as to the culture from which they arise." In the view of Dave Jones, "Gilgal is totally unique to Utah and unique in the United States. ... It's also open space that we lack on the east side of Salt Lake City. It would be a tragedy to lose it." Commissioners said they would consider the request, though they were unsure where the money would come from and said they would make no promises.

■ The first annual Single Mothers' conference was held in Salt Lake City on September 11, 1999. It drew more than 400 people. Conference topics included budgeting, returning to school, finding quality day care, and keeping children from drugs. The goals were to provide emotional support to single mothers and to help them attain decent jobs, health benefits, affordable housing, and day care. Many people do not realize how difficult it is to raise children alone, said Karen Mecham, conference director, especially with little education or money and a scant job history. Many single mothers feel alienated, she continued, because society tends to be hard on them as a group, especially those on public assistance. "We want to serve as mentors," she explained. "And we want to always provide positive reinforcement. They get plenty of negative reinforcement from everyone else."

■ In September 1999 the National Low Income Housing Coalition published a study of seventy metropolitan areas throughout the United States entitled *Out of Reach*. Using the U.S. Department of Housing and Urban Development's definition that affordable housing did not consume more than 30 percent of a person's income, it concluded that throughout the United States rental housing was less and less affordable for low-income residents, a large percentage of people paid more than they could afford for rent, and at the same time apartment rental rates were rising faster than wages. The situation in Salt Lake City was similar. "Everyone knows there's a crisis for those of very low income," said Steve Erickson, director of the Utah Housing Technical Assistance Program. "But it's pretty much a problem across the board for lower-wage earners, even those who might be considered lower-middle class." According to the study, more than 45 percent of Salt Lake's renters paid at least one-third of their income for housing. The previous year, 38 percent had.

In 1999 minimum wage workers in Salt Lake had to put in 89 hours a week to afford a two-bedroom apartment. A year earlier they would have had to work 80 hours. Nowhere in the United States, including Salt Lake City, could a person in a minimum wage job pay for even a one-bedroom apartment at the fair market rent for that area. According to Heather Tritten, affordable housing advocate for the organization, Utah Issues, the study showed that "the economic growth we are seeing in Utah has not reached everyone. It's leaving a whole sector of our community behind, in a spot where they can't afford to make rent." Especially hard hit, according to Linda Hilton, director of Salt Lake's Coalition of Religious Communities, were single women with children, who were the city's fastest growing homeless population, and the elderly.

■   On Sunday, October 3, 1999, from noon until 2:00 p.m. between sessions of the Mormon church's general conference, close to 200 people stood outside the south entrance of Temple Square to protest the church's financial support of California's Knight initiative, a March 2000 ballot proposal designed to strengthen that state's prohibition against same-sex marriages. They held signs bearing such slogans as "Hate Is Not a Family Value," "Choose to Love," "We Just Want to Get Married," "Keep Your Bigotries to Yourself," and "America Equals Equality." A counter-demonstration of about a dozen or so people took place across the street.

■   National Coming Out Day was celebrated in Salt Lake City on Sunday, October 10, 1999, at Sugarhouse Park. "It's an opportunity to break down the horrific stereotypes that have been put upon the gay and lesbian community. Besides, it's a great party," said state representative Jackie Biskupski. The event attracted more than 400 people and featured food, music, dancing, soccer games with a bright pink ball, and speeches. The next night a candlelight vigil and march from the steps of the State Capitol Building was held to mark the first anniversary of the death of Matthew Shepard, a gay University of Wyoming student who was beaten to death.

■   On October 23, 1999, a "Police-State Protest" was held on the grounds of the City and County Building from noon until 4:20 p.m. In publicizing the event, its organizers said, "Let Your Voices Be Heard. Salt Lake City will be getting a new Mayor. We need to let him know that we will not tolerate the Police State legacy that Deedee [Corridini] had left us. No more Drum Circle beatings; no anti-cruising laws; no more gay/lesbian discrimination; no more anti-medical marijuana; no more gun war; no more anti-polygamy; no more POLICE STATE. No more Chief [Reuben] Ortega clones. JUST SAY NO to violent cops and a government out-of-control. ... If you belong to a persecuted minority, you need to be at this rally. If we do not stand up for the rights of others who are different from ourselves, no one will stand up for us! Until we do, we are not freedom fighters, but privilege seekers."

A significant aspect of Salt Lake City's recent history is the bitter controversy over gay rights. It is perhaps the deepest and most bitter divide in the city today, as it is throughout the United States as a whole, forcing residents and elected officials alike to confront their moral consciences and consider how the city's professed ideals compare to its realities. Additionally, it is an important subject for all to consider because, as Martin Duberman, Martha Nicinus, and George Chauncey, Jr., say in the introduction to their important collection, *Hidden from History: Reclaiming the Gay and Lesbian Past,* "[P]ersonal sexual behavior is never simply a private matter, but is always shaped by and shapes the wider social and political milieus." Examining the subject can thus provide considerable insight into a society and culture at particular times and places and over time. With one or two exceptions, Utah historians have written little about gay and lesbian history, even though nationally in the last decade or so there has been an unprecedented outpouring of scholarship on the subject.

Utah's gays and lesbians became increasingly active and visible in the late 1980s and 1990s, in spite of a powerful stigma against homosexuality "reinforced," says Linda Sillitoe, "by the attitude of many churches, including Utah's predominant religion." But the city's gays and lesbians have long had a public presence. In 1948 the Radio City Lounge (or "R.C."), reportedly one of the oldest gay bars west of the Mississippi, opened in downtown Salt Lake and remains at the same location today. In the summer of 1969, Gay Liberation fronts were founded in cities throughout the United States. The group in Salt Lake City had a membership of about thirty people. According to Ben Williams, while they worked to form a coalition with other groups, including Vietnam Veterans Against the War and the National Organization for Women, initially they concentrated on "raising awareness among themselves about what it meant to belong to an oppressed minority. They instinctively knew that to survive individually, out of the closet, they had to collectively support one another and continually foster the concepts of Gay Pride among the homosexuals of Utah." In 1970 the Gay Rap Group, today known as the Lesbian and Gay Student Union, was organized at the University of Utah. Two years later the

262

The Gathering Place

Metropolitan Community Church (MCC) began its ministry in Salt Lake, and Utah's second gay bar, The Sun Tavern, named after a San Francisco bar, The Midnight Sun, opened. It quickly became a kind of community center for many of Salt Lake City's gay men and women, "a home, a place to feel comfortable," said Marshall Brunner, who began working at The Sun soon after it opened. "We've had weddings and wakes and everything in between here. The only thing we haven't had is a christening." According to Nikki Boyer, a bartender at The Sun for many years, and later one of its owners, "I've seen most everyone in this town in there, although not everyone will admit it. But the politicians can breathe easy. I'm not going to write my memoirs." In 1975 Utah's first gay newspaper, the *Salt Lake City Gayzette*, began publication. In 1977 the State of Utah denied the Metropolitan Community Church the right to hold a ball in the Capitol Rotunda. After the church sued and won, the legislature banned all dances in the Capitol and the State of Utah filed a motion to force the MCC to disclose a list of its members to law enforcement officials so they might compare it with their records on "known homosexuals." The motion was denied. That same year a group called Affirmation, "a non-profit fellowship serving gay, lesbian, bi & transgendered Latter-day Saints," was formed. According to its April 1999 newsletter, its goal was "to provide a safe, inclusive space for gay men and lesbians from Mormon backgrounds who live along the Wasatch Front. We affirm that a gay/lesbian lifestyle can be a positive one and that homosexuality is not incompatible with spirituality. At the same time, we are a diverse group who embrace a variety of life styles and hold a variety of attitudes toward spirituality, religion, morality, and politics."

In 1978 gays and lesbians protested the appearance of singer and anti-gay activist Anita Bryant at the Utah State Fair. That same year a Gay Pride Fair was held at the Northwest Multi-Purpose Center. In 1979 a protest and all-night candlelight vigil was held on the steps of the Salt Lake City and County Building during Gay Pride Week to draw attention to gay and lesbian struggles in Utah, and a radio program, *Gayjavu*, known today as *Concerning Gays and Lesbians,* began broadcasting on radio station KRCL. Also that year 20 Rue Jacob, a lesbian book store and coffee house, opened, and the group Older, Wiser Lesbians (OWLS) was formed. In 1982 the first Gay and Lesbian Day at Lagoon amusement park drew 2,500 people, and the Salt Lake Men's Choir was organized with thirteen members. By 1997 it had grown to forty-three mem-

263

As Complex a Place
as Can Be Imagined

bers, was the Choir-in-Residence at All Saint's Episcopal Church, and presented four concerts during its 1997-98 season. According to its vision statement, as an organization it valued "a safe haven of friendship, support, and unity; a high standard of musical excellence; a high level of commitment; opportunities to learn and grow through choral music; and building bridges of understanding and tolerance between diverse communities." In 1983 the Tavern Guild sponsored a "Basket Social" in Fairmont Park that evolved into an annual Gay Pride Day celebration. In 1986 *Triangle* magazine began publication, and the next year the Salt Lake Gay Community Council, today the Gay and Lesbian Community Council of Utah, was organized, and the People with AIDS Coalition of Utah was established. In 1988 at least four organizations were founded: Gay Fathers; the First Thursday Women's Group; the Utah AIDS Foundation; and the Gay and Lesbian Youth Group, which sought to discourage drug or alcohol use, increase self-esteem, provide a friendly social climate, and issue information through guest speakers and peer counseling. Yet, as Linda Sillitoe says, the group's founders and leaders "acknowledged, at root, a grimmer goal—to prevent teen suicide, which to them seemed astronomical among teens who believed they were homosexual." The next year the Desert and Mountain States Lesbian and Gay Conference was held in Salt Lake, and the Gay and Lesbian Historical Society and the Utah Gay Rodeo Association were both organized.

In 1990 Salt Lake's first Gay and Lesbian Pride March drew 200 people (the 1999 Pride Day march and celebration attracted a reported 18,000 people); a Utah chapter of Queer Nation was formed; Utah Gay and Lesbian Utah Democrats was organized; the Utah State Democratic Party included sexual orientation in its anti-discrimination policy; and when the Anne Frank Holocaust Exhibit opened at the City and County Building, local gays and lesbians and their supporters rallied to protest the exhibit's exclusion of homosexuals as Holocaust victims. In 1991 the University of Utah added sexual orientation to its non-discrimination policy, the *Womyn's Community Newsletter* began publication, and the Utah Stonewall Center opened. The center closed in the fall of 1997, after six years of operation, amid a financial crisis but reopened a year later with a new name, the Gay and Lesbian Community Center of Utah.

Informal surveys had revealed a general unawareness of the significance of the center's original name, which was intended to commemorate the three-day civil disturbance in New York City in June 1969 following a police raid of The Stonewall Inn. Police periodically raided the inn, as they did other gay establishments, but this time patrons fought back, rather than acquiesce, and the resulting "Stonewall Riot" marked an important episode in the gay rights movement in the United States. But, as Alan Ahtow, at the time deputy director of the Gay and Lesbian Community Center, said, gay and lesbian history received little attention in Utah. "People didn't know what Stonewall was. And the board felt it was time to include 'gay and lesbian' in our name and not hide behind a generic." According to Monique Predovich, the center's director when it re-opened in 1998, its mission was twofold: "To provide a safe and comfortable environment for people. And to be a voice for the gay community of the state, to challenge the discrimination that goes on here." In her view, "The general community has been used to us being hidden, and many of us have been told: 'Stay in the closet and be quiet, and you won't get hurt.' Well, we are not going to remain invisible and be quiet. We are this community's doctors and lawyers, and your [sons and] daughters. We are speaking out." As part of that mission, the center housed the Stonewall Library. "Believe it or not," Ahtow said, "Utah has one of the largest libraries dedicated to the literature of gays and lesbians."

In 1993 the Lesbian and Gay Chorus of Salt Lake City was formed, the *Pillar* began publication, and the Utah Coalition of Gay, Lesbian, and Bi Union Activists and Supporters was organized. According to Calvin Noyce, one of the latter's founders and its president in 1998, the group was formed "because there didn't seem to be anything in the labor movement for us. Obviously there were gay people in the labor movement here like anywhere else who had nowhere to turn." Noyce was also co-chair of Pride at Work (PAW), a national organization of gay, lesbian, bi-sexual, and transgendered labor activists. It had three broad goals: equality for gays at work; acceptance of gays within the labor movement; and more understanding within the gay community of working class concerns and issues. Founded in 1994, PAW received official recognition as a constituency group of the AFL-CIO in August 1997. Gay and lesbian workers were vulnerable to job discrimination and harassment, Noyce said, and were often without legal recourse, and PAW was a group to which they could turn for help in claiming the rights awarded to their heterosexual co-workers. By 1999 eleven of the fifty states specifically prohib-

265

As Complex a Place
as Can Be Imagined

ited the firing of workers on the basis of sexual preference, and PAW wanted unions around the country to insist on the same protection in contracts they negotiated with employers. Its main priority, though, Noyce said, was "working on the Federal Employment Non-Discrimination Act (ENDA), and health care for domestic partners. Without ENDA it will continue to be completely legal to discriminate against gay and lesbian workers." Asked during an interview, "Are you encouraged by the accomplishments of Pride at Work?" Noyce replied, "I think this is a hard struggle, and it's very far from being over both in the trade union movement and out of the trade union movement. When you're involved in something like this and something doesn't go the way you want it to go, and you think: 'God, we just don't seem to get anywhere.' That's when you can reflect back over what's taken place. Five years ago no one thought we were going to have an organization in the trade union movement called Pride at Work; ... Or looking at domestic partnership benefits. Back ten, fifteen years ago it was almost unheard of, but now many companies have them. The rest of the world considers Utah a very conservative state, yet here we have the fourth official gay and lesbian trade union organization. I think that's a pretty big thing. I'm proud of that."

In 1994 Utah Log Cabin Republicans, for politically conservative homosexuals, was founded. When the 1995 Gay and Lesbian Pride Parade wound its way from the State Capitol to the Gallivan Center in downtown Salt Lake City, it included twenty-eight entries and 600 participants, and after the parade 5,000 people attended Gay Pride Day events. In 1996 the *Salt Lake Xchange* began publication and the Mountain West Women's Chorus was founded. In 1998 Inklings bookstore opened. Its mission, according to co-owner and manager Liz Bracken, was to provide books for the gay and lesbian community and to attract others as well. The customer base, co-owner Stephanie Fulton said, was almost equally men and women, ranging from students to older men and women. "We're seeing a spectrum of ages, and that's great. We don't just want to cater to a certain population," she said. By fall 1999 new gay organizations included the Queer Utah Aquatic Club (QUAC); Friends of Thelma and Louise Lesbian Terrorists and Sewing Circle; the Utah Gay Latino Association; the Gay and Lesbian Political Action Committee (GOLPAC); the Utah Stonewall Historical Society; the Gay and Lesbian Opera Club; the

Alternative Garden Club; Gay Volleyball; Utah Gay Latino Association; and Utahns for Fairness.

In the winter of 1995 a group of students at Salt Lake's East High School asked permission to form a club that would provide peer support to gays, lesbians, and their straight friends. Their request polarized the community and was one of the defining moments of Salt Lake City's recent history. "The purpose of the club," the students wrote, "would be to increase awareness about homosexuality in high schools, to decrease homophobia, and to help gay, lesbian and bisexual students feel safe and welcome in their school environments." One of the organizers had seen two homosexual friends drop out of school and others who had become deeply depressed. "It's not about sex," she said. "Our club is more about stopping the suicide and the drug use and the dropping out of school. It's more about leading a safe and healthy lifestyle than a destructive one." The Salt Lake City School Board's inclination was to ban the club, but a federal equal access law, originally sponsored by Utah senator Orrin Hatch to

267

protect Bible study groups, prohibited doing so—no club could be banned if any were allowed to meet. Utah governor Michael Leavitt and Senator Hatch advocated that schools ban gay clubs anyway and then contest the federal law in court. One legislator argued that the state should simply give up the more than $100 million in federal aid it received annually in order to prohibit the club. Ultimately, rather than allow it, the school board, after a heated four-and-a-half-hour meeting, voted to ban all clubs not formally tied to school curricula. Forty-six clubs in all were excluded, ranging from hockey and mountain bike clubs to Native American and Polynesian associations.

Following the decision, hundreds of students boycotted classes and held protest rallies both on the school grounds and at the State Capitol Building, where a few adults joined them, and petitioned the school board to reconsider its decision. For weeks local newspapers were flooded with letters both supporting and opposing the ban. School board members appeared on local radio and television programs to explain their decision. An ultra-conservative citizen's group, the Eagle Forum, charged that "outside agitators," including the American Civil Liberties Union (ACLU), were using the students to advance their own agendas. On Capitol Hill state senators held a secret, closed-door meeting to discuss the issue. The 90-minute meeting drew a lawsuit from the

On March 2, 1996, East High School students and their supporters, numbering in the thousands, marched from the Federal Building in downtown Salt Lake City to the State Capitol to protest the school board's ban on all "non-curriculum related" clubs, rather than allow a gay club to be formed. The club's organizers said its purpose would be to provide support for gays, lesbians, and their straight friends.

ACLU on the basis that it violated Utah's Open and Public Meetings Act. In February 1997 the case was settled out of court, with the Senate admitting its violation of the law and agreeing to pay the ACLU $10,000 in legal fees. At a news conference, one lawmaker likened homosexuals to "animals." Another termed homosexuality a "perversion" that destroyed individual lives and threatened society as a whole. The legislature passed a bill prohibiting teachers from "promoting illegal activities" either at school or in their private lives. Governor Leavitt vetoed it, fearing it violated the First Amendment, but suggested that legislators write it more narrowly during a special session. The re-written bill, which became law, allowed school boards in all forty Utah school districts to prohibit specific clubs. At its September 15, 1998, meeting, the school board voted to let stand its original decision to ban the clubs and not re-open the issue for discussion.

Meanwhile teachers announced the formation of a local chapter of the Gay, Lesbian, and Straight Teachers Alliance (GLSTA) at a rally and press conference and participated in talk shows and media coverage locally and nationwide. "To not stand up now, when there are so many misconceptions and questions concerning gay issues, would go against everything I have tried to teach," one of its members said. "This is why I feel I have to come forward. There is too much hope in the world not to come forward. I owe it to my profession and to my students."

In April 1997 several students and their parents, backed by the ACLU and a number of national gay rights organizations, filed a federal law suit against the school board. A mediation hearing failed to resolve the suit, and the case proceeded. In the meantime the club, under the sponsorship of the Gay, Lesbian and Straight Education Network of Utah (GLSEN), continued to meet, not as an official school group, but under state and federal laws that allowed groups with outside sponsors to rent space in schools for meetings.

East High student Kelli Peterson, who led the push for the gay club, became a national celebrity. Filmmaker Jeff Dupre's documentary, *Out of the Past*, linked Peterson's struggles to those of lesbian and gay figures from the American past, including seventeenth-century Puritan minister Michael Wigglesworth, novelists Sarah Orne Jewett and Annie Fields, and civil rights activist Bayard Rustin. According to Peterson, she would not have felt so alone and so different for so long if she had known of such people because, as Dupre said, "The past is one place we find ourselves." The film won the Audience Award for Best Documentary at the Sundance Film Festival and was shown throughout the United States and on public television, and in a number of other countries, including Brazil, Australia, England, and Spain. After its screening at the San Francisco International Lesbian and Gay Film Festival, audience members asked about Peterson. "Kelli's going to school," said the film's co-producer, Eliza Starr Bayard, "and staying put in Salt Lake. I teased her on the phone last week, saying, 'So, when are you moving to San Francisco? Are you moving to New York?' She said, 'Are you kidding? I'm staying here in Utah. This is where I belong. This is where I'm needed.'"

The controversy at East High continued in April 1999 after the Gay Straight Alliance, with the approval of the school's principal, Kay Peterson, gave a six-minute slide show presentation during the school's annual multicultural assembly. The presentation defined terms such as gay, lesbian, and bi-sexual; discussed events and symbols of importance to the gay community, such as Pride Day, the rainbow flag, and the Stonewall riot of 1969; identified cities and towns in the United States more "gay-friendly" than others; and included a list of famous people who were gay, lesbian, or bisexual. Reaction to the slide show demonstrated how divisive the issue still was. Several days after the assembly, a small group of people gathered across the street from East High to protest the inclusion of the presentation in the assembly. They carried signs, waved American flags, and held a large banner proclaiming gays and lesbians to be "anti-species." That night nearly 300 people packed a meeting of the East High School Community Council to protest the inclusion of the presentation in the assembly. According to *The Salt Lake Tribune*, "Parent after parent stood at the Monday meeting and said GSA's presentation did not belong in the assembly at all and that a sensitive administration would have provided an alternative activity for students who were offended," and many parents called on the principal to resign. "This is propaganda," said one parent who was a member of the America Forever Foundation, whose theme was "United in Righteousness We Will Continue to be Great." Other parents said the slide show should have shown the downside of the gay lifestyle and were angry that students were told the assembly was mandatory and once the presentation began were not allowed to leave. Some students saw the very presentation itself as divisive, while students in the Gay Straight Alliance viewed it as a step for-

271

As Complex a Place
as Can Be Imagined

ward. "We just wanted to express our culture," one said. "People are going to be opinionated, and that could hurt us. ... We're going to go down for a little while, then come back up even more strongly. It betters us. We've taken another step." The Utah chapter of GLSEN applauded Peterson for approving the presentation. "The struggle for gay rights is a continuation of the civil rights movement into the new century," it said. "The climate still exists where many perceive that it is still OK to harass and exclude people who are gay. Some day, gay, lesbian, and bisexual students will be safe and included in our schools."

The National Conference for Community and Justice (NCCJ) issued a strong statement of support for the original decision to allow the presentation. "It is through the actions of people like Mr. Peterson that others can learn to overcome the destructive barriers of prejudice and discrimination, to recognize our shared humanity," it said, and called for a community-wide dialogue on the issue. It cited the findings of a 1995 study conducted by the Center for Disease Control in 1995 of 4,000 high school students nationwide: 37 percent of gay students had attempted suicide (in contrast to 9 percent of the total student population); 20 percent had skipped school in the prior month because they felt unsafe (compared to 4.5 percent of all students); and 67 percent had been threatened or injured by a weapon at a school in the prior year (compared to 29 percent of all students). "It is too easy to discriminate against an individual when he/she is merely a label (i.e., homosexual)," the statement concluded. "Open dialogue forces us to overcome our obstacles to see the human being before the label. ... The people of Utah can confront homophobia by continuing to educate our community about the challenges faced by gays and lesbians. ... only then, will we move toward having a community that allows all of our members to live in an area that respects each individual for who they are. Assemblies like the one at East High bring that day closer to reality."

Over the next several weeks the *Tribune* printed more than a dozen letters to the editor on the subject. One argued that the presentation did not belong "in the school's multicultural assembly along with groups from Africa, Fiji, Tahiti and Samoa. ... By claiming that the gay rights movement is an extension of the civil-rights movement, groups such as the Gay Straight Alliance pressure some, like Kay Peterson, into accepting the notion that homosexuals are a special group, deserving of special privileges." In the view of another,

"Enriching opportunities like East High's cultural awareness assembly can only better prepare students to harmoniously coexist with their co-workers, employers, neighbors and even family members. The verbal attacks on the gay children by students after the assembly and previous physical assaults of their parents and vandalism of their property exemplifies the need for such experiences now. I look forward to the day when the use of the 'F' word (faggot) is as socially unacceptable as the 'N' word is today." Another letter broadened the discussion: "I am a senior in high school. ... I wish Utah parents would quit making fun of the 'other'—the gays, the African Americans, the Latinos, the Goths, people who do not make as much money as they do, and anyone else whom they feel superior to because of some image they have of themselves. I promise if you do just this it will reflect onto your children and make high school a better place for everyone, not just a good experience for the 'popular crowd.'" A fourth letter said, "As a parent who has a student attending East High School, I want to offer my full support to Principal Kay Peterson for including a presentation by the Gay Straight Alliance at the school's multicultural assembly last week. Perhaps if there were more understanding and tolerance of differences among people, Matthew Shepard, of Laramie, Wyoming, would not have had to die an inhumane and senseless death, after being brutally assaulted, strung up on a fence and left to die last fall." Another asserted that those who demanded the principal's resignation "demonstrated the kind of ignorance from which fear and hatred is bred. ... My suggestion to those of you who are always at the forefront of protests to rid East High of anything related to GSA is to investigate the meaning of multiculturalism and try embracing all people instead of shunning those who are different and going on yearly witch hunts."

Several weeks later school officials announced that in the future participation in the multicultural assembly would be limited to groups representing particular geographic areas and cultures and, thus, the gay club would not be allowed to participate. A *Salt Lake Tribune* editorial criticized the decision, saying, "It is regrettable that the East High School community could not summon more tolerance for some of its outcast students, namely the members of the Gay Straight Alliance. Prohibiting their presentations at school assemblies does not advance the cause of greater understanding." And it recalled a statement by U.S. district judge Bruce Jenkins a year earlier as he heard motions on a lawsuit filed against the original ban on the club: "I sometimes wonder if school boards at more levels ought to add to their curriculum a class in tolerance, a class in compassion, a class in human dignity, a class on recognizing that not everybody's the same." Nevertheless, the school stood by the ban.

In May 1999, a month after the controversy about the assembly began, the Salt Lake School District rejected an application for a "Rainbow Club" at East High School. In their application, organizers said that it would "provide any interested student a forum to understand the contributions of gay, lesbian, and bisexual people. Textbooks and everyday discussions in the classrooms do not include this. Role models have been overlooked." District officials said they denied the application because the club was not "curriculum-related," though even if it were, the application would still have been rejected because "sexual orientation is not the proper organizing subject matter of a curriculum-related club."

The controversy at East High had implications beyond the boundaries of the school. It helped fuel an anti-gay backlash that enabled Republican Merrill Cook to ride his Democratic opponent Ross Anderson's support of same-sex marriages to political victory in the November 1996 election for the U.S. House of Representatives. A year later, in the 1997 Salt Lake City election for the district 5 city council seat, "Word was spread in one LDS ward," *The Salt Lake Tribune* reported, "that candidate Jackie Biskupski is gay and her election would be a blow against good family values." Her narrow loss, by forty-three votes, had significant implications when the new city council voted on January 13, 1998, to overturn an ordinance passed only the month before by the outgoing city council prohibiting discrimination against city employees on the basis of sexual orientation, and her victorious opponent voted with the majority.

Salt Lake City had been the first Utah municipality to adopt such an ordinance, though Salt Lake County and the University of Utah had similar policies—as did several hundred cities and towns in the United States, including Seattle, Portland, Ann Arbor, and Detroit—as well as a number of companies doing business in Utah, including Levi Strauss, Microsoft, Nordstrom, U.S. West, and REI. *The Salt Lake Tribune* supported the new ordinance, while the Mormon church-owned *Deseret News* editorialized against it. There was much public outcry against the decision to overturn it, and also much support. One letter to the editor said, "I support the recent decision of the Salt Lake City

Council to repeal the ordinance including 'sexual orientation' as a specially protected characteristic of employees or prospective employees of Salt Lake City. ... The city council's vote is not and should not be taken as denigration of the worth of any person or support for employment discrimination. That vote is and should be taken as the rule of the majority regarding a question our democracy reserves to the people—whether promotion of homosexuality has a proper place in Salt Lake City ordinances." Another letter made a telling point. "The decision to rescind the previous council's action," it said, "which extended protection from discrimination to include gays is both shameful and curious—shameful because it was a reactive and negative action taken against a specific group of people, and curious because of the zealousness with which certain members of the council pursued the issue. ... Because this action was the new council's first substantial piece of business, it placed an exclamation point behind the issue, in essence saying this is important, a priority, and requires our immediate attention."

In response to expressed concerns that if the ordinance remained in place, children would come in contact with gay employees, one letter to *The Salt Lake Tribune* said: "They already do. We are your family, your friends, your fellow employees, your teacher, your grocer, your postal carrier, your insurance agent, and even your minister. Get used to it. We are not hiding any more." *The Tribune* published a strongly worded editorial against the decision, characterizing it as "misguided," "shortsighted," "a tremendous disservice," and called on Mayor Corradini to veto it. She refused to.

Following Biskupski's announcement the next year that she would run for the Utah State House of Representatives, Gayle Ruzicka, president of the Eagle Forum, said that in an effort to defeat her she would inform voters that Biskupski was a lesbian. "She is living an illegal lifestyle," Ruzicka said. "In Utah sodomy is against the law." In a September 18, 1998, editorial, *The Salt Lake Tribune* called Ruzicka's position "a pernicious viewpoint" and "quite simply, bigotry—that is, the intolerance of another for her very identity, not simply the disagreement with her views on campaign issues. ... Gayle Ruzicka's position in Jackie Biskupski's race is immoral in itself. To reject a person's candidacy for public office on the basis of her identity is unacceptably intolerant in a democratic state." The week before the election a group calling itself Citizens for Strong Families mailed fliers to 6,000 residents of Biskupski's district urging

275

them "not to elect a lesbian as our standard-bearer." Even so, she won the election by a margin of more than three to two.

~

Recommended Readings

Barber, Phyllis. "Culture Shock." *Utah Holiday*, Nov. 1981, 31-40. Reprinted in McCormick and Sillito, *A World We Thought We Knew*, 393-406.

Edison, Carol A., Hatch, Anne R., and Miller, Craig R. *Hecho en Utah: Una Historia Cultural de Las Comunidades Hispanas de Utah/ Made in Utah: A Cultural History of Utah's Spanish-Speaking Communities*. Salt Lake City: Utah Arts Council, 1992.

Hoskins, Shannon R., ed. *Faces of Utah: A Portrait*. Layton, UT: Gibbs Smith, Publisher, 1996.

O'Donovan, Rocky. "'The Abominable and Detestable Crime Against Nature': A Brief History of Homosexuality and Mormonism, 1840-1980." In Corcoran, Brent, ed. *Multiply and Replenish: Mormon Essays on Sex and Family*. Salt Lake City: Signature Books, 1994.

Papanikolas, Helen Z. "Utah's Ethnic Legacy," *Dialogue: A Journal of Mormon Thought* 19 (Spring 1986): 41-8. Reprinted in McCormick and Sillito, *A World We Thought We Knew*, 241-48.

EPILOGUE

Salt Lake City is rooted in a complex and compelling past, rich and textured, multi-layered and multi-faceted. Formed from a process of conflict involving an intricate interplay of racial, class, ideological, cultural, and gender issues, its history is the account, not of one people, but of many. There has been much to uphold the authority of a white, heterosexual, middle-class, able-bodied, and patriarchal social order, and also much to challenge it and advance other visions. Increasingly shaped by, and reflecting, the values and practices of the larger society, Salt Lake's history is complicated and ambiguous, a story, in a sense, not of paradise lost, but of possibilities lost, a history as much of suffering as of fulfillment. A variety of experiences and processes has constituted its life. There have been many lives and many realities to be accounted for. Various groups have experienced the city in different ways. In a sense, each has inhabited a different city.

Salt Lake's residents have always been, in Richard Sennett's phrase, "people in the presence of others." As Roland Barthes says of cities in general, Salt Lake has been "the place of our meeting with the other." And the context of that meeting has been uneven distributions of advantages and disadvantages, privileges and marginalization, power and a relative lack of power. Rich and poor, black and white, male and female, Mormon and non-Mormon, disabled and abled, heterosexual and homosexual, native-born and immigrant, have all experienced the city differently. Thus, for example, it has always been a safer city in a variety of ways for men than for women, for white than for black or Hispanic, for straight than for gay.

This means that in order to understand the history of Salt Lake City, it has been necessary to take difference seriously, to be sensitive to it, to attend to it. As part of that, it has been important to focus on power relations. When that is done, arrangements of privilege and marginalization come into sharp focus. The interests of some groups have clearly been advanced and those of others slowed or subverted. Particular groups have been defined as "inside" and others as "outside" the community, and for the most marginal, even the interstices of urban space have often been denied. Hassled and policed by the various agents of law and order, they have found it difficult to enjoy even the right to their own limited space let alone to have the cultural capital to negotiate an expanded place. For many people, James Baldwin's comment, as he surveyed his own New York City in 1963, has echoed across Salt Lake City's streets: "You know—you know instinctively—that none of this is for you. You know before you are told. And who is it for and who is paying for it? And why isn't it for you?"

What of the future? The meaning of Salt Lake history is inseparable from the question of who the people of the city actually are and whether they can live and work together with all of their class, gender, ethnic, and cultural differences. Perhaps the central question this book has been concerned with, both explicitly and implicitly, is, "What does it mean to be a Utahn?" That is to say, "To whom does Salt Lake's past, present, and future belong? Whose city is it? Who has a right to find their histories here? Who has the right to appropriate space and participate in decision making?" In the end, it is this question that emerges repeatedly from the historical record. It is the fundamental question the city has always faced, and it remains the crucial question facing it today. The old definitions, prevailing for so long, are inadequate. New ones are necessary, and the search for them is underway. Utah, as historian F. Ross Peterson says, is a state seeking contemporary definition. Much is at stake. Past definitions have tended to be narrow and exclusionary. New ones, whatever they may be, must allow for other ways of seeing and thinking. They will have to include more expansive images, ones that will more accurately take into account the diverse society that Utah really is, always has been, and will continue increasingly to be, and that will resist, rather than uphold, monolithic, one-dimensional, stereotypical representations, that will allow resistance to proceed against exclusion and marginalization, that will make possible greater understanding of the society to which we belong, the history of the people and traditions with which we interact, and the meaning of the ideas and experiences we encounter. The right to, and respect for, difference and diversity in the city must become, as it now is not, an integral aspect of social citizenship. In an emancipatory practice, the "right to the city" would not be preserved mainly for the privileged. The unoppressive city would be open to what might be called "unassimilated otherness." It would lay down institutional and ideological means for recognizing and affirming differently identifying groups in two basic senses: giving political representation to the interests of various groups, and celebrating the distinctive cultures and characteristics of those groups.

At a regional humanities conference held in Salt Lake City in the fall of 1996, five panelists discussed the lives of women in the western United States. Three were white females, including a member of the Mormon church and a member of the Catholic church. A fourth was a Native American woman of Klamath and Shoshoni ancestry, and the fifth a Japanese Buddhist woman. Many in the audience were surprised to find that the person whose roots in Utah went back the farthest, and the only native born Utahn, was the Japanese woman. I envision a future where our view of the past does not lead us to be surprised by that fact—nor to deny or resist its implications. As Kathryn L. MacKay and Larry Cesspooch say in their introduction to the series of oral interviews with Utes contained in Leslie G. Kelen and Eileen Hallet Stone's important collection, *Missing Stories: An Oral History of Ethnic and Minority Groups in Utah*, "We have asked *Nuche* [the Utes] to speak to us. We must behave properly and listen."

279

INDEX

281

The Gathering Place

About the Author

John S. McCormick, Ph.D., University of Iowa, is a professor of history at Salt Lake Community College. He is the author of *The Historic Buildings of Downtown Salt Lake City*; *Past, Present, and Future: The History of Utah Power & Light Co.*; *The Utah Adventure*; and *The Westside of Salt Lake City*. He is the co-author of *Discovering Utah* and *Saltair*; co-editor of *A World We Thought We Knew: Readings in Utah History*; and a contributor to *Differing Visions: Dissenters in Mormon History*. He has published in *Dialogue: A Journal of Mormon Thought*, *Southwest Economy and Society*, and *Utah Historical Quarterly*.